Palgrave Politics of Identity and Citizenship Series

Series Editors: **Varun Uberoi**, Brunel University, UK; **Nasar Meer**, University of Northumbria, UK and **Tariq Modood**, University of Bristol, UK

The politics of identity and citizenship has assumed increasing importance as our polities have become significantly more culturally, ethnically and religiously diverse. Different types of scholars, including philosophers, sociologists, political scientists and historians make contributions to this field and this series showcases a variety of innovative contributions to it. Focusing on a range of different countries, and utilizing the insights of different disciplines, the series helps to illuminate an increasingly controversial area of research and titles in it will be of interest to a number of audiences including scholars, students and other interested individuals.

Titles include:

Parveen Akhtar
BRITISH MUSLIM POLITICS
Examining Pakistani Biraderi Networks

Heidi Armbruster and Ulrike Hanna Meinhof (*editors*)
NEGOTIATING MULTICULTURAL EUROPE
Borders, Networks, Neighbourhoods

Peter Balint and Sophie Guérard de Latour
LIBERAL MULTICULTURALISM AND THE FAIR TERMS OF INTEGRATION

Fazila Bhimji
BRITISH ASIAN MUSLIM WOMEN, MULTIPLE SPATIALITIES AND COSMOPOLITANISM

Jan Dobbernack and Tariq Modood (*editors*)
TOLERANCE, INTOLERANCE AND RESPECT
Hard to Accept?

Romain Garbaye and Pauline Schnapper (*editors*)
THE POLITICS OF ETHNIC DIVERSITY IN THE BRITISH ISLES

Nisha Kapoor, Virinder Kalra and James Rhodes (*editors*)
THE STATE OF RACE

Peter Kivisto and Östen Wahlbeck (*editors*)
DEBATING MULTICULTURALISM IN THE NORDIC WELFARE STATES

Dina Kiwan (*editor*)
NATURALIZATION POLICIES, EDUCATION AND CITIZENSHIP
Multicultural and Multi-Nation Societies in International Perspective

Aleksandra Maatsch
ETHNIC CITIZENSHIP REGIMES
Europeanization, Post-war Migration and Redressing Past Wrongs

Derek McGhee
SECURITY, CITIZENSHIP AND HUMAN RIGHTS
Shared Values in Uncertain Times

Nasar Meer
CITIZENSHIP, IDENTITY AND THE POLITICS OF MULTICULTURALISM
The Rise of Muslim Consciousness

Tariq Modood and John Salt (*editors*)
GLOBAL MIGRATION, ETHNICITY AND BRITISHNESS

Ganesh Nathan
SOCIAL FREEDOM IN A MULTICULTURAL STATE
Towards a Theory of Intercultural Justice

Therese O'Toole and Richard Gale
POLITICAL ENGAGEMENT AMONGST ETHNIC MINORITY YOUNG PEOPLE
Making a Difference

Momin Rahman
HOMOSEXUALITIES, MUSLIM CULTURES AND MODERNITY

Michel Seymour (*editor*)
THE PLURAL STATES OF RECOGNITION

Katherine Smith
FAIRNESS, CLASS AND BELONGING IN CONTEMPORARY ENGLAND

Paul Thomas
YOUTH, MULTICULTURALISM AND COMMUNITY COHESION

Milton Vickerman
THE PROBLEM OF POST-RACIALISM

Palgrave Politics of Identity and Citizenship Series
Series Standing Order ISBN 978–0–230–24901–1 (hardback)
(*outside North America only*)

You can receive future titles in this series as they are published by placing a standing order. Please contact your bookseller or, in case of difficulty, write to us at the address below with your name and address, the title of the series and the ISBN quoted above.

Customer Services Department, Macmillan Distribution Ltd, Houndmills, Basingstoke, Hampshire RG21 6XS, England

Homosexualities, Muslim Cultures and Modernity

Momin Rahman
Trent University, Canada

© Momin Rahman 2014
Softcover reprint of the hardcover 1st edition 2014 978-1-137-00295-2
All rights reserved. No reproduction, copy or transmission of this publication may be made without written permission.

No portion of this publication may be reproduced, copied or transmitted save with written permission or in accordance with the provisions of the Copyright, Designs and Patents Act 1988, or under the terms of any licence permitting limited copying issued by the Copyright Licensing Agency, Saffron House, 6-10 Kirby Street, London EC1N 8TS.

Any person who does any unauthorized act in relation to this publication may be liable to criminal prosecution and civil claims for damages.

The author has asserted his right to be identified as the author of this work in accordance with the Copyright, Designs and Patents Act 1988.

First published 2014 by
PALGRAVE MACMILLAN

Palgrave Macmillan in the UK is an imprint of Macmillan Publishers Limited, registered in England, company number 785998, of Houndmills, Basingstoke, Hampshire RG21 6XS.

Palgrave Macmillan in the US is a division of St Martin's Press LLC, 175 Fifth Avenue, New York, NY 10010.

Palgrave Macmillan is the global academic imprint of the above companies and has companies and representatives throughout the world.

Palgrave® and Macmillan® are registered trademarks in the United States, the United Kingdom, Europe and other countries.

ISBN 978-1-349-43409-1   ISBN 978-1-137-00296-9 (eBook)
DOI 10.1057/9781137002969

This book is printed on paper suitable for recycling and made from fully managed and sustained forest sources. Logging, pulping and manufacturing processes are expected to conform to the environmental regulations of the country of origin.

A catalogue record for this book is available from the British Library.

A catalog record for this book is available from the Library of Congress.

Typeset by MPS Limited, Chennai, India.

Transferred to Digital Printing in 2014

*To Sean and to Jess
who are my (mixed species)
double consciousness*

Contents

Acknowledgments x

Introduction 1
   The conceits of modernity and modernization 2
   Muslim homo-eroticism in historical and
   contemporary context 4
   Political possibilities 6

1 In Search of My Mother's Garden: Reflections on Migration, Gender, Sexuality and Muslim Identity 9
   Introduction 9
   History, narratives and narrators 10
   Migration 13
   Identities 15
   Gender 17
   My mother's garden 21
   Not quite Muslim, not quite gay, towards a queer intersectionality 24

2 Islam *versus* Homosexuality *as* Modernity 27
   Introduction 27
   The drumbeats of Islamic 'otherness' 29
   Democracy as Western exceptionalism 34
   Equality and secularism versus multiculturalism
   in the context of gender 37
   Sexual diversity as *the* marker of Islamic otherness? 42
   The conceits of the West and the resistance of the East 47

3 Problematic Modernization: The Extent and Formation of Muslim Antipathy to Homosexuality 49
   Introduction 49
   Muslim regulation of homosexuality at the national
   and international level 51
   The attitudes of Muslim majority and minority populations 56
   Explaining Muslim antipathy through the
   modernization thesis 59

	The complexities of modernization and reactions to homosexuality	62
	Understanding Muslim homophobia in the contexts of modernity and Islamophobia	66
4	**Traditions and Transformations of Muslim Homo-eroticism**	**70**
	Introduction	70
	Homo-eroticism in traditional Muslim cultures	72
	The transformation of Muslim homo-eroticism through the 'Gay International'	78
	Modernity misunderstood? Colonialism, post-colonial cultures and the regulation of the sexual	82
	Connected histories: the wider sociological basis of homosexualization during modernity	88
	Homosexualization beyond westernization and the politics of Muslim identity	92
5	**Queer Muslims in the Context of Contemporary Globalized LGBTIQ Identity**	**94**
	Introduction	94
	The world 'they' have won	95
	Connected contemporary histories: queer Muslims in Muslim majority cultures	102
	Connected contemporary histories: queer Muslims in the West	108
	From connected histories to queer Muslims as modern intersectional subjects	111
	Towards an intersectional modernity?	115
6	**The Politics of Identity and the Ends of Liberation**	**118**
	Introduction	118
	The triangulation of Western exceptionalism: homocolonialism, Muslim homophobia and monoculturalism	119
	The political presumptions of homocolonialism: 'coming out' and the essential context of political identity	125
	Beyond homocolonialism: the ends of liberation and equality as resource	130
	Arriving at the terrain of dialogue and recognizing queer as privilege	135

7	**Beginnings**	**137**
	Introduction	137
	The homocolonialist 'test' for internationalized Western queer politics and consciousness	138
	Homocolonialism in multiculturalism	144
	Embracing Western exceptionalism through homocolonialism: challenges for Muslim consciousness and politics	149
	The past and future imperfect, tense	154

Appendices   156

Notes   189

Bibliography   213

Index   228

Acknowledgments

Many people help with the process of writing a book by discussing the ideas and themes in various circumstances and over varying time periods. I have been giving talks on some of these chapters for a few years now and I am grateful for the feedback and criticism those presentations have produced. Colleagues in Sociology, Women's Studies and International Development Studies have invited me to do talks at 'small but mighty' Trent University where we all ply our trade and their interactions are particularly welcome. I have also received much support from colleagues in the queer caucus of the International Studies Association, which is similarly small and equally mighty in the range of research, activism and argument that it contains, all of which have impacted upon how this project has developed. I have also benefited from more direct and sustained discussions with the following; Mike Bosia, Gerald Hunt, Stevi Jackson, Sean Lockwood, Barb Marshall, Tariq Modood, Abouzar Nasirzedah, Wim Peumans, David Rayside, Walid Saleh and Matthew Waites. David Rayside has been especially encouraging in my pursuit of these issues since my move to Canada (even though I am sure he means it as an insult when he describes me as a 'theorist'), largely through my almost immediate involvement in the Mark S. Bonham Centre for Sexual Diversity Studies at the University of Toronto, which David really got off the ground. The Centre continues to flourish and provides both a huge range of courses on sexuality and a 'hub' for research and activism. Thanks also go to Lucy Marshall-Kiparissis and Ben Peel who did some research for me. I also want to acknowledge my family, who I am sure will never read this book, but in their compassionate, pragmatic (and sometimes angry) approach to dealing with *my* 'issues', they have unwittingly helped to develop some of the issues and themes contained within this study.

Introduction

On July 5, 2007, I emigrated from Britain to the New World. Arriving at Toronto's Pearson airport from Glasgow, Scotland, I was directed to immigration control along with my partner *du jour* (who shall remain nameless in deference to my current spouse). The immigration official was a young South Asian woman who was busy harassing a senior South Asian couple about their intended stay in Canada to visit their family. Both my white partner and I were distressed at this scene, partly I suspect, because of our anxiety about how we would be treated as next in line, and partly because the couple were obviously infirm, with one (the woman, I think) in a wheelchair and using some breathing assistance apparatus (I'm not making this up, reader). When our turn came, the official asked sharply why we were even approaching her together, assuming that *we* could not possibly be a couple. Whether this was primarily heteronormative or racially based, I cannot know, but once we had established that we were indeed immigrating together, the atmosphere changed almost immediately. At first the official was obviously embarrassed at her assumption and flustered, and covered this up by printing off our visas from her computer. Soon, however, she was all smiles and pleasantries, having established that I had employment and my partner was coming in as a common law spouse, with all the relevant documentation. She then asked if we would mind if she called in a group of trainees to watch her process our case, and talk them through it as a useful example (I'm really not making this up). They duly arrived and were talked through the details of our status, and we simply went along with it all, not daring to complain about the previous couple's treatment but rather anxious to get through this final barrier. I was also particularly anxious to pick up Jess, our dog who had arrived on the same flight and was waiting for us to claim her from an animal immigration depot somewhere else in the airport.[1]

We might think of my arrival in Canada as a micro-example of Puar's homonationalist embrace (2007), whereby my queer identity rendered me free from the scrutiny apparently accorded to South Asians/Muslims. Within that broad discourse, moreover, perhaps there was a specific assumption that *I* could not be gay, because of my ethnicity. I have no way of knowing what would have happened if I had approached alone but I suspect that given my occupational class status, I would have eventually (and perhaps rather quickly) been given more courtesy than the previous South Asian couple. The assumed mutual exclusivity of queerness and Muslim and/or Asian cultures is the personal and analytical impetus to this study, although it expands beyond that core question. I begin, therefore, with an auto/biographical narrative in Chapter 1[2] – 'In Search of My Mother's Garden: Reflections on Migration, Gender, Sexuality and Muslim Identity'. This chapter explains my own social location as a gay, Western, Muslim man and thus renders visible my own investment in this project.[3] It charts the issues and difficulties that arise in trying to reconcile homosexuality and Muslim culture, but also reminds us of the lived experience of such issues and the relevance for me of an intersectional theoretical and epistemological approach to these questions – a theme that is pertinent throughout this study. This chapter therefore provides an opening bracket to frame the more academic discussions in subsequent chapters, and is partnered by a brief return to personal experience in conclusion to the study. In the rest of the book, I present a detailed study of the issues surrounding homosexuality and Muslim cultures that construct the possibilities of lived experience that are discussed in the first chapter. I organize this discussion through the three broad themes of the conceits of modernity and modernization; Muslim homo-eroticism in historical and contemporary context; and political possibilities. Of course, none of these are mutually exclusive but I do aim to build an argument that weaves them together based on this linear construction of the text.

The conceits of modernity and modernization

I deal first with the political context to current oppositions of homosexuality and Muslim cultures in Chapter 2 – 'Islam *versus* Homosexuality *as* Modernity'. My central argument here is that we are living within a discourse of Islamic otherness that positions Islam against homosexuality because homosexuality has become deployed as *the* marker of the superiority of Western modernity. No one can doubt that Muslim cultures and identities are under intense scrutiny in the West, anchored in the premise of incompatibility with Western forms of governance, citizenship and cultural values. Many have detailed the role of gender politics in this putative 'civilizational clash' (Phillips, 2007; Razack, 2008) but there is only an emerging field of work on issues relating directly to homosexuality, despite the fact that there is a public discourse of Muslim antipathy to individual and public homosexuality that has become part of the wider discourse of Muslim 'otherness'.[4] Indeed, both Lesbian, Gay, Bisexual, Transgendered, Intersexed, Queer (LGBTIQ) groups and mainstream policy makers have increasingly used the public acceptance of homosexuality as a marker of the superiority of Western societies, in contrast to Islamic values and Muslim attitudes (Mepschen et al., 2010). I demonstrate that when sexual diversity is present in civilizational debates, it is cast as a defining feature of Western exceptionalism, thus drawing it into the core of definitions of Muslim incompatibility with modernity. I argue, however, that this positioning is based on a number of conceits about modernity that are unsustainable. First, homosexuality is not accepted universally in the West and so its identification with Western exceptionalism – defined with reference to liberal democracy, individualism and social equality – is highly problematic. When it is deployed thus, the argument is that – like gender equality – the conditions for homosexual public acceptance and rights are possible *only* in liberal democratic conditions of governance and citizenship. In contrast, I argue that the relatively recent appearance of LGBTIQ and gender equality in the West suggests that either democratic principles are not inherently favorable to such issues or that other political and social structures are much more important in how sexuality changes within modernity. It is important, therefore, to question both the identification of homosexuality with modernity and particularly to be aware of how such an equation can be deployed to serve the racist orientalist dialectic of Islam versus modernity.

The challenge to such conceits of the 'West' provokes a consideration of a number of further issues, including a need to accurately assess the resistance of 'Eastern' cultures to homosexuality. In Chapter 3, therefore, I discuss the available evidence on Muslim antipathy to homosexuality. I cover the regulations at both national and international levels, drawing on collated data presented in the Appendices[5] that summarize regulations, socio-economic and governance status, colonial history, and any indication of group LGBTIQ activity in Muslim majority countries. I go on to assess the ways in which the evident antipathy to homosexuality is explained using broad modernization arguments that position Muslim populations and cultures as 'lagging behind' Western modernity – hence the title of the chapter: 'Problematic Modernization: the Extent and Formation of Muslim Antipathy to Homosexuality'. I argue that whilst broad modernization arguments are convincing in describing overall Muslim resistance to sexual diversity, we must attend to the complexities in modernization analyses that undermine characterizations of Muslim religious identity as somehow exceptional in its homophobia, but rather confirm an entirely conventional picture of high religiosity in any grouping as an impediment to accepting homosexuality. Moreover, in comparing a range of analyses that use a modernization frame, I demonstrate that a complex sociological picture is needed when accounting for Muslim identity; one that is less concerned with religion and more with the socio-ethnic dimensions of contemporary Muslim political consciousness. I do not dismiss modernization factors out of hand, therefore, but rather point to their complexities and argue that we must constantly bring those to the fore to prevent any lazy deployment of modernization within the orientalist Islamophobic discourse described in Chapter 2. In conclusion, however, I raise the question of whether modernization logic can be sustained in the contemporary context of both Islamophobia and the internationalization of queer rights. I argue instead that we must accept that the Muslim experience of sexual diversity politics is significantly different from the Western one and that this reality undermines any assumption that the processes of Muslim modernization will inevitably lead to the same outcomes around sexuality as those experienced in the West.

Muslim homo-eroticism in historical and contemporary context

In a sense, the preceding two chapters have focused on the ways in which queer politics and Muslim identities are respectively drawn into the broad civilizational dialectic. Moving beyond this critique, the remaining chapters are more focused on how to challenge these common sense political understandings, using queer Muslim experience as a starting point to challenge the apparent exclusivity of Western modernity and Islam. In Chapter 4 – 'Traditions and Transformations of Muslim Homo-eroticism' – I begin with a survey of the historical evidence on Muslim homo-eroticism and discuss the ways in which it has been transformed during modernity. I argue that colonization certainly narrowed the acceptable definitions of sexual diversity, mirroring the creation of the 'homosexual' in the 'home' colonizing states. I move on to discuss the two broad explanations for post-colonial regulation of sexuality, dealing first with Massad's characterization of contemporary queer politics as a continued form of colonization by the West (2008). Whilst I critique the empirical basis of his putative 'Gay International', I agree that current forms of queer political strategies contain a Western bias in terms of the possible outcomes of sexual diversity in modernity. However, I reject the characterization of this internationalization as exclusively a new form of Western colonialism, drawing on the second set of explanations for post-colonial regulation that demonstrate the investment that Muslim states have in continuing the regulation of homosexuality and, in doing so, consider a wider sociological basis to 'homosexualization' than is evident in Massad's analysis. I argue that post-colonial analyses such as Massad's are in danger of reinstating a Eurocentric view of modernity by ceding the construction and regulation of homosexuality as exclusively 'Western'. Moreover, this characterization in large part permits and perhaps encourages Muslim resistance to the recognition of Muslim cultural homo-eroticism and to homosexuality in general as 'Western'.

In order to develop an alternative perspective, I draw upon the idea of 'connected histories' (Bhambra, 2007; Subrahmanyam, 1997) that asks us to interrogate modernity as specific conjectural phenomena that illustrate interconnections of processes rather than to reify distinct cultures or concepts. In particular, the challenge such a perspective addresses is whether we accept modernity and its consequential formations as exclusively Western phenomena, and I suggest that the historical evidence on colonial and post-colonial regulation of sexuality indicates that we must think of modernity as having connected global impacts, whereby the 'forces of homosexualization' may have been imposed by Western colonialism, but have not been subsequently disowned by post-colonial cultures. In conclusion, I discuss the viability of challenging Muslim homophobia in part by recognizing the traditions of Muslim homo-eroticism, but I suggest that the evident lack of this strategy in contemporary Muslim politics indicates that something more is needed to bring us onto a shared, rather than oppositional, terrain of Islam and sexual diversity. A large part of other strategies depend on recognizing the continued manifestation of 'homosexualization', both in the West and in Muslim cultures, and I therefore continue with the idea of connected histories to further explore the contemporary interconnections around Muslim homo-eroticism in Chapter 5 – 'Queer Muslims in the Context of Contemporary Globalized LGBTIQ Identity'. I begin with a discussion of the contemporary globalized culture of queer identity, drawing heavily on Jeffrey Weeks' optimistic account of *The World We Have Won* (2007). I suggest that his approach rightly identifies contemporary connections in sexual modernity, but that his analytical framework relies too heavily on a positive account of expanding reflexive globalization, missing out the regulatory ways in which Western queer subjectivity is constructed. I go on to discuss the limited evidence we have available on queer Muslims in Muslim majority countries and within Western minority populations. Whilst there are obvious differences in these experiences, I argue that there are indications of a connectedness around sexual identities and politics that do speak to a globalized gay culture and its local adaptations, but that these need to be understood within a more astute framework of power divisions than is evidenced in Weeks' approach. I propose using an intersectionality perspective to help us understand the complexities of contemporary queer Muslim experience, arguing that such a framework retains an emphasis on power divisions and oppressions, whilst allowing us to incorporate multiple vectors of identity formation and directing us to include the socio-political as a key context of 'intersection'. In this sense, my use of intersectionality is a translation of the idea of connected histories into the contemporary era, wherein sexual modernity is a complex, interconnected range of intersecting identities and socio-political deployments of regulation.

Political possibilities

In adopting this perspective, I raise the implication that modernity must be understood as intersectional. I explore this implication throughout the final two chapters, as the beginning point of how we translate the preceding critiques into practical politics. I do not, however, suggest a resolution to this question, or indeed propose a new model of modernity but rather I suggest that this is one of many 'beginnings' that need further exploration but that, first and foremost, must be based on more research on queer Muslim experience. In Chapter 6 – 'The Politics of Identity and the Ends of Liberation' – I therefore return to my core argument that specific understandings of modernity underpin the discourses of opposition between Muslim cultures and sexual diversity, but I reframe these politics through an intersectional analysis. Specifically, I argue that the idea of Western exceptionalism is the primary political idea that is legitimized through a process of *triangulation*. A key component of this process is what I call 'homocolonialism'; the deployment of LGBTIQ rights and visibility to stigmatize non-Western cultures and conversely reassert the supremacy of the Western nations and civilization. I describe the intersecting formations of both the positioning and the processes of triangulation and argue that such an intersectional appreciation permits the beginnings of a disruption to this triangulation, both in terms of the positioning of monocultural civilizations and the reiterative processes at work.

I then go on to consider the implications of this disruptive intersectionality for the dominant Western queer politics of identity, arguing that we must rethink the assumptions behind Western politics, both in terms of its current construction as 'identity' politics linked to human rights, and its assumption of what outcomes to sexual liberation look like. I frame the problems with identity politics as 'homocolonialist' presumptions based on Western forms of political and sociological subjectification and I suggest that we must start to consider the differential outcomes of 'equality' that are possible in contemporary socio-political contexts. I suggest that we focus more on equality as a set of discursive and institutional resources rather than as a teleological, pre-formed universal outcome which is, in reality, based on Western experiences of coming out and Western forms of political engagement which are, moreover, grounded in a Western essentialist understanding of sexuality. As a way forward, I suggest that we recognize the assumption that sexual liberation is understood as the liberation of essential 'true' selves, and instead start to think about 'possible' sexual selves and how they are able to shape their own meaningful versions of equality using the available political resources in their cultures and communities. The second major disruption we can achieve through an intersectional analysis is to illuminate the ways in which Islamophobia and homophobia reinforce each other through the processes of triangulation. For queer Muslims, I argue that we cannot have 'liberation' from one of these hierarchies without liberation from the other and this means that whilst we can point out the ways Muslim homophobia reinforces Islamophobia, we also need to think about the ways in which the reverse is true and thus how queer politics should be concerned with the effects of Islamophobia. In conclusion to Chapter 6, I discuss how my analysis can begin to move us towards a terrain of dialogue between queer and Muslim politics. I suggest that we must be aware that the routes to this dialogue are different for each, particularly because queer politics has a privileged position over Muslim politics in many contemporary situations. This means that there will be important differences in how practical political strategies can be developed to challenge the triangulation of Western exceptionalism and the dominance of homocolonialism within this process. I therefore turn to these more practical strategies in the final chapter.

In a somewhat transparent ruse, I claim that the final chapter is not one of specific conclusions, but rather one of 'beginnings', with that solitary word serving as its title. In large part this is because I discuss specific political strategies that might derive from the preceding analysis of broad political possibilities and in this, I am suggesting many shifts or breaks with contemporary practice from both Muslim and queer politics. Specifically, I propose a homocolonialist 'test' for Western queer politics, against which its contemporary strategies must be measured if we are to avoid reinstating the triangulation of Western exceptionalism. This involves mainstreaming the politics of development over and above an exclusive import/export model of queer rights, and querying the effectiveness of Western concepts of sexual orientation in the construction of laws and politics. Moreover, I suggest that these shifts are necessary both at home, in dealing with multiculturalism, and abroad, in engaging with Muslim majority cultures and argue that, above all, we have to begin by refusing 'pinktesting' of immigrant and foreign communities, because it reinstates the triangulation that ultimately harms the possibilities of equality for queer Muslims and for Muslims in general. I conclude with the more difficult route to 'testing' homocolonialism within Muslim politics, but I argue that Muslim politics *does* embrace homocolonialism because it provides a useful vector of resistance to Western imperialism and, in doing so, legitimizes Muslim national governments and dominant Muslim community organizations. I question whether this is productive for Muslim communities, precisely because this embrace ultimately reinforces Islamophobia, but also because it closes down one route to the reflexive engagement with issues of pluralism, gender equality and diversity, which, I suggest, are fundamentally needed to accelerate social justice for Muslims.

At a broader level, these strategies are only beginnings because they are interrelated with other critiques and suggestions that already exist in different areas such as development politics, multiculturalism, queer national citizenship politics and progressive Muslim politics, and as such, contribute to and merge with these other, already begun projects. As Said argued in his analysis of literary openings, a beginning is the intentional method for what follows and thus 'a beginning is really nothing more than the created *inclusiveness* within which the work develops' (Said, 1985: 12). This introduction hopes to mirror that function but, in truth, the overall study can only claim this function as well, hoping both to be inclusive in its interdisciplinarity and also to be part of more creativity that develops around the issues of Muslim cultures and sexual diversity, to help in enabling what follows.

1
In Search of My Mother's Garden: Reflections on Migration, Gender, Sexuality and Muslim Identity

Introduction

In Search of Our Mothers' Gardens is Alice Walker's 1983 collection of essays and reminiscences, in which she focuses on her intellectual and personal journey as a feminist, writer and, as she puts it, womanist:

> Womanist, as she defines it, means many things: first, most definitely, 'a black feminist or feminist of color' ... wanting to know more and in greater depth than is considered 'good for one'. Second, 'a woman who loves other women, sexually and/or non-sexually. Appreciates and prefers women's culture, women's emotional flexibility (values tears as the natural counterbalance to laughter), and women's strength.'
>
> A womanist also loves; 'Loves music. Loves dance. Loves the moon. *Loves* the spirit. Loves love and food and roundness. Loves struggle. *Loves* the folk. Loves herself. *Regardless.*'(1983: xi–xii)

Following somewhat erratically in her footsteps, I offer a few reflections on issues of migration, gender, sexuality and identity. The original impetus for this chapter was a public lecture delivered in 2005 on women's history, in which I used my autobiographical narrative to think about questions of gender and sexuality in the context of Muslim identity.[1] Since then, I have thought more directly about my location as a gay man in provoking the initial choice and formation of topic. In revisiting this history with a keener sense of my queerness, I therefore weave a different narrative from the initial talk, but a central thread remains the topic of women in my family and the wider community of Bengalis and Muslims that I am connected to.

This alerts you to that fact that aspects of this narrative are a history once removed and, therefore, whilst these aspects are indeed part of my autobiography, I cannot claim any 'truth' for them except as *my* standpoint on gendered experiences and identities. I mention this at the outset because it is important to say that I am not speaking for women even – *particularly* – those in my family. How could I? Ontologically and experientially I do not share their existence, their social constitution or their social histories – I am an educationally and materially privileged British-born Bengali male, one who is both physically and culturally absent from most of the everyday aspects of the women's lives I discuss. Rather, my aim is to explore how my narrative, my standpoint as a gay man, is inextricable from the lived experiences and political dimensions of gendered Muslim identity: how queerness is inevitably defined in relation to gender norms and their disruptions but how these norms are also ones of culture and ethnicity. I am not simply a gay man, but a gay British Bengali, irreducibly racialized in my queerness and thus occupying an intersectional location in terms of gender, race, class and sexuality.[2] My hope is that I can usefully explore this queer intersectionality to understand its dimensions and also whether it can contribute to untangling some of the contemporary controversies of Muslim 'difference'.

History, narratives and narrators

My assumption is that history, by definition, only exists in the present. By this statement, I remind myself that narratives, particularly autobiographical ones such as mine, are constructions in the present, even as they seek to be reconstructions of the past. Whilst the methods of narrative are varied, they have in common a reliance on subjective sources, whether that is memory, personal visual or written documents, and the extended in-depth interview. This qualitative approach is in fact the inevitable option when attempting to understand personalized stories, but it just as inevitably throws up the questions of epistemology, ontology and authenticity by placing the narrator at centre stage of our methodological nexus. The act of telling the tale is in full measure, constitutive of the tale that is told: it is a crucial part of those interactions around telling 'stories' (Plummer, 1995). And so we need to know something about the narrators of history to assess to what extent their stories, their narrative constructions, are governed by their present social locations and motivations. Hitherto, I have tried to be honest about my position as a socially privileged and largely westernized male, removed from the everyday life of my family. Moreover, the most

Western aspect of my character – or so Bengalis and Muslims would have you believe – is my homosexuality. Momin means 'believer' and 'faithful one' in terms of the Islamic religion, and a homosexual identity is certainly a breach of this faith, regarded as a sin – moreover, one that we can choose *not* to commit. I have chosen that sin, chosen to come out and live as a gay man, an identity that has pushed me away from a Bengali and Muslim community both geographically and culturally, whilst simultaneously – in common with most homosexuals who 'escape' their localized culture – it has provoked a constant awareness of gender conformity and non-conformity amongst that culture.

Part of that awareness has been that the women in Bengali culture carry much of the burden of cultural integrity, although I am loath to accept that as a purely 'Eastern' phenomenon.[3] In many everyday ways, this means that they also carry the burden of history, of the changes brought about by migration, political events and discourses and the cycles of the economy. My failure to be a 'faithful' Bengali male has allowed me space to reflect on these issues of gender division, what it is to be a man or woman, but it has also forced me to reflect upon the privileges of masculinity within culture and how I still receive some of them, despite moving away from the culture, and, perhaps worst of all, having chosen to be gay.[4] But the truth is that I have never focused directly on these issues in my academic work, despite that being largely about sexuality and gender. Literally too close to home? Perhaps, but also partly because I failed to inhabit an assumed academic identity by failing to engage with issues of ethnicity. What changed was a change of academic location for a while – a semester as a visiting lecturer in a Women's Studies program at the University of Maine – where they invited me to do the annual Women's History lecture, thus provoking a more disciplined reflection upon issues which had been circulating for a while. A first telling of the tale that was not reflexive about epistemology in its content. This second telling of the tale has constituted the narrative differently because I am trying to be more reflexive about the knowledge I produce through my narrative, and how that knowledge is fundamentally governed by intertwined neglected narratives, and thus intersecting explanations of oppressions and ontology. The skills an academic training has given me have been used to reflect upon the personal; my existence as a gay man, the oppressions I felt within that identity, how and why gender politics and divisions create controversies of sexual difference and above all, what it means to be Muslim, gay, Muslim *and* gay.

Epistemological consequences occupy and exercise me precisely because the ontological is what I am at heart attempting to understand.

A relativist epistemology is by definition the basis of autobiographical narrative methodologies and I am secure in those implications, but I am aware as well that they raise uncertainties, ambiguities about claims to authenticity and perhaps validity. For example, I am removed from the early experiences of migration simply because I wasn't born until my family had been in Britain for some time. As a narrator, I am therefore dependent upon the oral histories provided within the family – mostly, it has to be said, by my mother and eldest sister. And so another dimension of standpoints becomes involved which requires attention to the relationship between me, as narrator, and the memories I deploy of others' memories and how they serve the authenticity I am trying to access, or construct. In this sense, this narrative is not autobiography but auto/biography, a term introduced by the feminist theorist Liz Stanley 'to contaminate the idea that a narrative produced by a self writing about itself, and one produced by a self writing about another being, were *formally* distinguishable from each other' (Broughton, 2000: 242). Whilst the deployment of memories in the narrative that follows is an attempt on my part to perform some kind of audit of the self (Stanley, 2000) of my ontological dimensions, it is also an auto/biography of the Muslim women I know, and how my thinking and writing of gender determines my thinking about sexuality.

Broughton goes on to discuss how feminist interventions in this genre have shown that writing biographies of other and self have often masked the social location and epistemology of the writer; something I hope I am rendering visible. However, in my uncertainty about these questions of epistemology and authenticity, I think that I can only claim that I am producing a 'queer' narrative, one that acknowledges and embraces the uncertainties of identity categories and explores how I am located within, against and outside these categories as historical and political phenomena. Whilst there are different dimensions to queer theory, I am focused on its challenges to ontological foundations, challenges made to universal categories of gender and sexuality often deployed within feminist and gay movements and ideas.[5] As Seidman argues in his review of queer theory, it has contributed to the elaboration of those 'disenchanting' ideas which propose that the 'subject' is an unstable and arbitrary construction, forged out of multiple and historically contingent intersections of ways of thinking about self-identity (1996: 11–12). I am proposing that you understand this story as a queer narrative precisely because that framework allows for the uncertainty the narrative displays and thus shows affinity with the intersectionality that I am trying to reach for. In presenting this history, I am made aware that it is a story of intersectionality and how that intersectionality renders me queer – there are never quite solid or definite identifications with Muslim, Bengali, or gay identity – a history of deferred ontology. Perhaps histories are never the whole story about the past, but they are often much of the story about where we are in the present.

Migration

And the present day is somewhat amazing to me – here I am, the son of first generation immigrants, inhabiting a position of social and economic privilege as an academic, having used that profession to migrate recently myself, from the UK to Canada.[6] Unfortunately, I am an exceptional case, in that Bengalis are still very near the bottom of the socio-economic heap in Britain, despite four generations of presence.[7] Like many others, my family emigrated to the United Kingdom, or rather, East London, back in the 1950s, from Bangladesh. Monica Ali's 2003 first novel, *Brick Lane*, is named for the area in East London which became home to many Bengalis, congregating together as immigrants sensibly do, for the security of knowing that there are others around you, like you, who may give you work and housing and, indeed, treat you as fully human. The family lived in this area before I was born, but we still have relatives there and indeed, the area is now called not only Aldgate, but also Banglatown, in recognition of the now well-established Bengali community and culture. However, my particular Indians moved west. Of course, not very far west, given the narrowness of England's waistline, but far enough to live in a community in Bristol, a city which was ready for the spice of Indian cooking – or so my parents' generation hoped. And there they still reside, having been there for almost 50 years, now in a well-established community with several mosques, wonderful grocers and butchers, and so-so tailors, but not widespread economic or educational success.

Migration is of course a rich story and it has many different dimensions, both positive and negative histories intertwined. My interest here is to think through migration as a movement through identities. Who traveled, and what were their identities, and what did we and I become by living within and against those identities? You see, in truth, although we describe our 'selves' as Bengali, my parents were born in India, and more properly under the colonial rule of British India. Partition occurred in 1947 and although Nehru – the first Prime Minister of India – eloquently described the moment as part fulfillment of 'a tryst with destiny', it turned out to be a bloody and wrenching event, creating two states – India and Pakistan – allocated along majority religious identification. Muslim Pakistan consisted of Pakistan as we know it today – that burden on the left shoulder of India – and East Pakistan, a geographically separate landmass, which became the independent state of Bangladesh in 1971 after a war of independence from Pakistan. So, although we are now officially Bangladeshi in British audits, that State-derived identity did not exist until the early 1970s. We have always been self-identified as Bengali – relating to the region in North-East India which is a wider expanse than the state of Bangladesh. My Bengali father was born and raised in Calcutta, the former colonial capital of India and still an important city, but in India after partition and, more recently, officially renamed Kolkata to match its Bengali pronunciation. And it was my father who came to Britain first, working in and running restaurants, going home occasionally to East Pakistan, and my mother arrived only after the first few years, with my eldest sister in tow. My brother was born here, eight years after my sister. By the time I was born, trips 'home' were to Bangladesh, although I went only once in my life, when I was around four years of age, and I will probably never go again; home, for me, is the West. Now living in Canada, when I think of 'home' I think of trips back to Britain where my family and most of my friends remain.

Migration is of course about journeying. But it is not enough to understand it as simply journeying from one land to another. Post-colonial migration is definitively about journeying through time – traveling from third to first worlds involves not only a change of economic choices but also a change of culture – how societies and labor are organized and how that impacts upon the possibilities of cultural practice and identity. If, as we sociologists like to claim, the ascendance of the 'West' has been defined by all that is modern, migrating to the West has meant traveling into the future, from rural, agricultural and most of all, traditional, lives, to a system of wage labor, commodities, and smaller kinship networks. This traveling through time is a migration into structures of modernity, both economic and bureaucratic. And, as Stanley (2000) reminds us, the bureaucratic imperative to modernity creates the need to account for our 'selves', through official audits of self. We travel into the future, and our 'selves' are remolded, reimagined in this future-present. My family's engagement with such structures is defined both through economic location – as with many from the subcontinent – work was the aim, over and above the welfare available – but such work is low skilled, low paid and often, in the catering and service trades where many Bengalis end up, subject to wider economic factors that determine disposable incomes. But for the generations that followed, the welfare state in its various forms provided the hope of springboard out of this situation: from maternity and infant care through the National Health Service (NHS),[8] through primary and secondary education through the local state, through the benefits system, from public housing provision and supporting and supplementing incomes. What a litany of socialized provision! When it used to be called social security. But state, or rather collective, provisions are now much less secure than they were, and regarded suspiciously in our contemporary neo-liberal or Thatcherite political discourses of low taxation and minimal public provision, as they have been since the late 1970s fiscal crises of Western capitalist states.[9] But I guess the point is that these bureaucracies, at a general level as well as individualized ones, created identities, or at least defined them to a large extent, both negatively – the immigrants scrounging of the welfare state, and taking 'Western' jobs – and positively; by creating personalized routes for the self. Identities now wedded to welfare provision, social housing, income support, all in support of low wage jobs (with low expectations of moving out of such socio-economic sectors) but security in the social provision so fundamentally absent in countries of origin. Such fundamental changes in the way that lives are structured, represented and lived can but impact upon how those lives are inhabited.

Identities

During this journey through modernity, my family have always identified as Bengali. Thus, whilst migration is a journey through time, that journey is undertaken within and against categories of identity. I do not think that any of us were ever actually Bangladeshi citizens since, by 1971–1972, those of us who were already around in Britain were all subjects of the Crown – as British citizenship is charmingly defined. But were we ever really British? Not, I would think, in any full measure – it took until 1997 for British Muslim to become an official identity – in the sense that our head of state mentioned the British Muslim as a new and welcome part of British identity on a trip to Pakistan and India.[10] Forty years after my father first arrived!

There is little point in rehearsing the specifics of legal racism – how Britishness has been defined in opposition to particular ethnic identities. Suffice to say that whilst we may now see British South Asians as indeed British, and whilst we see curry as something of a national dish, British political and popular culture has agonized its way through the process of understanding and accepting difference. Indeed, we have the irony now of a political discourse which criticizes British multiculturalism from the centre left (whence it came) long after multiculturalism has become embedded in everyday life in many cities and towns across the UK. What seems to underlie such anxieties are more traditional concerns of social integration, social order and social inequalities, but in accepting differences, we seem to have lost sight of how to articulate that some difference still can be mapped accurately onto social inequalities. Ghettos are not just ethnic, cultural choices to separate, but have historically been the way to survive economically. They may be a feature of urban British life, but the inequalities and separation they signify are not caused by those that inhabit these spaces. And separation from the wider populace is also, seen from the 'other' perspective, a logical social reaction to lack of provision, and a lack of acceptance of differences. But of course, the crucial issue now is how these spaces also have become mini-cultures of their own (as if multiculturalism could mean anything else in practice!), particularly in relation to Muslim identities and the practices that these communities engage in. It is also not a wild claim to make when I say that the British Muslim is now a vilified character, less than ten years after its emergence into the discourse of Britishness. I am sure I don't even have to iterate the spiraling descent of this discursive transformation but think of the horror at the 7/7 bombers[11] being British and of the recent controversies around women wearing the veil in Western societies, exemplified in Britain.[12]

My experience of this identity is governed by my own semi-detached attitude to identification as a British Muslim. I have never been comfortable with that explicitly religious identification, although certainly these days it is used to define and characterize a culture even though many within that group are divided by national identities such as Pakistani and Bangladeshi. My own memories of growing up in Bristol also mark out more of a cultural identity rather than religious one. Furthermore, although we were different in many ways – what food we ate at home, what language we spoke, and of course, our skin, we were also largely westernized, going to school, learning English as our first language, playing with the other kids on the street and in each other's homes. My only concerns around identity would have been whether I was going to be Starsky or Hutch in playground re-enactments.[13] Not so, I think for my parents' generation. They of course were concerned for us to do well in school, although they themselves had neither the experience nor the cultural resources to participate much in helping with either our homework or parent-teacher relationships. However, they were also concerned to make us aware of our ethnic culture, and in particular, my memories evoke my mother taking on this responsibility.

Needless to say, as a student I was a failure – neither motivated nor respectful of the need to learn the written Bengali language, or to speak Bengali consistently at home. And my imagination of the future had no particular direction, but was certainly not working in restaurants or running a shop, which seemed to be all that the Bengali men did. But I was pretty much left alone, a second son having nowhere near the expectations of a first, and regardless, not expected to carry the burden of family respectability as the girls were. As I grew older – I hesitate to say matured – I could, and did, cut my hair into the required buzz cut, stay out late, even drank with my friends, all in that void of parental half-knowledge and denial. But I also became aware of the divisions between genders, divisions mostly of different types of labor: domestic labor, emotional labor and the labor of responsibility. Identities, sociologically speaking, are twofold: they are both the self-representation we choose to adopt, inhabit and mould, and cultural historical categories that are assigned to us. Although it is right to distinguish 'identities' from the traditional sociological concept of 'roles' precisely because they signify a self-description first and foremost, they do not exist solely as interiority. Identities do not simply come from or exist solely within; they are a social resource, dependent on the possibilities of politics, culture and time and, in their very act of declaration, they become part of these social possibilities. And the current possibilities of Muslim identity are not positive ones; particularly in Britain, it seems that there has been a remarkably quick shift from embrace to abjection. If identities are historically specific, they must also change through time, particularly as we inhabit them and as the possibilities of history affect us. History, it seems to me, has moved in opposite directions when it comes to Muslims, particularly in relation to women's identity.

And this is interesting to me because my own identity as gay and Bengali has also pushed and pulled me, shattering any expectations of linear progression I had towards liberation, towards integration, towards the secular equality that democracy promises. Rather, in the current political climate, it has rendered me unable to exist comfortably as 'Western', when I had thought all along that as a gay man, I could not exist as Bengali, as Muslim.

Gender

The idea that circulates in the West is that Muslim identity is inherently repressive for women. The debates on the veil over the last few years can be understood in this way since one element of this discourse is that the veil represents patriarchal control, both within the marriage and wider community. From Susan Moller Okin's query 'is multi-culturalism bad for women?' (1999), to the deployment of the 'imperiled Muslim woman' in justifications for the War on Terror (Razack, 2008), we have seen a steady iteration of women's freedom and equality with Western 'values'. Certainly, through most of my young adulthood, I thought the same, although in truth I am not sure I could articulate that as Muslim as opposed to Bengali culture. Women were the barometers of cultural practice, and they were always two steps behind men in their freedoms. That is how I saw it, and I felt conversely distanced from the expectations of masculinity – providing, marrying, having children, being tough, stoic, leading (or controlling?) the women. I identified with the emotional openness of women, with the domestic labor they performed, with their abilities and duties to keep life going, by providing, managing, raising the children and, most of all, as we grew to adolescence, struggling to communicate, struggling to understand the very different lives we led or tried to lead, as teenage and westernized youth, but still Bengali, still part of our culture.

In preparing the original talk in 2005 I tried to think through some issues that had been evident to me for some time but are absolutely refracted through my development of an intellectual career focused on sexuality and the inequalities of sexual identities. Being a PhD student supervised by the materialist heterosexual feminist Stevi Jackson gave me enormous time and guidance to read and absorb the theories that linked institutionalized heterosexuality with the stigma and oppression of homosexuality. The vast wealth of academic literatures in this area and producing my own research contributions have helped me to make sense of my youthful identification with women, with women's writing such as Walker's and with the lives I saw being led in my family; how not wanting to become a 'real' man may have led me towards homosexuality. However, there has been a change in how the women I know identify, and that has affected my sense of identity, suggesting to me that my youthful self-definition against the Bengali/Muslim identity was too simplistic and remained unrefined during my initial intellectual career when I was focused much more on how *I* was oppressed. Let me talk now through some of these reasons.

First, gender is a social division – it is relational and depends absolutely on the notion that we have two groups which are defined through an exploitative relationship. Even as I saw the oppressions for Bengali women, I derived much freedom from being a Bengali man.

I have fled the constraints of that culture – or so I liked to think – but I did so by taking the freedoms I could expand as a man. Furthermore, as most feminisms have always understood, 'woman' is not a unitary or universal experience, and it is similarly important to understand that masculinity is not monolithic, but is divided through class and ethnicity, and men have to become men, as women are compelled to become women. Thus, men have the same impetus to inhabit their identity – the same power of expectation operates, although of course, the routes to masculinity largely depend on the exploitation of women. Beauvoir was correct to say that one is not born a woman (1949) but the point was to focus on how culture compelled women into femininity. In Bengali culture, it seems to me that women could not but become women – there was no other choice, but I had thought less about what happens when men fail to become men. What happens when structures of globalized capitalism and racism deny routes of advancement to whole ethnic groups of men? How does their power in relation to women become affected?

Was I wrong to reject the whole culture and religion? Certainly it has constraints and responsibilities, but these are of gender and culture, not of religion; or rather, religion often becomes the post hoc rationalization of existing cultural norms. And these seem to be changing. Women in my family now have expectations of women's rights, of women's access to education, jobs, and independence, and this occurs from within the cultural framework of being both Bengali and Muslim. Is this the benign influence of the West, or is it the sensible adaptation to resources and opportunities that were not there before the politics of feminism? For example, in common with many other ethnic groups and whites, Bengali boys are doing less well adapting to the new post-industrial nexus of education/employment. Whilst they hang tough, speaking hip hoplish about BMWs, bitches and bling, the girls drive past them in both expectations and achievement.

Do women inhabit the power of identity differently – are women better, because they have always had to be, at resistance? Creatively merging slivers of power to accelerate their lives beyond the apparent limits of 'femininity'? For the women in my family, across generations, the possibilities were seemingly contradictory – I do recall the identities of the 1970s and 1980s, and they were, by and large defined in terms of our extended family identities; Western adoptive, perhaps not completely assimilative, but certainly freer in the sense of there being fewer traditional constraints for women, and more encouragement to explore and mix in the new culture – indeed, there was little alternative since communities were not strong enough in number or voice to create much more than social gatherings at houses and restaurants. My mother smoked – how terribly modern – and she dressed in Western clothes as well as traditional saris; she often went out with us socially, but she always had the dinner ready as well. My sisters went out, but more circumspectly.

I failed to become a man, a proper Bengali man, in the most fundamental way possible. But in fact, I had privileges over the other men, the other boys of my age; a private school scholarship education and eventually university (both funded by the national government in stark contrast to the current austerity-justified withdrawal of the state from liberal arts education in the UK); an overwhelmingly white, English and Scots world when I experienced it but one where I could fit in relatively easily, having learned the middle class liberal codes, knowledges and cultures at my private school and absorbing them more at university. In the absence of wanting to be a real Bengali man, it was possible for me to become gay, not to choose homosexuality in some casual performative way, but to live in a culture which had begun to provide space for association and recognition of existence. But the existence is a totalizing identity – not just a sexual preference, so, although I am sure I was not born a homosexual, I certainly had no choice but to become one, or rather, wholly 'one', once I had stepped through the veil of heterosexuality. Although homo-sex exists in Bengali culture, it does not exist as a social identity, one which individuals can identify with and inhabit. Moving across culture, space and most of all, through time – a journey from a pre-modern world to one about to enter post-modernity has had consequences for my family and for me, allowing me to become something they could not have imagined as Bengali.

Those who migrate do so in search of a better life, particularly for economic opportunity, but mostly for security, not to deny indigenous people or established settlers their own means of getting by. But they did not bargain for the world to change as much as it has in the latter half of the twentieth century, for fiscal crises in Western states heralding the withdrawal of the state from social provision, from the routes to success through education being affected so much by this issue. And of course, culture has gone from being, literally, black and white, to bursting out in full color – multiculturalism exists not simply as a political goal, but as everyday lived experience. Concurrently, gay culture has emerged in the West, as have public debates and expectations of women's equality. Whilst they may welcome the latter, as I see women doing in Bengali culture, they must resent the former – that identity that I embody – easily, or lazily, understood as the corruption of the West.

I cannot imagine how different this world must seem for those of my mother's generation, those from 'pre-modernity', but neither am I seduced by the notion that the journey through modern time is linear, or, put it another way, that the advent of difference is simply liberal democratic progress in its inevitable motion so that we will, eventually, just all 'get along'. Along with the explosion of sexual and ethnic and racial difference has come the inevitable normalizations within those communities – establishing and practicing their cultural norms in more institutionalized ways. The advent of settled, secure Bengali communities, with generations of families, links with institutions such as councils and police, and the money to help fund Mosques, extra schooling in the Quran and Arabic, and a stronger political identification as Muslims can but inevitably produce greater challenges to other differences that have been establishing themselves during this same period – most pertinently gay culture.

I saw this change – this active present normalization of 'tradition' in my own family and the wider community in Bristol, both of Bengalis and, in my later home town of Glasgow, within the Pakistani community there. Women look different, wearing less Western clothing and more traditional Eastern attire, covering their heads more and less prone to wearing saris as well. It seems that these communities, including my family, have become much more Muslim. Some of my aunts would not have their photos taken at my brother's wedding a few years back – a very traditional Muslim idea that only Allah should create the human image. My nieces learned Arabic when younger and they were forbidden junk food treats – once my main method of bribery. Are all those women I looked up to, all those women who helped me, even when I became the ultimate other, are they all now Muslim, over and above being Bengali?

My mother's garden

It would be easy to say that this Islamification occurred due to 9/11. But that is not quite true. Whilst it is true that the searing heat of that murderous act has burned Muslim identity powerfully into Western consciousness, the consequences for Muslims globally are nuanced to the political context in which they live. Thus, in Britain, whilst many of the women I know see the War on Terror as a cultural and literal war on Islam and the poor who make up the majority of Muslims worldwide, they also understand it as a continuation of the decades-old racism around immigration in the UK. Furthermore, those that I know see their Muslim dress and identity as a positive point of resistance to such discourses – as in so many histories of turning the screw – instead of obliteration, the result is stronger, more confident identification. Moreover, the economic and cultural establishment of Muslim institutions predates the terrorism of 9/11 – it is more accurate to think of the transformation into Muslim identity as an inevitable outcome of time and immigrant integration – this is of course the established and now expected path of immigrants in the West.

The consequences of integration, of multiculturalism are numerous and increasingly difficult, generating controversies of difference between majority/minority and minority/minority communities. One such debate is about state-funded religious education in Britain.[14] Do we deny money based on the separation of church and state and the underlying concerns about the institutionalized schooling of gender divisions? Or do we accept that institutionalized racism within the state system has failed specific ethnic communities, such as Bengalis? Some see the establishment of Muslim schools as a way of guaranteeing educational success, for boys and girls, a haven from the commercialization and sexualization of childhood within Western capitalist culture, a place where the rigidity of religion can be used to achieve the investment of a good education.

I find myself uncertain on such issues, conflicted by my Western liberal secularist instincts and my knowledge that I am the only member of my wider family to make it to college level education, and that was largely due to a private, although publicly funded, high school education. Conflicted by my childhood experience of the culture as expecting less public achievement of women and my knowledge that now, the expectations of girls is that they will and should achieve, both educationally and in work – perhaps this just makes them more like Western women with the famous double burden to achieve good jobs and skills and also to keep their female cultural identity and integrity intact. But the expectations and sense of entitlement is good – my youngest niece announced that she wanted to be class president – but would have to wait until she got to a school that had such American-influenced structures. (Somewhat gloriously, she now has a scholarship to the private school I also attended in the 1980s, where she has enlarged her ambition to be 'head girl' of the whole school). And the difference, I note, is not that women should be or are Muslim for their husbands, for their families, although that is undeniably part of the context, but that women choose adherence, and this sense of identification goes hand in hand with their expectations, of themselves and their daughters, beyond the support or presence of men. I hear them talk about domestic violence, the failure of men in work and education, the need for women to be together, rather than isolated, to rely on themselves and each other, rather than men.

But I find it difficult that I have to understand these issues from the point of view of women who have adopted a stronger sense of Muslim identity within their ever-held Bengali identity. In respecting their choices and resisting the resurgence of racism that Islamophobia has brought, I have also chosen to identify as Muslim in particular circumstances but, in truth, I prefer the vision of us living in multicolored harmony in the 1970s – when the sun always seemed to shine, instead of the dour days of official audits compelling us, interpellating us, as 'Muslim' – what do they really mean? Brown? Arab? Immigrant? Or just this era's 'other', as Turner argues (2002)?[15]

During this time in the 1970s, my father failed in business, and failed in health, carrying with him the effects of what we charmingly call third world afflictions, such as tuberculosis, although I hear that this disease is making a comeback in the West. Of all the places we have lived, my mother talks about this house and time fondly. She talks about the house where we lived, the small council house, with her garden where she grew vegetables, hung out the washing and could manage to clean and house us all, whilst my father was sick, idle and on social security and we were all at school, except my eldest sister, who was working and preparing for the inevitable, at that time, arranged marriage. When she talks of this time and place, it is of the space – how it was manageable, peaceful and my recollections are similar. Apart from the usual childish fears (the large dog at the end of the street), we roamed around the neighborhood at will, afraid neither of strangers or traffic, those twin anxieties of contemporary urban parenting, although I guess now we think of them as pedophiles and SUVs.

And peace. My mother talks of this as a stable time, and I know that she defines it against the recent past and present, one ravaged by deaths and disappointments and the unending worry of the future, the lack of stable marriages, the lack of tradition – of which I have become, in person, both a symbol and reality. After all, which Bengali, which Muslim, would want a gay son? But as I mentioned earlier, we were not particularly Muslim at that time, when I was growing up and later, when I came out. I don't recollect regular praying, only abstaining from foods and drink that are forbidden, and communal cultural events and gatherings that were amongst Bengalis, not all other Muslims. Now this has changed; conformity to dresscodes and religious observance are much stronger, and the identity is much more 'traditional' Muslim, although not, in my understanding, traditional South Asian. And the discourse of 9/11 with its stark oppositions of the West and Islam has produced a double movement – as the Muslim identity becomes more stigmatized, so more people are moving into it, partly through the progress of history and communities, partly through self-identification and reaction to disappointments of the West.

Is the best irony that Muslim identity is giving women a sense of security? A sense of their own potential, and allowing them to articulate demands and expectations, both from Muslim men, and from the wider world so obsessed with their identity? When my mother talks of the time and space of that house, and her garden, she talks of security, but what she means, I think, is the peace of mind that security brings. I have had to accept, that after journeying myself through cultures and time, perhaps the peace the women I know need can be found in a space where religion, culture, self-respect and self-worth grow side by side. Perhaps contemporary Islamophobia renders mainstream cultural spaces uncertain and insecure, and they need to seek out their own gardens, their own Islam. Whilst I may not be able to give meaning to being the 'faithful one', I remember that Islam has many meanings. Whilst the literal translation of the word 'islam' may be 'submission' to the will of God, it can also mean – and invokes such meaning in its universal greeting 'salaam' – quite simply, peace.

Not quite Muslim, not quite gay, towards a queer intersectionality

It's a peace I cannot share. I am not quite Muslim, although I have become much more ready to identify as such in those official audits of self that Stanley describes; going through airports has become a fascinating game of identity interpellation and resistance, for example. My interactionist sense tells me that the official 'they' are often just as uncomfortable with seeing that totalizing identity – I am, after all, a fully fledged label-wearing homosexual and therefore 'Western' – but inevitably, resistance on both sides crumbles or dissolves into the easy, or secure two-step of interpellation and then identification as Muslim. But I won't ever be the 'Momin' my father named me for because of my gayness, especially when the political opposition of the West and Islam associates the former with women's equality and as Waites points out, more hesitantly with sexual diversity (2008). I may feel more often interpellated as Muslim, and react positively, as a mode of resistance by being Muslim for that interaction, but that consequence of the War on Terror does not negate or dissolve the memories of other terrors; the terror of coming out, causing pain to those I love and terrifyingly, risking the loss of their love, as well as continuing to live detached from their everyday lives.

But am I quite gay enough? In truth, being gay has indeed meant being Western in my experience. Perhaps not inevitably being white, but certainly being 'modern' – having to choose and socially construct a life in opposition to tradition, religion and institutionalized heterosexuality. And by default, modern culture has been 'white' modern culture: Western societies during multiculturalism and gay liberation have not easily accepted either, but gay culture has often mirrored the uncertainties of valuing ethnic difference even as it claimed the validity of sexual difference. Our desires, our icons, our lifestyles represented within commercialized gay culture have been and remain overwhelmingly a hegemonic version of white, youthful masculinity. Whilst existing in that culture has not provoked terrors on the same scale as being racialized or coming out, I have always known that I am 'different' from the 'norm', different from the expected.

But I believe that being gay, along with an academic career focused on sexuality, has given me the experience and intellect to understand and challenge 'norms' and sometimes to resist them. Being a gay academic has allowed me to be a 'queer theory' intellectual, but then, perhaps my becoming gay could only be so with the inflections of my ethnicity, even or particularly when I was resisting those identifications. So my narrative is a queer narrative, illuminating the inability to be ontologically secure but thus being productively problematic, akin to the way Cosslett et al. characterize feminist engagement with autobiography as 'disruptive interdisciplinarity' (2000: 1). Disruptive as a queer identity would be, should be – but, entwined within my narrative, or rather constituting it, are those issues of gender norms that render me gay, and my gayness so problematic. And journeying through those norms have made me reflect upon the disruptive identities that Muslim women now seem to embody, challenging both secularism and feminism as Motha puts it (2007). The women I discuss would not see themselves as 'queer', but in the presentation of agency I have given, they are challenging the negative stereotypes of Islam and women and disrupting the totalizing oppositions of West/East, freedom/oppression, white Western feminism/Muslim female subordination.

That is not *my* story, but my narrative directs us towards these issues, suggesting, I claim, how narratives can illuminate the intersections between realms of the social, how understanding these intersections of identity dimensions is also inevitably about the possibilities and limits of identity within the historical political contexts of what Islamic identity means in our post-colonial, multicultural, post-9/11 world. In this world where totalizing identities are being used to mark Muslims in opposition to the West – and its rights for 'humans' – interventions of this 'queer' kind, that disrupt such binaries are ever more urgent. Whilst I rage against the gradual but steady iteration of Muslim abjection, I see in my experience – limited, dislocated, removed from Muslim identity – complexities, differences, resistances to what being a Muslim woman might mean, or what being a Muslim might mean to women and how that 'queer' perspective has been developed through my gayness or more properly, my queerness. And that brings me peace of a sort. Peace in the knowledge that I, and perhaps those similarly in my position, can productively illuminate the intersections and complexities of current oppositions and binaries within Muslim communities and families, gay communities and culture, and wider Western political culture and discourses; caught as we are – at every level – between terror, belonging and love.

2
Islam *versus* Homosexuality *as* Modernity

Introduction

Can we really doubt that Islam is opposed to homosexuality? Even if we cannot pin down *why* we think this, I am pretty certain that most of us *do* think this. The 'we' here is perhaps uncertain, but I have in mind most Muslims, most LGBTIQ[1] people, Western and Eastern publics and politicians. I discussed my complicity with aspects of such beliefs in the previous chapter but I also reflected upon how personal experiences derive from the difficulties of negotiating a social world where racism, Islamophobia, and homophobia intersect. Thus, as with the individual struggle to be a queer Muslim, so too do general populations use wider culture to make sense of their identities and beliefs. The plural 'we' therefore derives understandings from the 'why', and so in this chapter, I unpack the ways in which contemporary political discourses ultimately frame the opposition of homosexuality and Muslim cultures. This is not to ignore the historical differences in Western and Eastern cultures but it is a rejection of using those cultural divisions as a starting point. Instead, I argue that the contemporary *political* is a dominant framework through which the cultural and historical is currently understood. Moreover, this politics is widely conceived, drawing on issues of civilizational 'clash' between 'Western' nations and Muslim societies; characterizations of what progressive governance means within this context; assumptions about the inherent values of democracy; the relationship of religion to democratic governance and cultural values and the problems of multiculturalism in the West. I argue therefore, that we have to understand the social significance of sexual diversity and LGBTIQ rights within this intersecting political context; a context that is tautologically creating the cultural divides it purports merely to describe and thus structuring the perceived opposition of Islam and sexual diversity.

The underlying theme that weaves this politics together is a conceptualization of the modern world as a Western one, initiated by the Enlightenment exclusively in the West, and resulting in a dynamic movement, a momentum of *progress* towards more rational governance that has inevitably led to greater political and social equality, underpinned (often implicitly) by wealthy capitalist economic systems. Moreover, the fundamental assumption about modernity as Western is that its social formation is exceptional and that is the reason why it has pushed European societies (and their offspring white settler societies) to surpass other civilizations in their inevitable triumph over the rest of the world (Bhambra, 2007; Callinicos, 2007). I begin, therefore, with a discussion of how Islamic 'otherness' has come to dominate Western political and cultural discourses, demonstrating the key aspects of its development and how these connect to historical accounts of fundamental differences in modernity between the West and East. I focus on the primacy given to notions of democracy and equality within such accounts, showing how the historical inconsistencies in the emergence and development of both are ignored in favor of creating a narrative that positions these as inherent values and inevitable outcomes of Western modernity. I move on to discuss gender equality because it has become a key test of democratic credentials, both in rendering Muslim cultures other to the West and in doing the same to Western Muslim immigrant populations. I suggest that these contemporary debates about multiculturalism versus gender equality are important not only because they derive from the wider political discourse of Islamic otherness, but because issues of sexual diversity are subsequently derived from this understanding of gender politics. I point out, however, that LGBTIQ issues in general, but particularly homosexuality, have a less certain and less consistent presence in accounts of Western democratic equality and therefore we must remember that *absence* is the most common condition of LGBTIQ issues in the West. Perhaps precisely because discussions of LGBTIQ equality are uncommon in Western democracy, I demonstrate that when sexual diversity is present in civilizational debates, it is cast as a defining feature of Western exceptionalism, thus drawing it into the heart of definitions of Muslim incompatibility with modernity. In conclusion, I suggest, that we should not ignore that gay rights discourses and identities in particular, and LGBTIQ issues more generally, are drawn into a civilizational and racialized discourse of opposition to Muslim cultures. This is not to excuse the homophobia in

Muslim cultures but to argue that we must recognize that gay rights can be used to promote Islamophobia and to question how useful or productive that is for the goals of sexual diversity, particularly if we want to challenge homophobia within Muslim cultures. I am conscious that I do not spend most of the chapter discussing sexuality; discussions of homosexualities in both Muslim and Western cultures, and of Muslim homosexualities in the West, occupy the subsequent chapters. However, my aim in this chapter is to precede those analyses with an understanding of the contemporary political formations that are the defining context for them, so that we might better work towards resolutions of the positioning of Islam versus homosexuality.

The drumbeats of Islamic 'otherness'

I do not think that anyone can doubt that Islam as a religion and Muslims as its adherents are under intense global scrutiny. Nor is this a sympathetic enquiry when conducted by Western culture but an examination that is, above all, attempting in various ways to explain the 'otherness' of Muslims. Indeed, Muslim identity has become *the* semiotic marker for all that is opposed to Western values. For example, during the 2008 American Presidential campaign, the *New Yorker* magazine published an issue with a cover that depicted Barack and Michelle Obama celebrating in the Oval Office dressed as radical, Osama bin Laden-worshipping, American flag-burning Muslims. Both Obama's campaign and that of John McCain – the Republican contender – simply described the cartoon as tasteless and inappropriate to the tenor of the contest for the Presidency and thus avoided any recognition of the satire in the image and the discourse that made the satire so sharp: that to be thought of as Muslim in the USA had become a cultural accusation of 'un-Americanness' *and* that 'Muslim' could serve as a trope for general racialization in a cultural era where people could not directly attack Obama's ethnicity.[2] Despite their disdain, the Obama campaign did make it clear that their candidate was not a Muslim, but a good old-fashioned Christian. The drumbeats of this discourse of Muslim otherness have obviously been louder since 9/11 but they have existed for some time, perhaps, indeed, for most of 'modern' time and not just within popular and political culture,[3] but within academia as well. I hesitate to cite Weber in the context of this discussion, given that he was the most skeptical of the idea of progress of the classical sociologists, but his description of Islam, Hinduism, Buddhism and Taoism as 'impediments' to the development of the modern rational capitalism – in contrast with ascetic Protestantism in the West – demonstrates that the identification of Muslim culture as inimical to the development of modernity is there at the very beginnings of sociological thinking on what constitutes modern life (Weber, 2002: 200). Of course, Said's critique of orientalism included academic knowledge produced during Weber's time as central to the legitimizing projects of Western powers over their colonial possessions and peoples, constituting the latter as the subordinate 'other' (1978), and Bhambra points out that whilst Weber did attempt 'to move beyond a unilinear, directional interpretation of historical progression, [he] did not escape the evaluative bias of the West being understood as being at the highest point of development ...' (2007: 34). Indeed, Bhambra argues that the very episteme of sociology was inevitably geared towards understanding modernity as a rupture that put Western civilization on a fundamentally different trajectory than that of other regions. These intellectual traditions of sociological understanding have informed the more recent historical and political academic writings on Islam and Muslim culture, ideas that preceded 9/11 but whose legitimacy has been bolstered by that attack and Western responses to it. Throughout, the overriding Western political argument has been consistent with the drumbeats of 'otherness'. As Turner puts it in his critique of these discourses of civilizational opposition:

> With the collapse of organised communism in 1989–92, western politics lost its Other. During the last decade, Islam, and in particular fundamentalist Islam, has been constructed as the unambiguous enemy of western civilization. For Samuel Huntingdon (1993, 1996), the clash is inevitable and deeply embedded in two different cultural systems, one that separates God and Caesar, and one that pulls them together. (Turner, 2002: 109)

In his original article and subsequent book (1996), Huntingdon proposed that 'culture' would be the new source of conflict post-Cold War, manifested through opposing 'civilizations' which he defined as 'Western, Confucian, Japanese, Islamic, Hindu, Slavic-Orthodox, Latin American and possibly African', defined by history, language, culture, tradition and religion (1993: 23). This academic perspective has found political expression in the subsequent discourses used to frame the War on Terror, distilled to focus exclusively on Islamic culture versus the West. As Turner demonstrates, Huntingdon shares this thesis of civilizational clash with Fukuyama's argument in *The End of History and the Last*

Man (1992) which focused more precisely on the values and practices of liberal democracy and a secular state tied to modern capitalism.[4] Huntingdon also drew upon scholarship about the Islamic world, most obviously the work of historian Bernard Lewis, who described Muslim resentment of the West as a reaction to the historical decline of Islamic cultures during modernity, and therefore the current enmity as '... no less than a clash of civilizations – the perhaps irrational but surely historic reactions of an ancient rival against our Judeo-Christian heritage, our secular present, and the worldwide expansion of both' (Lewis, 1990: 59).

Turner challenges these academic arguments in three ways: he criticizes the monolithic view of Islam and Muslim culture they contain; he identifies the absence of any understanding of contemporary globalization and migration as structural forces that are as powerful as 'civilizational cultures'; and he excavates the contradictory political inheritance of these ideas. On this last point, he demonstrates that 'While American policy is clearly influenced by the Huntingdon thesis, it may be that contemporary politics owes more to Schmitt and Strauss than to Huntingdon and Fukuyama. The language employed by the Bush administration closely parallels the political philosophy of Schmitt and Strauss, who have had a direct impact on American conservative republicanism.' (2002: 104). Turner dissects the political philosophy of the early twentieth century German legal scholar and philosopher Carl Schmitt at first, demonstrating how it is heavily influenced by his Roman Catholicism and focused on the sovereignty of a state as defined by its ability to act decisively, something Schmitt thinks is compromised in liberal democratic systems, because of their pluralism and 'deliberative and consultative approach' (2002: 104). In developing this position, Schmitt drew upon Weber's argument for plebiscitary democracy, embodied in a strong leader as a way of overcoming political bureaucratic inertia, identifying the Reich president as the key position to promote in the context of the crisis-ridden Weimar republic, eventually joining the Nazi party and supporting their regime (Callinicos, 2007: 174–177; Turner, 2002). Turner shows how these conservative theories of the political paved the way for the emphasis on the friend/foe dichotomy that has been so central to the War on Terror. It is political struggle, against a common enemy, that provides coherence and legitimacy to a sovereign state and so the requirements of strong sovereignty are that there are 'friends' and 'enemies'.

Liberal democracy is therefore a problem for sovereignty and decisive leadership in Schmitt's ideas and those of Leo Strauss, who was influenced by Schmitt and was subsequently influential in the development of contemporary neo-conservative thought exemplified by Huntingdon and Fukuyama.[5] Strauss was a contemporary of Schmitt's who went into exile in the USA, teaching at the University of Chicago and influencing a large part of American neo-conservative thought with his views, similar to Schmitt, that the pluralist and thus relativist politics of liberal democracy needed to be replaced with strong state, morally grounded, policies that recognized the fundamental superiority of capitalism and democracy. Strauss is credited with a direct influence on a whole generation of American conservatives, including those who were involved in the think tank Project for a New American Century and those within the cabinet of George W. Bush's presidency (Kepel, 2006). Moralism, based on a civilizational distinction, is therefore at the heart of contemporary political orientalism and it has a problematic relationship to the values and practices of democracy, particularly the secularism that liberal democracy represents.

Western modernity is identified with the Protestant work ethic, whereby individuals came to believe that both working hard and receiving the rewards of industrious individual accumulation were a sign of salvation, of being one of the 'chosen' who would go to heaven. Although Weber clearly argued that the widespread secular diffusion of this idea is what provides the critical mass cultural shift to a modern work ethic, it is nonetheless derived from an ascetic, puritan, individualized form of Reformation Christianity. The irony became that this Protestant individualism actually undermined a moral collective framework in its affinity with capitalism because the rewards of the work ethic became more important to wider populations than its initial motivation, thus accelerating secularism in modern life, albeit as an unintended consequence. Modern capitalism therefore spread beyond the confines of puritan Protestant nations, cultures and populations and, moreover, this secular diffusion of the work ethic was bolstered by the 'scientific' revolution of the time, whereby empirical methods and technologies were gradually discovering understandings and explanations for the physical world that displaced the need to believe in a supernatural 'creator'. Increasing secularism eventually breeds cultural relativism because dominant norms such as a country's historical religious ideology are rendered less important, and ideas of liberal neutrality take hold, thus permitting the recognition of differences like multiculturalism and indeed, sexual diversity.[6] In contrast to these developments in modernity, Schmitt wanted the return of an ethical life: 'It was political struggle itself that promised the restoration of an ethical life. Schmitt wanted to criticize liberalism on the grounds that it created a life without values in which individuals were seduced by the amusements and entertainments of modern culture. Without the political, life was merely an amusement and lacked seriousness. Religion, which was pre-eminently the serious life, has been undermined by a secular culture of amusements.' (Turner, 2002: 107). Thus, whilst the friend/foe dichotomy is mapped onto civilizations and thus constitutes the discourse of Islamic otherness and Islamophobia, there is actually a contradiction at the heart of the clash of civilizations thesis, since it derives from a conservative political philosophy that actually values religion as central to a moral political life, and decries democratic deliberation, inclusiveness, and secularism.

This contradiction is not dealt with in the academic arguments that propose the 'clash', but rather it is ignored in favor of mapping the friend/foe dichotomy onto assumptions about Western civilization, capitalist culture and liberal democracy as a fundamental teleological aspect of modernity. Indeed, it is those aspects of Western decline that Schmitt and Strauss most despised that are brought to the fore in the civilizational dialectic: liberal pluralist democracy and modern rational capitalism. Turner suggests that Barber's book *Jihad vs McWorld* (2001) captures the opposition of secular capitalist consumer life and the resurgence of 'tribal' identities (including religious fundamentalism) more clearly than either Huntingdon or Fukuyama. Whilst Barber is not part of the neo-conservative strand, and he is clear that he uses Jihad only as an exemplar of global non-rational, anti-democratic politics,[7] he nonetheless replays the oppositions about Islam and modernity, assumptions that are there throughout the more directly conservative works by Fukuyama, Huntingdon and Lewis that have been discussed above. Indeed, they all are champions of democracy or rather, liberal democracy, but Barber is more astute in recognizing the dangers of liberal democracy allied to rampant capitalism, describing the danger as a new form of totalitarianism: 'As once political totalism rationalized *its* dominion by reference to its supposed association with freedom – the government of the proletariat was to usher in a communist age of pure freedom – so today markets rationalize their dominion over every other sector of life by appealing to the supposedly manifold liberties of consumer choice.' (2001: 295). Barber thus recognizes the sociological context of contemporary Western modernity as economic as well as merely political and recognizes that there may be tensions between these aspects, something which is not critically dealt with by neo-conservative thinkers in their current invocation of Western modernity versus the orient.

Many others have demonstrated the historical development of orientalism that underpins the focus on Islamic otherness and its manifestations and I cannot add anything useful to these welcome critiques[8] although I return to them in the chapters below. Rather, I want to focus on the assumptions about modernity, modernization and democracy that are central to this orientalism because those aspects more directly affect the ways in which gender and sexual politics get drawn into the drumbeats of Islamic otherness.

Democracy as Western exceptionalism

Orientalist assumptions in the service of neo-conservative frameworks do not acknowledge the sociological complexity of modernity but rather emphasize the political aspects of Western governance, either taking for granted the capitalist context in which this developed or subordinating it to the development of secularism in the relationship between state and civil society. Current Western democratic systems are cast as having a consistent, principled lineage dating from *before* the transformations of modernity, and thus their pre-existence permits the correct management and development of the rupture that modernity entails. The Age of Enlightenment in Europe from the eighteenth century onwards is identified as a central formative precursor to modernity. Often referred to as the Age of Reason, historians of politics, philosophy and sociology regard this period as providing the intellectual basis for the subsequent attempts to understand modernity. The significance of the Enlightenment is that it culminated in a fundamental shift in ways of thinking about societies, politics and human nature, particularly in identifying the limits of previous dominant knowledge on these topics, largely derived from the Renaissance rediscovery and interpretation of Classical texts. The influence of Enlightenment thinking impacted attempts to understand significant changes in European societies, but also suggested that these changes were a fundamental break with previous historical development, and thus, it was 'a new age that no longer seeks to derive its legitimacy from principles derived from the past, but rather offers its own self-justification'. (Callinicos, 2007: 13). This age was understood by Enlightenment thinkers as a definitively different, 'modern' period. Modernity itself remains a theoretically contentious term in various disciplines but, sociologically speaking, it is empirically defined by the expansion of Western imperialism (begun in the sixteenth century), the advent of modern rational capitalism through thoroughly commercial societies, complex divisions of labor, industrialization, urbanization and the application of rationalization to bureaucratic organization, particularly in the realm of government expansion (Turner, 1990). On the side of knowledge, it is also identified with the development of scientific approaches to studying the physical world, subsequently applied to the study of human societies (exemplified in the first wave of sociological theory). Intellectually, what characterizes modernity is therefore an orientation towards its present and future, rather than its past, and an assumption of exceptionalism in the direction that social development takes in the West. As the Marxist historian Hobsbawm puts it:

> ... the global triumph of capitalism is the major theme of history in the decades after 1848 ... a society which believed that economic growth rested on competitive private enterprise ... resting naturally on the sound foundations of a bourgeoisie ... ever-growing enlightenment, reason and human opportunity ... a world of continuous and accelerating material and moral progress. (Hobsbawm, 1975: 1)

Considerations of democracy and equality are notably absent from any empirical description, with both arriving in gradual stages and in particularistic forms of franchise, procedures and application. Indeed, in his historical review of *Models of Democracy* (1987), Held points out that whilst democracy has become the dominant and popular form of governance by the late twentieth century, its existence is less than a century old in terms of modern, mass-franchise representative government. This historical reality does not undermine the claims that modernity represents a radical historical rupture, and may indeed reinforce it, but it does suggest that democracy is a relatively new aspect of the momentum of modernity and not necessarily inherent within its origins. Given that democratic governance has emerged gradually and in specific socio-economic contexts, we must think about the Western form of democracy that exists as a *particular* form, one that is now described as liberal democracy and involves limited participation and limited intervention by the state in the civil and economic realms.[9] Arguments that posit democracy as an inevitable part of modernity are only convincing if they acknowledge that the needs of a newly emergent bourgeoisie produced political pressure for change in governance, and that consequent changes emphasized liberalism over and above social equality. Liberalism is in fact a more consistent part of democracy than what we think of now as equality in the West (which only recently includes gender and ethnic equality and, less consistently, sexual diversity). Liberalism began essentially as a philosophy that wrestled with the nature of the relationship between the state and its citizens, developed largely in reaction to absolutist monarchies and indeed drawing upon rediscovered accounts of ancient democracy in Athens in particular (Callinicos, 2007; Held, 1987). Whilst equality as a principle is there from early liberal thought, it is framed narrowly, as equality of franchise to participate in governance, rather than as forms of social equality and thus liberal equality excluded women for its early existence (Held, 1987, Phillips, 1993), notwithstanding claims for their inclusion (Wollstonecraft, 1792 [1972]). Moreover, liberalism was concerned with the reform of government by monarchs who derived their authority from religious legitimizations, the keystone of absolutist rule from the demise of the Classical era through to the Enlightenment.[10] Thus, challenges to clerical power in both governing institutions and as a source of legitimacy for these, produces secularism as an inevitable part of liberalism, much more so than concerns for social equality. Finally, we must remember that this secularism was heavily influenced by the challenges of Protestant Reformation theology that provided both an emphasis on the individual's relationship with God, rather than their relationship to the institutions and representatives (including monarchs) of the Catholic Church and that this individualism converged with liberal principles demanding the freedom of individuals from absolutist rule. And where was this 'freedom' to be practiced or exercised? In the emergent commercial societies of modern northern Europe as Weber identified.

The history of democracy and equality is therefore a partial rather than universal development; it is in fact, the history of Western liberal capitalist democracy (Held, 1993) and proponents of the clash of civilizations ignore these complexities within modernity, focusing instead on providing a narrative of coherent principles and implementation, with inconsistent acknowledgement of the sociological aspects to their development.[11] They also ignore the difficulties of more recent history, particularly how Western colonial powers refused to apply democratic principles and laws to their colonial subjects when it threatened their imperial power, and how they have consistently supported undemocratic post-colonial regimes throughout the Muslim world because of strategic interests, illustrating again that democratic principles did not override issues of social power.[12] Contemporary political accounts of Muslim cultural otherness that rely heavily on understandings of modernity choose their emphasis politically rather than including the broad sociological picture, and thus include democracy and social equality as key components of both the empirical description of the modern West, and the momentum of modernization, however inaccurate and partial these accounts are. The wider political positioning of Muslims is part of this dialectic of otherness that frames the West as modern, as Muslims as outside of this modernity, both literally and culturally/politically. I go on to consider how within issues of the sexual – both gender and sexuality – these assumptions are to the fore in framing Muslims as outside the rational, reasonable, modern world.

Equality and secularism versus multiculturalism in the context of gender

If democratic governance has become the overriding factor in the discourse dividing the West and the Muslim world, then gender equality has become the major wedge issue that encapsulates this division because it is seen to symbolize secularism, the principle of equality for all individuals, and the openness of Western civil society to social activism and political change. Gender equality is thus a core aspect of the liberal democratic practices and values that Huntingdon cites as definitive of the West and its modernity despite the historical reality that rights for women are very recent additions to the Western democratic settlement. Lewis similarly proposes that Muslim civilizations are incompatible with modernity, but in his historical description of the West's ascendance over the Islamic world during modernity, he recognizes that gender equality was entirely absent from European concerns about those 'other' cultures, both during initial cultural engagements and during the period of colonization (2002: 67–73). This should not surprise us since a reorganization of gender divisions into rigid binary forms was a product of modernity, if that is understood as the impact of industrialization, urbanization and the consequent separation of home and workplace. There was a significant consolidation of gender divisions into hierarchical and exploitative forms during the emergence and consolidation of modernity in nineteenth century European societies (Engels, 1942 [1884]; Gilman, 1998 [1898]; Weeks, 1989) and the liberal extension of political equality embraced men first and women later. Gender *inequality* is therefore a more consistent feature of Western modernity than gender equality. Lewis recognizes these limits of liberal democracy in the West but he also argues that many 'liberal' Arab regimes have not promoted women's rights because they have deferred to male public patriarchal opinion instead. Moreover, he suggests that whilst many Muslim cultures sought to modernize to compete with the

West, there was been a cultural rejection of modernization when it is seen as Westernization, and that gender equality has been seen as the latter:

> The emancipation of women, more than any other single issue, is the touchstone of difference between modernization and Westernization. ... The emancipation of women is Westernization; both for traditional conservatives and radical fundamentalists it is neither necessary nor useful but noxious, a betrayal of true Islamic values. (2002: 73)

There is now a dominant discourse that frames gender equality as an inherently Western value. The impact of the gender equality aspect of the 'clash of civilizations' discourse has been significant within the public realm, with controversies of difference on this issue throughout Western countries and in debates about Muslim nations (Fekete, 2006; Phillips and Saharso, 2008; Rizzo et al., 2007), particularly in the political justifications for pre-emptive invasions of Afghanistan and Iraq (Kepel, 2006; Razack, 2008). Razack demonstrates the ways in which 'the policing of Muslim communities in the name of gender equality is now a globally organized phenomenon' (2008: 20), arguing that 'three allegorical figures have come to dominate the social landscape of the "war on terror" and its ideological underpinning of a clash of civilizations: the dangerous Muslim man, the imperilled Muslim woman, and the civilized European ...'(2008: 5). She illustrates the ways in which contemporary discourses of gender inequality within Islam have an orientalist history, particularly during colonialism when the claim of gender emancipation was one part of the justification for colonial suppression and control of less civilized native cultures (McClintock, 1995), regardless of the actual historical inconsistency of action. Gender equality has thus become the marker of the modern West, rendering Muslim cultures outside modernity by virtue of their resistance to this momentum of equality, a resistance both of their patriarchal religious views and their inability to develop secular, liberal state governance. Of course, this ignores the historical and contemporary evidence on how Muslim women in different cultures have managed to engage in debate, resistance and reform of the patriarchalism within their cultures (Rogan, 2009; Yamani, 1996) because that would not serve the politics of the global 'War on Terror'.

The crusade for gender equality is not, however, simply directed outward from the bastions of the West. Indeed, it is within the West that the wedge of gender has become more pointedly drawn into a debate about the problems with multiculturalist developments of secular liberal democracy, echoing the skepticism about the relativism of Western democracy that runs through neo-conservative thought. Discussions of gender have therefore been to the fore in debates on the acceptability of Muslim immigrant populations and the need for a coherent, unified Western culture. As Phillips and Saharso put it in their review of European policy initiatives:

> Across Europe, the discourse and practices of multiculturalism are in crisis ... When we consider what is most commonly offered, in both popular and policy discourse, as evidence of a conflict over fundamental values, we find issues relating to the treatment of girls and women figuring large: women wearing hijab; girls subjected to genital cutting; young people forced by their families into marriage with unknown and unwanted spouses; young women murdered by family members for behaviour said to offend principles of community honour. (Phillips and Saharso, 2008: 291–292)[13]

Within feminist thinking, this incompatibility was a subject of debate before 9/11, controversially raised by Okin in her essay, 'Feminism and Multiculturalism' (1998), in which she focused on religious minorities in the West in general but illustrated this with a consistent emphasis on Muslim communities.[14] Introducing her premise that recent decades have seen a shift from assimilationist policies in the West to multiculturalism (for both immigrants and indigenous peoples) and acknowledging the variety in different national contexts, she argues that nonetheless '... one issue recurs across all contexts, though it has gone virtually unnoticed in current debate: what should be done when the claims of minority cultures or religions clash with the norm of gender equality that is at least formally endorsed by liberal states (however much they continue to violate it in their practices)?' (1999: 9). As a democratic theorist, Okin is focused on the recent shift in democratic practices in Western societies, which has seen the largely contemporaneous advent of gender equality legislation and multiculturalist policies. She argues that proponents of the group rights model of multicultural policies have ignored two key issues: first, that minority cultural groups have gendered divisions within them and second, that these group cultural rights ignore what happens in the private or domestic sphere, where many gendered inequalities are practiced and experienced. In arguing this case, she concurs with the understandings of democracy as Western exceptionalism and she locates the possibility of gender equality firmly within this form of governance:

> While virtually all of the world's cultures have distinctly patriarchal pasts, some – mostly, though by no means exclusively, Western liberal cultures have departed far further from them than others. Western cultures, of course, still practice many forms of sex discrimination ... But women in more liberal cultures are, at the same time, legally guaranteed many of the same freedoms and opportunities as men. In addition, most families in such cultures, with the exception of some religious fundamentalists, do not communicate to their daughters that they are of less value than boys, that their lives are to be confined to domesticity and service to men and children, and that their sexuality is of value only in marriage, in the service of men, and for reproductive ends. This situation, as we have seen, is quite different from that of women in many of the world's other cultures, including many of those from which immigrants to Europe and North America come. (1999: 16–17)

Okin is therefore setting up the potential incompatibility of these two recent democratic developments, essentially arguing that the range of laws and policies designed for gender equality may conflict with and should take precedence over cultural rights for immigrant groups: 'It is by no means clear, from a feminist point of view, that minority group rights are "part of the solution". They may well exacerbate the problem.' (1999: 22). She goes on to muse whether it might be better if an oppressive patriarchal culture become 'extinct'. Okin thus positions any religious ethnic culture that she deems to be patriarchal as evolutionarily redundant, unwelcome in comparison to the formal evolution of Western liberal democracy as the preferred model, and seems to welcome any help to encourage this social selection (though she wrote before gendered justifications of the 'War on Terror'). I confess to still being offended every time I read this essay. As I discussed in Chapter 1, the realities of women's lives in Muslim cultures are much more complex than Okin admits, or even attempts to consider. Moreover, her understanding of how minority cultures exist within majority societies is simplistic in its dichotomy. In her response to criticisms published collectively after her initial essay, she reins in her comments to suggest that she was not 'recommending the active extinction or wholesale condemnation of cultures' (1999: 117), but rather that she was thinking about how assimilation changes cultures, particularly when individuals interact with and adopt 'alternative' cultures. This, in my view, does not quite get her off the hook of effectively ignoring the power relationships between dominant and minority cultures, or of ignoring the reasons why 'minority' women might identify more strongly with their ethnic cultures rather than gender politics in this context.[15]

The responses to Okin's argument have been numerous, both within her book (1999) and more broadly within democratic theory and there are a number of key issues that they raise in relationship to how we think about Islam and issues of the sexual. The central issue of how group rights may privilege the power of men within an ethnic community is one that remains valid and urgent. For example, Anne Phillips attempts to develop a multiculturalism focused on the rights of individuals, not on groups, whilst not denying that ethno-cultural groups have a right to state funding and support but accepting that they will not be representative of all members of that particular culture (2007).[16] Phillips engages in sustained examples to illustrate that the rights of individuals to pursue aspects of their lives in accordance with cultural (as ethnic and/or religious traditions) should be protected, with the usual limits applied in all cases – protection of minors, violence, and those that have been decided by democratic political processes (and she puts acceptance of sexual diversity in this category).[17] However, as Brahm-Levey points out, this challenge to multiculturalism does not mean that multicultural policies have failed, but rather that reified essentialist notions of minority cultures are being interrogated, whilst policies of cultural recognition (including anti-racist and anti-discrimination statutes) have remained as an accepted part of contemporary liberal polities (2009: 77).

He agrees, however, that current concerns with multiculturalism are absolutely identified with reactions to Muslim communities, thus part of the dialectic discussed above, and also how they are largely focused on the regulation of women, and particularly the sexuality of those women.[18] Thus, in the frame of gender, multicultural policies have become a synonym for Muslim cultures and are then positioned against liberal values of equality and, ultimately these policies are seen as potentially subverting the secularism at the heart of liberal democratic systems.[19] These are different concerns than those focused on governance discussed in the previous section, but the point is that this emphasis is still part of the same overall discourse of Islamic otherness, suggesting that the political needs of this current orientalism are more important than any internal consistency on what actually constitutes 'good' democracy. Just as the broad equation of Western culture with a democratic exceptionalism renders Muslim culture as 'other' so too does the framing of gender politics. Indeed, we might say that gender becomes the key wedge issue that separates Muslim from modernity, permitting the exclusion of both Muslim majority cultures from 'civilized' international culture and Muslim immigrants from the citizenship of their Western 'host' nations. We must remember, moreover, that the use of gender equality against multiculturalism in the West serves to critique certain types of democratic practices and versions of social justice; those that stretch beyond formal liberal individual rights to attempt group recognition and cultural pluralism, often based on established evidence that ethnic groups are socially and economically disadvantaged in liberal capitalist societies. The version of gender equality being deployed in the West is therefore a discourse that structures Muslim otherness and a particular version of Western democracy.

When we consider the actual history of gender politics the inconsistencies in this discourse become starkly apparent. The expansion of liberty is linked first and foremost to the development of modern rational capitalism (Held, 1993) whereby preventing state interference with faith and finance took precedence over social equality, despite some early feminist claims for the emancipation of women in the first era of modern democracy (Wollstonecraft, 1972 [1792]). Notions of social justice and equality for specific groups began with working class political organization in the late nineteenth and early twentieth centuries, and only expanded to include women and homosexuals in the last third of the twentieth century, and then only with their self-organization rather than through state-led politics (Dahlerup, 1990; Altman, 1980; Rahman and Jackson, 2010). Gender equality is therefore a relatively recent addition to our self-image as Western, modern and democratic, with the subordination of women in the gender hierarchy being a consistent feature of modernity in the West, in common with non-Western cultures. Moreover, the apex of this hierarchy – masculinity – was constructed in opposition to both femininity and homosexuality, confirming the wealth of research on the ways in which the identity of the stigmatized homosexual is a product of modernity and its gendered processes (Connell, 1987, McIntosh, 1996 [1968], Seidman, 1996). Nonetheless, the framing of Islam outside the West and its modernity is the discourse that conditions our understanding of gender equality and sexual diversity as integral to Western exceptionalism.

Sexual diversity as *the* marker of Islamic otherness?

The narrative of gender equality currently being deployed in the West is indeed a partial one, inevitably so as it is derived from the discourse of democracy, social equality and secularism as foundational elements of modernity despite the historical inconsistencies in this narrative. Moreover, I have argued that these narratives of modernity and gender equality must be understood as fundamentally political formations, primarily serving the needs of the current manifestation of orientalist views of Muslim cultures. In the realm of the sexual, most of these debates have centered on gender but there have also been discourses on the incompatibility of sexual diversity and Muslim culture. For example, Fekete illustrates a re-emergence of anti-immigrant right-wing politics in her analysis of immigration policy prescriptions and public debates around multiculturalism in Europe since 9/11, commenting that:

> Most alarmingly, even some feminists and gay activists are now part of an overtly right-wing consensus that calls for immigration controls specifically targeted at immigrants from the Muslim world. Central to such a process is a generalised suspicion of Muslims, who are characterised as holding on to an alien culture that, in its opposition to homosexuality and gender equality, threatens core European values. (2006: 2)

The question in the heading for this section, however, marks out the difference in how issues of homosexuality are being drawn into the debates around Muslim antipathy to the West. Sociologically speaking, social changes in gender organization and identities have certainly been interdependent with those around homosexuality during modernity (Rahman and Jackson, 2010; Seidman, 1996; Weeks, 1989), but the political deployment of the gender equality discourse against multiculturalism does not fully explain the existence of homosexuality in this context. We may think of the difference as one of uncertainty of the acceptance of sexual diversity as compared to gender equality in liberal democracy. In their discussion of the ways in which gender equality is framed in opposition to multiculturalism, Phillips and Saharso acknowledge that Muslim antipathy to homosexuality also figures in the current European-wide retreat from multiculturalism, although less consistently so than gender equality, perhaps because '... it can be more readily assumed that "we" in the majority group all support gender equality, but not so easily asserted that "we" all regard homosexuality as fine'. (2008: 293). LGBTIQ rights are both more recent than women's equality and less evenly accepted across the West in general and within Europe, where they continue to provoke controversies in the European Union countries, despite more institutional success for LGBTIQ rights in the EU than the UN (Gerhards, 2010; Sweibel, 2009). In North America, Canada is at the progressive end of the scale, whilst the USA is resolutely conflicted over homosexuality (Rayside, 2008; Rayside and Wilcox, 2011a). This inconsistency has two manifestations within the civilizational dialectic: absence and presence.

The former is the more common occurrence, reminding us that Western liberal democracy has not *inevitably* produced the conditions that recognize sexual diversity and indeed that even if the *principles* of secular democracy can be usefully deployed to further such rights, the social and political contexts are more important variables. Butler has usefully critiqued these assumptions as the discursive deployment of 'secular time' as a momentum and outcome to modernity that permits the framing of Islam and Muslims as 'pre-modern' and thus justifies coercive state regulation of these subjects (2008), confirming Turner's argument above on the function of Islamic otherness as serving state sovereignty (2002). Furthermore, Puar's work identifies a crucial expansion of homonormativity into homonationalism whereby some homosexual identities are marshaled in the service of nationalist identities and discourses to disavow terrorist bodies, particularly Muslim and Arab ones (2007). The strength of her critique is her focus on the ways in which some contemporary queer identities are now identified with the bio-politics of life (marriage, families and the 'virility' of market participation) and how that shift permits their incorporation into nationalist discourses, which have always been underpinned by heteronormative bio-politics, emphasizing reproductive gendered sexual identities. She also argues that this bio-politics is inevitably a tradition associated with white dominance in the West and so it reinforces nationhood as 'whiteness', and so queer identities are now explicitly being assembled into a racial/sexual hierarchy that allows their deployment as markers of Western sexual exceptionalism in contrast to traditional – mostly Muslim – cultures of the 'terrorists'. Puar's analysis allows us to characterize new routes for the cultural production of some queer identities in the 'home' nation. It also allows us to think of the boundaries of this normative queerness – only those identities that fit into the dominant national identity discourse are given entrance since these are the ones that serve the projection of sexual exceptionalism outwards into the space of international relations. This has been a hugely influential analysis in terms of identifying an emerging tendency, but Puar also recognizes that 'homonationalism' is both limited and inconsistent, or in my terms, mostly absent. When LGBTIQ rights are currently deployed within the discourse of Islamic otherness we should query, therefore, whether they are there to serve the political elements of this discourse over and above the actual furtherance of sexual diversity, given that they are often, overwhelmingly, absent from nationalist politics and Western civilizational discourses.

This overriding absence of LGBTIQ equality makes it, however, all the more exemplary when it is present in civilizational debates. Just as the gender equality discourse promotes a particular version of Western democratic development so too does the presence of LGBTIQ rights imply a particularity to Western development, precisely because they are at the 'cutting edge' of human rights discourses in the West itself. Thus, it is not sexual exceptionalism that is being promoted here, but rather Western civilizational exceptionalism.[20] The acceptance of sexual diversity becomes an exemplary test of democratic cultural and governance credentials amongst Western nations themselves, remaining both controversial and inconsistent but trumpeted by those who have such rights as evidence of their accelerated modernity. Unlike gender equality, which is portrayed as an uncontroversial universal value, LGBTIQ rights will therefore be inevitably regarded as an exceptional marker when deployed in any civilizational dialectic – perhaps the new 'touchstone' of difference that Lewis describes above. As Mepschen et al. argue, gay politics[21] have undergone a 'remarkable shift' that have moved them center-stage in the civilizational defense of European and specifically Dutch culture against multiculturalism represented by Islam (2010). They argue that secularism and sexual freedom have developed as key aspects of contemporary Dutch identity, and indeed, that the progress of gay rights within this movement has been exceptional, resulting in a normalization of gay identity.[22] It is this exceptionalism, however, that permits the use of homosexuality to challenge Muslim cultures within the political discourse of modernity described throughout this chapter.

> Gay rights discourses have thus offered a language for the critique of Islam and multiculturalism – an idiom that underscores an Orientalist discourse that renders Muslim citizens knowable and produces them as objects of critique. Sexuality offers a prism through which cultural contrast comes to be perceived, temporally, as the difference between modernity and tradition. (Mepschen et al., 2010: 970)

The Dutch example also illustrates another consequence of the deployment of homosexuality as Western exceptionalism: the assumption of mutual exclusivity whereby the identities of 'gay' and 'Muslim' are seen as the product of mutually exclusive 'cultures': 'gay' is understood as

Western, and 'Muslims' as unable to accept gay public equality. This opposition is evident within the attitudes of Muslims and, therefore, feeds assumptions about Muslims as 'other' to Western culture and its values of democracy, secularism and tolerance of sexual minorities. For example, in small-scale research on public Muslim figures in the UK and their attitudes to multiculturalism, Modood and Ahmad (2007) demonstrate that sexual diversity is a key area of conflict:

> The issue of sexuality, then, is in fact one of the pivotal points of contention between secular liberals and 'mainstream', practising Muslims within Western multicultural societies, and among Muslims themselves. It, together with the wider theme of sexual freedom, is central to the political hostility against Muslims in, for example, the Netherlands, where gay sociology professor Pim Fortuyn led a popular movement to restrict Muslim immigration because the attitudes of Muslims were alleged to be threatening traditional Dutch sexual liberalism. (2007: 199)

This is but one example of a vast range of evidence that Muslims do see homosexuality as immoral but this religious perspective – enthusiastically shared by many Western Christians as Rayside and Wilcox point out (2011b) – is often extended to argue that a homosexual lifestyle is antithetical to Islamic cultures, evidenced in some recent survey analyses.[23] Not only do Muslim communities and organizations promote this view of their culture but an inevitable dialectical consequence has been that Western popular cultural and political discourses of Muslim otherness have focused on this intolerance. Even in countries where homosexuality remains controversial, gay identity is deployed to critique Muslims. For example, in August 2010, Fox News reported that one of its broadcasters was proposing to open a gay bar near the site of the proposed Islamic cultural center near ground zero in New York City ('Greg Gutfield wants to build gay bar next to "ground zero" mosque.').[24] His website elaborated on the idea:

> This is not a joke. I've already spoken to a number of investors, who have pledged their support in this bipartisan bid for understanding and tolerance. As you know, the Muslim faith doesn't look kindly upon homosexuality, which is why I'm building this bar. It is an effort to break down barriers and reduce deadly homophobia in the Islamic world. The goal, however, is not simply to open a typical gay

bar, but one friendly to men of Islamic faith. (http://www.dailygut.com/?i=4696)

Whilst this may be a satirical take on the siting of the Islamic center, it hits its target precisely because the mutual exclusivity of sexual diversity and Muslim culture is taken for granted, apparently illustrating an inevitable cultural conflict and fundamental difference between 'civilizations'. However, this argument is tautological, relying as it does on an assumption of Western modernity as the only possible social formation that permits homosexuality and inconsistently drawing upon various aspects of that modernity to support its claim, and, having already begun with an exclusion of Muslim cultures from that modernity, thus trumpeting the presence of sexual diversity in the West as evidence of the fundamental difference and inferiority of Eastern societies, beliefs and cultures.

The conceits of the West and the resistance of the East

Sexuality is mostly absent from Western discussions of modernity but when sexual diversity is present in civilizational debates, it is cast as a defining feature of Western exceptionalism, thus drawing it into the core of definitions of Muslim incompatibility with modernity. This positioning is based on a number of conceits about modernity and its putative cornerstones of liberal democracy and social equality that are, in fact, unsustainable. Homosexuality is not accepted universally in the West and so its identification with Western exceptionalism is problematic. When it is deployed thus, the argument seems to be that, like gender equality, the conditions for homosexual public acceptance and rights are possible only in the liberal democratic conditions of governance and yet both its absence from these models historically, and the relatively recent appearance of LGBTIQ and gender equality, suggest that either democratic principles are not inherently favorable to such issues, or that other political and social structures are much more important in how issues of the sexual change within modernity. Social equality of various groups is in fact much more contentious in Western democracy than formal liberal equality of individuals. It is important, therefore, to question the identification of homosexuality with modernity and particularly to be aware of how such an equation – like gender equality – can be deployed to serve the racist orientalist dialectic of Islam versus modernity. Common sense assumptions may be that challenging homophobia in general, and Muslim homophobia in particular, are distinct politics from questions of racialization, and thus that they do not aim to or in effect reinforce Islamophobia. I have argued, however, that the two are increasingly connected and we, both we in the West and we in Muslim communities, need to interrogate that connection if we want to prevent homosexuality becoming the litmus test for Muslim compatibility with the modern world, and through this, a legitimization of Islamophobia. The challenge to such conceits of the West that I have presented in this chapter is only a starting point, one which provokes a number of further issues which partly require a shift from the realm of political discourse to a more intersecting sociological appreciation of the social and political. First, we have to consider the 'Eastern' side of this dialectic; both the formation of Muslim homophobia as part of this dialectic of Islamic otherness to modernity, and the consequences this has for the visibility of homo-eroticism in Muslim cultures. Moreover, the overriding frame discussed throughout this chapter deploys not only a partial account of modernity and democracy, but also a partial sociological account of homosexuality as possible only within the governance structures of the West. This permits Muslim resistance to the recognition of Muslim cultural homoeroticism and to homosexuality in general because they become located as 'Western'. It is important, therefore, to investigate further the ways in which homosexuality has come to be seen as Western and the problematic consequences of this for how we understand LGBTIQ politics within the West and internationally. I turn to a deeper exploration of these issues in the following chapters.

3
Problematic Modernization: The Extent and Formation of Muslim Antipathy to Homosexuality

Introduction

Perhaps most people assume that Islam must be opposed to sexual diversity and gender equality because their first thoughts are of fundamentalist Islam based on rigid interpretations of the Quran. Muslims are not immune to this assumption either, with much of the evidence discussed below indicating a common sense understanding of Islamic prohibition of homosexuality.[1] There is, however, a wider public culture in the West in which we associate *all* of our present mainstream religious traditions with antipathy to homosexuality. The first wave of gay liberation analyses focused keenly on Christianity's contribution to ideologies of homosexual oppression (Altman, 1993 [1971]) and most accounts of the progress of LGBTIQ rights include the gradual secularization of Western societies as a key explanatory factor (Weeks, 2007). To this day, religiosity seems to be a key explanatory variable in accounting for homophobia amongst populations and, moreover, anti-gay prejudice often appears as the most extreme form of discrimination in religious populations (Leak and Finken, 2011). In many Western countries, conflicts between religious and queer rights groups have existed since the early days of gay liberation and continue in the present era of increasing queer rights. For example, in spring 2012, Catholic school boards in Ontario, Canada, reacted strongly against proposed provincial government legislation that would force Catholic schools to permit Gay-Straight Alliance student clubs as part of anti-bullying measures in schools. Whilst not condoning bullying, various Catholic leaders argued that allowing clubs that used the word 'gay' in their title, would threaten the specific cultures of their schools and undermine religious freedoms.[2] Given the historical and continuing political opposition between 'Western' faiths and homosexual citizenship, we should not be surprised to see religion as a constant and primary variable in both describing and explaining the general Muslim attitude toward homosexuality, either within Western minority populations or Muslim majority countries. This is not to argue that all Muslim identities are coherently or consistently religious but rather to point out that the assumption of religiosity as a dominant definition of what 'Muslim' means is still operationalized in much research on sexuality, despite the fact that, as Meer argues in the context of Britain, we have to increasingly understand Muslim as a socio-ethnic category that denotes identities that are much more complex than a prescriptive religious identity (Meer, 2010: 104–105).

Before I discuss the role of religion in these explanations, however, it is important to gain some empirical understanding of the extent of Muslim regulation of homosexuality. I therefore begin this chapter with an overview of actual laws relating to homosexuality (bi, trans and intersex rarely figure in these policies) in Muslim majority countries. I then describe the available evidence on Muslim populations' attitudes to sexual diversity, both in majority and minority communities. Taken together, these different levels of evidence portray a broad antipathy to homosexuality in Muslim cultures. My focus therefore turns to the modernization thesis that is the orthodox framework for sociological explanations of the acceptance of homosexuality, premised largely on the 'traditionalism' of religiosity, of both individuals and particular cultures, as a key variable in explaining progress and its lack in the realm of sexual diversity. Assessing the available surveys and theories, I suggest that there are limits in the data that encourage caution when considering modernization processes in relationship to homosexuality. I argue, however, that this caution does not undermine the broad sociological relationship between modernization and sexual diversity, but rather that we must attend to the complexities and contexts of modernization that indicate the specificity of likely contemporary Muslim reactions to homosexuality. Furthermore, we have to be clearer about the teleological equation of modernization processes with a uniform modernization outcome. I argue that the conceits of identifying Western modernity with sexual diversity are thus further challenged, precisely because we cannot take the Western experience of modernization processes as the blueprint for contemporary Muslim experience of modernization around gender and sexuality. Specifically, the progress of LGBTIQ visibility and citizenship in both Western countries and internationally is facing resistance from a specific formation of Muslim antipathy that is historically and politically distinct and is, in large part, caught up in reactions to Islamophobia and a resultant Muslim identity and consciousness that is not merely religious. In conclusion, therefore, I map out some key differences from the orthodox, Western model of modernization in the contemporary formation of Muslim antipathy to homosexuality and suggest how we may use this understanding to begin navigating our way through the evident and perceived opposition between Islam and homosexuality.

Muslim regulation of homosexuality at the national and international level

> When asked about the death penalty Iran imposed on homosexuals, Ahmadinejad discussed the death sentence for drug smugglers. When pushed by moderator and acting dean of the School of International and Public Affairs John Coatsworth, the Iranian president said: 'In Iran, we don't have homosexuals like in your country. In Iran, we do not have this phenomenon. I don't know who has told you we have that'.[3]

This is one account of the erstwhile Iranian President's famous denial of homosexuality during his 2007 visit to Columbia University in New York City, illustrating again the identification of homosexual rights with Western exceptionalism discussed in the previous chapter and, more pertinently, how such a discourse is used to judge Islamic nations such as Iran. The Islamic Republic has been a bête noire of the USA since its inception in 1979; subsequently featuring in the triumvirate of nations that President Bush characterized as an 'axis of evil' in his State of the Union address in 2002 and remaining a key constitutive other in 2012, when US Defense Secretary Leon Panetta reassured the public that the US would remain able to conduct wars against threatening states like Iran despite proposed half trillion dollar budget cuts to the military.[4] Iran is perhaps the exceptional Muslim nation in current times or rather, the exceptional *Islamist* one, but the use of homosexual rights to illustrate its 'otherness' is not limited to this one country. There is a common discursive reflex in Western mainstream and gay cultures and in Eastern Muslim cultures that sees homosexuality and Islam as mutually exclusive. We must, therefore, first understand the empirical basis of this putative opposition from the Muslim side.

At the level of state regulation, the picture of LGBTIQ rights is a bleak one in Muslim majority countries. Using the annual report from the

International Lesbian, Gay, Bisexual, Trans and Intersex Association (ILGA), *State-Sponsored Homophobia, a world survey of laws: criminalization, protection and recognition of same-sex love* (Itaborahy and Zhu, May 2013), we can see that 31 out of a total 47 Muslim majority countries criminalize homosexual acts, although eight of these only criminalize male/male sex (see the tables in Appendix A – Queer Rights in Muslim Majority Countries by Region). Based on the ILGA report on 192 countries (and territories of disputed status), homosexual acts are illegal in 76 countries, and so Muslim nations constitute almost half of these states (and the legality of same-sex relations is unclear in only two countries – Bahrain and Iraq – both Muslim majority nations). All of the five states in which homosexuality is punishable by the death penalty are also Muslim majority nations (Iran, Mauritania, Saudi Arabia, Sudan, Yemen). Regional jurisdictions within Nigeria and Somalia apply the same penalty and the latter is a Muslim nation, whilst the former is currently 48% Muslim and has the sixth largest national Muslim population and will be a Muslim majority nation by 2030 (see Appendix B – Queer Rights in Countries with Significant Muslim Populations). The ILGA report does not specifically discuss Muslim culture as a variable, although many of the summaries about the situation in each continent do mention conservative religious and cultural traditions as obstacles to LGBTIQ rights. Rights themselves do not make for recognition or full citizenship but the legal framework within a state is important as a basis for the activities and safety of LGBTIQ identities as individuals and communities. The criminalization of homosexual acts makes the first step almost impossible. As Adam et al. argue in one of the first comparative analyses of national movements:

> As a basic prerequisite for the emergence of a lesbian and gay organization, individuals must be able to find a social space where they can develop lesbian and gay identities, and they must be able to construct a rudimentary organization beyond private circles of friends. Once this space is carved out, lesbians and gays can start making political demands. (Adam et al., 1999: 344)

Leaving aside national regulation for the moment, we must consider the internationalization of LGBTIQ rights as a contemporary context for Muslim cultures, since the last decade has seen the emergence of discussions of sexual orientation within international human rights discourse, although the European Union (EU) is currently the only intergovernmental organization (IGO) that includes LGBTIQ issues in its regulations (Hamzic, 2011; Sweibel, 2009). The EU began discussions of sexual orientation discrimination in 1981 through a Court of Human Rights ruling but widening the debate took time with anti-discrimination measures only fully adopted by 2000 (Hamzic, 2011). These are, however, now mainstreamed to the extent that criminalization of homosexuality was abolished by those states wishing to accede to the EU by 2004 (Sweibel, 2009).[5] This does not affect any Muslim majority nations and Turkey is the only Muslim country that is an official candidate for future EU membership, where homosexuality is already decriminalized.[6] Perhaps the most significant international declaration subsequent to the EU's adoption of an anti-discrimination agenda is the Yogyakarta Principles that emerged from a working group of international jurists and activists,[7] and in particular a seminar held in Indonesia in 2006 (http://www.yogyakartaprinciples.org/principles_en.htm). These principles affirm the relevance of applying human rights to sexual orientation and gender identity, addressing the inconsistency and ambiguities that surrounded human rights legislation and providing a clear, legal justification in the 29 principles affirmed. The statement of principles is directed first and foremost at the United Nations, which has been a more difficult venue for LGBTIQ agendas than the EU (Sweibel, 2009; Waites, 2009). Sweibel points out that the UN really only recognized such issues as late as 2006 and, moreover, that much of the institutional opposition within the UN bureaucracy has come from 'right-wing Catholics and fundamentalist Islamic states' (Sweibel, 2009: 25) and others support this analysis of an alliance of primarily patriarchal religious viewpoints expressed by states in their resistance to both LGBTIQ rights and women's reproductive rights and sexual equality in international forums (Chappell, 2006; Hamzic, 2011; Houston, 2012). It is clear, moreover, that Muslim majority nations have not been not supportive of the recent legitimization of LGBTIQ rights within the Human Rights Council. For example, the United Nations clearly signaled support for ending discrimination in a joint statement by 85 states in March 2011 to its Human Rights Council, followed by a resolution for the same in June, which also commissioned a report from the Human Rights Commissioner on the extent of discrimination and violence based on sexual orientation and gender identity.[8] There were only two signatories of this statement from Muslim majority nations (Albania, and Sierra Leone – which still criminalizes male/male sex) and only three from those countries with significant Muslim populations – all of which have already decriminalized same-sex relations (Cyprus, Guinea-Bissau and the Former Yugoslav Republic of Macedonia (FYROM)).

It is therefore not surprising to see the absence of sexual diversity issues in those IGOs that are composed of Muslim nations. Habib points out that the 1981 Universal Islamic Declaration of Human Rights[9] prioritizes Sharia law over the perceived Judeo-Christian and secular provenance of the UN's 1948 Universal Declaration of Human Rights, and thus does not provide scope for including sexual orientation (Habib, 2010a: xxiii). The subsequent 1990 Cairo Declaration on Human Rights in Islam made by the contemporary 45 states of the Organization of the Islamic Conference (OIC) reiterates this position[10] (http://www.oic-oci.org/english/article/human.htm). On their website, there are numerous references to combating Islamophobia and many useful publications but nothing referring to sexuality. The OIC currently has seven members who are also part of the third largest IGO which is the Commonwealth of Nations, established in 1931 to formalize continuing relations between the United Kingdom and the increasing number of its former colonies, although its present 54 members include those not colonized by Britain. The Muslim majority nations are: Bangladesh, Brunei, the Gambia, Malaysia, Maldives, Pakistan, Sierra Leone, but three countries with very significant Muslim populations – India, Nigeria and Tanzania – are also part of this organization, with the first two comprising 177 million and 76 million Muslims respectively, the third and sixth largest national Muslim populations in 2010. It is a rather more informal IGO than the others but nonetheless engages in many cultural forms of cooperation. Its statement of principles made in Singapore in 1971 was the closest document to a constitution until March 2013, when the Charter of the Commonwealth was published, which includes affirmations of democracy and individual rights, but no mention of issues surrounding sexuality or homosexuality (http://thecommonwealth.org/our-charter). More recent statements on human rights are the same, although mainstreaming rights is now a key mission of the organization (http://www.thecommonwealth.org/subhomepage/190707). Waites and Lennox demonstrate that human rights as a general tool and discourse did not appear until the 1991 Harare declaration (made at the Commonwealth Heads of Government Meeting) and that sexual orientation remained absent at that point and remains outside official policies today, although they document the increasing activism within various sections of the Commonwealth on sexuality (2013a: 35–37).[11]

All Muslim states in Africa except Morocco are also members of the African Union (AU) which has a Court of Justice and Human Rights to oversee the African Charter on Human and People's Rights (www.au.int/en/about/nutshell). This document does not refer to the rights of LGBTIQ people but rather prioritizes the heterosexual family as the basis of society.[12] The Arab League nations are all Muslim majority states and similarly have adopted a Charter on Human Rights since 2008 but again, there is no mention of sexuality, homosexuality or LGBTIQ persons and instead emphasizes the family.[13] Asian IGOs include the Association of South East Asian Nations (ASEAN), founded in 1967, which counts the Muslim majority states of Brunei, Indonesia and Malaysia amongst its members, but does not address human rights issues, sexuality or homosexuality in its activities which remain mostly regional economic cooperation and development (www.aseansec.org). The Shanghai Cooperation Organization (SCO) was established in 1996 by China, Russia and the Muslim states of Kazakhstan, Kyrgyzstan and Tajikistan and then adding Uzbekistan in 2001. Although the founding states have decriminalized homosexuality (the Muslim states since 1998), Uzbekistan still criminalizes male homosexuality (Appendix A, Table 2) and there is no evidence that SCO membership impacts the regulation of homosexuality. As with ASEAN, the main purpose of SCO seems to be regional security and economic cooperation rather than governance or social justice issues (http://www.sectsco.org/EN/) and the same appears true for the South Asian Association for Regional Cooperation (http://www.saarc-sec.org). This IGO numbers Afghanistan, Bangladesh, the Maldives and Pakistan amongst its eight members and these four Muslim nations all criminalize homosexuality (Appendix A, Tables 2 and 5). It also includes India – currently containing the third largest national Muslim population at an estimated 177 million (Appendix B, Table 1) and which has decriminalized homosexuality since 2009 (pending High Court decisions). The same focus on development is true for the Economic Cooperation Organization (ECO), whose 10 members are all Muslim nations amongst which five have decriminalized homosexuality (Azerbaijan, Kazakhstan, Kyrgyzstan, Turkey, Tajikistan) but the remainder not (Afghanistan, Iran, Pakistan, Turkmenistan, Uzbekistan) (http://www.ecosecretariat.org/). There are also a majority of Muslim nations in the Commonwealth of Independent states (CIS)[14] – the successor IGO to the USSR since 1991 – but these six (out of 12 total members) include the latter two from the ECO that have not decriminalized homosexuality (http://www.cisstat.com/eng/cis.htm).

There is, of course, a broader question about whether international and intergovernmental agreements are really that relevant in promoting and enforcing LGBTIQ equality issues, particularly since the evidence demonstrates that the topic is mostly absent anyway as, indeed, they are in the politics of most Western nations. I discuss these critiques in Chapter 6 but for our purposes here, we need only focus on the fact that

LGBTIQ issues are tentatively emerging as a presence on the international level. Hamzic argues that, at the very least, the categories of 'sexual orientation and gender identity are firmly established in international human rights law' even if they are not explicitly included in specific treaties (2011: 251). This means that they are forming part of a discourse of international human rights that is debated and contested by different nations and, more broadly, may therefore be drawn into the dialectical characterization of the West and Muslim nations or, at the very least, be seen as a marker of Muslim resistance to international standards of human rights, as in the case of the UN (Sweibel, 2009; Waites, 2009).

The attitudes of Muslim majority and minority populations

As Adamczyk and Pitt point out, there is very little research on attitudes to homosexuality in non-Western nations (2009). This also means that there is little evidence on Muslim attitudes to homosexuality and what there is available is largely directly associated with their religious views. Beckers' analysis of the World Values Survey[15] (WVS) remains one of the few available comparisons, and he shows that there is a lower average level of acceptance of homosexuality in Muslim cultures (2010). His analysis of data is taken from the integrated comparison of datasets from 1981 to 2003 (waves 1–4), which includes only 11 Muslim majority nations, and the subsequent fifth round of surveys (wave 5: 2005–2008) that included only seven Muslim countries. Beckers thus cautions us as to the generalizability to all Muslim nations but nonetheless suggests that the similar results for Muslim nations across these different waves of research suggest the possibility of tendencies that are common to Muslim cultures (Beckers, 2010: 77). He demonstrates that the 11 Muslim countries surveyed up to the fourth wave of the WVS have the lowest average acceptance of homosexuality (mean of 1.2) in comparison to other religious traditions, but that there is also the least variation between Muslim populations in comparison to other groups. We must bear in mind the overall scale here, since Beckers points out that in this fourth wave, only seven overall countries had acceptance levels above the mean of the scale (5.5 on a scale of 1–10). This pattern is repeated in the fifth wave of the WVS, with the seven Muslim nations demonstrating a mean level of acceptance at 1.9, still the lowest in comparison to other religious traditions. Beckers' analysis broadly confirms the modernization thesis on tolerance and acceptance of non-normative identities, developed by Inglehart and colleagues in their sustained analysis of the WVS data (Inglehart and Baker, 2000; Inglehart and Norris, 2003; Inglehart and Welzel, 2005) which essentially argues that economic development leads to increased concerns with, and wider acceptance of, issues of self-expression whereas in less developed countries, the emphasis is more on economic survival and correlates with less tolerant attitudes. Adamczyk and Pitt's analysis of the same data in the fourth wave of the WVS focuses on the 'self-expression' versus 'survival' thesis and they conclude that Muslims appear to be the least tolerant of homosexuality but in this they share similar levels of disapproval with Protestants, particularly when the 'survivalist' culture predominates over 'self-expression' values in nations that have significant Protestant populations (2009: 349). In common with other analyses, more liberal attitudes were found amongst women rather than men, younger cohorts, and more educated groups but national regulations were found to be statistically insignificant in predicting intolerance, perhaps indicating that cultural orientation, religion and tradition are more important (2009).

Turning to the similarly limited evidence on Muslim minority populations, a survey of Muslims in the USA (0.6–1% of total US population) by the Pew Research Center showed that 61% thought homosexuality should be discouraged compared to 38% who thought the same in the general population (Pew, 2007: 45). Only 27% thought it was acceptable compared to 51% in the general population and 75% of those Muslims with the highest religious commitment (23% of the total Muslim sample) were opposed to homosexuality, mirroring the 75% of native born African-American Muslims who did not accept homosexuality.[16] Native born Muslims opposed homosexuality by 61%, only slightly more tolerant than those born outside the USA – 67% of those from the Arab region, 65% of those from Pakistan, and 70% of those from the rest of South Asia were opposed to homosexuality. As Rayside (2011) points out in his analysis of this data, however, there seems to be the potential for generational differences, given that 32% of those aged 18–29 accept homosexuality in comparison to 26% of those aged 30–39 and those aged 40–54 and only 22% of those aged 55 and over (Pew, 2007: 45). Canadian Muslim attitudes to homosexuality were partially assessed in a 2006 Environics survey, which found that only 10% of Muslims expressed strong agreement with same-sex marriage (legal in Canada) whilst 58% expressed strong disagreement with these rights (Rahman and Hussain, 2011). Survey evidence from a report on British Muslims' attitudes found that the most disapproving of homosexuality were those in the 16–24 age cohort (71%) comparing to 61% overall, supporting the overall picture that religiosity is stronger in younger British Muslims (Policy Exchange, 2007: 47).[17] However, a YouGov poll conducted on 600 Muslim students found only 25% who had no respect for homosexuals, comprising 32% of males and 19% of females (Thorne and Stuart, 2008).[18] This might indicate that those in higher education are more tolerant supported by the fact that 53% indicated that they had the same respect for homosexuals as 'anyone else', although on both questions Muslim students vary significantly from non-Muslim students, at 4% who had no respect and 77% who had the same respect for homosexuals as anyone else (2008: 60). There is no clear indication of the age of respondents, however, although we can assume that the majority are in the usual 18–24 undergraduate cohort. A Gallup report in 2009 in the UK and in Germany and France found none of the 500 British Muslims interviewed showing any acceptance of homosexuality (compared to 58% of the general public); only 19% in Germany showing acceptance (compared to 68% of the general public) and only 35% of French Muslims showing acceptance in comparison to 68% of the general population (Gallup, 2009: 31).[19] However, a poll in 2011 gave evidence that almost 20% of British Muslims strongly agreed that they were 'proud of how Britain treats gay people' although this compares with 46% of the overall sample (Wind-Cowie and Gregory for Demos, 2011: 91).[20]

There are similar limitations in the quantity of data when looking at more qualitative evidence. In her research on heterosexual Muslims in Glasgow, Scotland, Siraj concludes that their attitudes to homosexuality are influenced mainly by religiosity, with educational levels, age and gender showing no discernible effect in her sample,[21] although she does point out that the vast majority of her respondents were highly educated (Siraj, 2009). She points out that whilst attitudes amongst the general British population seem to have shifted towards more acceptance of homosexuality, her participants 'did not perceive being homosexual as a legitimate social, personal or religious identity ...' and so '... for the most part, Muslims exhibit disproportionately negative attitudes towards homosexuals and homosexual relationships'. (2009: 55). In their comparative study of adolescents in Canada and Belgium, Hooghe, Claes et al. found that Muslims were overall less accepting of gay rights activism than other religious groupings and, moreover, that variation within the Muslim adolescent groups in both countries correlated to their frequency of religious engagement with more religiosity indicating less tolerance (2010: 392). By controlling for other factors within their analysis, Hooghe et al. conclude that religiosity is a significant predictor of intolerance, even in countries where LGBTIQ rights have been enshrined in the period of childhood and early adulthood socialization of their sample. They caution, however, that the single most important variable still seems to be gender, with Muslim adolescent males showing significantly less tolerance than females, and that this confirms the well-established gendered pattern of homophobia across all cultures, classes and religions (Hooghe, Claes et al., 2010).

Explaining Muslim antipathy through the modernization thesis

The first observation we can surely make is that we need much more thorough empirical data on attitudes to sexuality, homosexuality and sexual diversity amongst Muslim populations, both minority and majority cohorts. The next, sixth, wave of the WVS being conducted from 2010–2012 may produce such data, given that the aim is to survey 40 of the 47 Muslim majority countries identified in Appendix A (Comoros, Djibouti, Afghanistan, Bahrain, Brunei, the Maldives and Kosovo are the exclusions), and 12 of the 14 countries with significant Muslim populations listed in Appendix B, Table 1 (Benin and Turkish Cyprus are not included).[22] Nonetheless, what survey data does exist, taken with the picture of state and intergovernmental regulation, clearly indicates an opposition between Muslim cultures and homosexuality. It is important, therefore, to consider the explanations for this opposition and to assess both the credibility of particular components within such explanations and to point out problems within these perspectives.

The 'face' of Muslim opposition is obviously seen as religion, both in terms of a broad social heritage of Islamic values creating a culture of homophobia, and religiosity amongst individuals deriving from these specific national or minority belief systems. As discussed in the introduction to this chapter, the established body of evidence considering other religions supports the view that mainstream religious traditions have historically contributed to the oppression of homosexuals (and women) (Altman, 1993 [1971]) and provided focal points for resistance to the advance of LGBTIQ visibility, organizing and rights during the period of gay liberation both in the West (Weeks, 2007) and internationally (Sweibel, 2009; Weeks 2007). Research on attitudes has consistently confirmed that personal religious affiliations and beliefs and the related wider religious culture impact negatively on the acceptance of homosexuality (Adamczyk and Pitt, 2009). This picture is also confirmed by research on LGBTIQ individuals who are religious, demonstrating that they experience severe conflict in attempting to reconcile sexual identity with their religious traditions (Anderton et al., 2011); a problem that is evident in those from a Muslim background as well (Yip, 2004, 2005, 2007). This evidence points us towards two connected conclusions. Yes, Islam is problematic in its acceptance of homosexuality but also that *Islam is therefore not extraordinary* as a religious tradition but rather in step with its monotheistic precursors in terms of the difficulties it creates for homosexuality (indeed, ultimately relying on the same scriptural narrative for its condemnation as does Judaism and Christianity[23]).

Nonetheless, the issue in survey approaches remains one of the perception of Islam's continuing influence in majority societies and minority communities and thus the related impact it has on Muslims' belief systems and attitudes, in comparison and contrast with the already 'modernized', secularized West. In the WVS analysis, two major axes are put forward to explain cultural values; the scale from traditional values to secular-rational ones and the scale from survival values to those of self-expression which, taken together, account for 70% of the cross-national variations in values (Inglehart and Welzel, 2005, 2010). Above all, the data from the WVS have been used to describe the progress towards democratization but with a significant emphasis on how socio-economic development links with other factors and particularly how mass attitudes in populations contribute to democratic development (Inglehart and Welzel, 2005, 2010; Welzel and Inglehart, 2008). In making this last point, Inglehart and Welzel are revising the standard modernization thesis that has overwhelmingly prioritized economic development. They argue for the significance of how transitions from agrarian economies to industrial, and industrial to post-industrial, produce stable shifts in attitudes that correlate with democratic development: 'Evidence from many societies indicates that modernization-linked values and attitudes show sufficient stability over time to be treated as attributes of given societies. Moreover, the self-expression values syndrome shows remarkably strong linkages with a wide range of societal phenomena such as civil society, gender equality and democratization' (Inglehart and Welzel, 2010: 563). Values matter, and can contribute or hinder democratic development over and above economic structures. In this analytical frame, Muslim societies fall overwhelmingly into the traditional (primarily religious) and survivalist 'corner' of modernization, graphically demonstrated in the cultural maps produced by Inglehart and Welzel (2005, 2010 but also accessible at http://www.worldvaluessurvey.org/wvs/articles/folder_published/article_base_54).

At first glance, such large-scale survey data seems to clearly confirm the broad civilizational clash described in the previous chapter and, indeed, those essentially political arguments are given credence through this more sociological account of political development. We should remember, however, Inglehart and Welzel are putting forward a revision to the standard modernization thesis that prioritizes economic development and thus that they are challenging some previous assumptions, many of which underpin the characterization of Western modernity and Islamic 'otherness' described in Chapter 2. In the sense that modernization *processes* are taken to be inevitable consequences and criteria to the formation of modernity in standard orientalist accounts, we can understand their critique of classic modernization arguments as a challenge to the assumption of a singular momentum to or formation of modernity, since they point out that modernization is neither temporally linear nor a deterministic set of processes. Rather, they acknowledge that national political, religious and historical contexts are important variables in how processes of modernization occur and so we cannot claim that economic modernity automatically begets democracy (Inglehart and Welzel, 2010: 552), again adding some cause for skepticism towards those conceits of the West discussed in the previous chapter, whose logic is premised on a linear development of modern capitalist economies, democracy and queer liberty.

Of course, in making their arguments, they are putting forward the case for the relevance of mass attitudes or values to be taken seriously as a factor that provides a causal link between economic development and democratization and so their analysis *does* confirm the 'traditionalist' and 'survivalist' character of Muslim societies, permitting a more complex but nonetheless potentially oppositional account of civilizational difference through stages of progress. Drawing on both their data and thesis, Beckers' (2010) analysis of attitudes to homosexuality in Muslim societies broadly confirms the more complex modernization thesis proposed by Inglehart and Welzel that looks beyond economic development as the sole engine of democratization. He argues that it is the interplay between socio-economic development (including gender equality) and the existence of some forms of responsive government (broadly understood as democratic practices) that combine to help create conditions for the acceptance of homosexuality. Moreover, he suggest that these factors are more important than the specific religious beliefs of a culture (Beckers, 2010: 88), again suggesting a more nuanced reading of Islamic influence than is presented in civilizational arguments but still suggesting the ultimate positioning of Muslim societies as lagging behind the modernization of the West. There are both complexities and contexts to the processes of modernization that are taken into account in the analyses above that challenge a simplistic political equation of Muslim religious identity as the central explanation to Muslim homophobia. What remains, however, is the broad premise of modernization as a set of processes that will lead to the outcomes experienced in the West, thus inevitably defining Muslim societies and the cultural values of their populations, as, if not quite as pre-modern, then certainly as problematically modern.

The complexities of modernization and reactions to homosexuality

In terms of attitudinal studies, the relationship between democratic governance and socio-economic development seems to provide a convincing thesis in relation to the acceptance of homosexuality. Nonetheless, there are complexities within such arguments, not least of which is the question of *what* is being measured in terms of 'homosexuality' and, of course, there are wider contexts to assessing modernization than simply attitudinal surveys. I take up the point about epistemological assumptions about homosexuality as an identity in the following chapters, linking it to how one thinks of sexuality in modernity. However, since this chapter has surveyed more positivist evidence, it would be premature to deconstruct its concepts before dealing with its internal logic. Let me concentrate, therefore, on the complexities within the modernization thesis. My aim here is not simple deconstruction or dismissal – since most analyses of Muslim antipathy confirm its premises – but to attend to caveats about its uniformity or momentum and thus to raise the question of how we should challenge some of the uses of modernization arguments in the discourse of Islamic 'otherness'.

As Jurgen Gerhards points out in his analysis of the European Values Survey (EVS) (part of the WVS), the majority of EU citizens do not support the acceptance of homosexuality, with large variations between the more socio-economically 'modernized' states and those more recently acceded as well as the candidate state of Turkey (2010). He concludes that both the socio-economic aspects of modernization (accelerated by the economic integration project central to the EU) and the cultural heritage (including religion) of individual countries therefore impact upon attitudes towards homosexuality, and predicts that further integration will make homosexuality more acceptable across the whole of the EU. Whilst he confirms a more nuanced modernization explanation, he also points out that EU non-discrimination policies were largely elite transnational directives, not necessarily reflective of national public values, as evidenced by the range of opinions within Europe. There are contradictions in national values and state regulation within Europe, despite the fact that we consider the EU as the most progressive IGO around sexual diversity. Stulhofer and Rimac's analysis of the EVS confirms that country economic modernization lowers the level of homonegativity, and that the lack of material security in post-communist Eastern Europe seems particularly significant in explaining disapproval of homosexuality, but this has to be taken into account along with the resurgence of traditional orthodox Christianity. They also demonstrate that variations exist within the 'old' EU, particularly in comparisons of the Nordic Protestant countries and the Catholic Mediterranean ones. This emphasis on religion is also why they argue that recent immigrants seem to be associated with higher levels of homonegativity within national samples, although there is no data on the ethnic, national or religious identities of the national immigrant samples, but rather they include a variable that simply counts the percentage of immigrants in the specific country (Stulhofer and Rimac, 2009). They also fail to account for the broad socio-economic position of immigrants in each country, thus failing to explain the relative importance of economic security and cultural heritage in combination. We may simply see this evidence as further confirmation of the 'time-lag' economic development modernization thesis, nuanced to include the relationship of cultural values as argued throughout WVS studies but this time applied within the orbit of the 'West'. However, these studies also illustrate a key point that is often ignored when the acceptance of homosexuality is cast as an inevitable aspect of Western exceptionalism: tolerance of homosexuality is neither uniform across the West, nor explained by economic development, religion and governance as individual variables, but by a context-specific combination of, at the very least, all three.

Furthermore, we should remember that a change in values towards homosexuality is relatively *recent* in the West, demonstrated keenly by the shift in the WVS data whereby as recently as 1981 (the first wave of the WVS, constituted as the EVS), 44% of the sample from the UK, Italy, France, West Germany and the Netherlands were at the zero tolerance end of the scale on homosexuality ('never acceptable') but within 25 years, less than half of this figure held the same opinion (21% in 2006) (Inglehart, 2008). Thus, whilst 'self-expression' values may have emerged as a direct result of the material security of Western European populations post-World War Two, their impact on attitudes to homosexuality have taken somewhat longer to emerge, and are not uniformly embedded within rich, democratic societies, again giving us cause to dispute the orientalist discourse that identifies queer rights with Western exceptionalism.

A further caveat is added by Adamcyk and Pitt's analysis of the fourth wave WVS data (1999–2001 surveys) in which they demonstrate that the influence of religion may actually *increase* for those who have high religious identification in societies in which self-expression values are also high (2009: 348). This argument suggests that when 'self-expression' values increase in rich, post-materialist countries, the consequent cultural and state liberalization (around homosexuality, for example) can actually increase the *relative* influence of conservative religious views on homosexuality in response to the new and increasing visibility of queer culture and rights. In their data, this was most evident for Muslims and conservative Protestants. The context of LGBTIQ public visibility and legal advances thus becomes important in assessing responses to homosexuality in any account of 'modernization'. Rather than assuming that increased political visibility of queer rights is a threshold of 'progress', we have to consider how their presence may provoke resistance where there was none before, something that is perhaps underlying the evidence on the 'new' EU cited above, and something that has been documented in various analyses of global homophobia (Weiss and Bosia, 2013).

In their analysis of the WVS data from Europe, North America and Australia from 1990–2002 (waves 1–3), Andersen and Fetner (2008) point out that while the broad post-materialist thesis is correct, there are nuances to its empirical evidence, particularly along class lines. They argue that increasing tolerance towards homosexuality is evident in societies with high GDP per capita, but that this is skewed towards professional and managerial classes with markedly less tolerance in working classes. Not only does class matter, but income inequalities within specific countries also seems to matter in predicting less tolerant attitudes, regardless of class, leading the authors to argue that the post-materialist thesis of the modernization argument needs further refinement, over and above that provided by Inglehart and Welzel. The impacts of both class position and overall wealth distribution within rich Western countries is an important factor in predicting levels of tolerance such that 'social tolerance is likely to be highest in rich societies where the benefits of economic prosperity are relatively equally distributed among all members' (Andersen and Fetner, 2008: 956).

We might say with some certainty that attitudinal change is neither uni-dimensional nor linear. Religion, class identity and broader class inequalities, political changes and visibility related to homosexuality will all provide the context within which homosexuality will be responded to within any given country. The limited qualitative evidence cited above speaks to this complexity in terms of beliefs and attitudes, and provides an indication that gender identity might be the most important variable in assessing reactions to homosexuality, over and above a religious or ethnic identification. Nonetheless, at a more general level of measuring groups of societies, political and value change *has* occurred, but so recently in terms of both the period and economic formation of Western modernity and the Enlightenment, that it becomes difficult to hold up sexual diversity as either inevitable or exclusively possible with Western democracy based on its actual historical emergence or wider social reactions to it unless, of course, we *begin* with that tautological assumption that the present time is the inevitable progress of modernity and democratization because LGBTIQ rights exist. This is not to dismiss the key factors that have become the orthodox explanation for the emergence of queer identities; open and free association; economic and cultural independence of women; law-based societies that are open to group influence through political practices. These are of course identified with the democratic societies in which gay liberation first emerged, and so we inevitably draw a causal link with these democratic 'modernized' systems, but the specific histories of national gay movements the West vary enormously and the current international spread of queer rights is not limited to stable or successful democracies.[24] What I think we have to consider is how far we are equating specific modernization processes with broad outcomes that are based exclusively on Western experiences of modernization.

We should remember that the specific modernization thesis of democratization drawn from large-scale surveys is hitherto based overwhelmingly on *non*-Muslim societies. If social economic and responsive government development are necessary (but not sufficient) conditions for the emergence of LGBTIQ visibility and its eventual acceptance, then we have to take into account the socio-economic and governance developments of Muslim majority societies, and the class position of Muslim minority populations. The tables in the Appendix illustrate the current picture of socio-economic development and, moreover, governance systems described in these tables offer a bleak picture in terms of what we currently understand as democratic in the West. Taken with the portrait of state regulation and Muslim intergovernmental disinterest in issues of sexual diversity, we can see that the conditions that might decrease the cultural and individual influences of religious orthodoxy seem to be lacking – or perhaps 'lagging behind' – in Muslim societies and thus would broadly explain the basis for the survey and qualitative evidence presented throughout this chapter in line with a simplistic modernization thesis. However, even if Muslim societies 'progressed' to similar levels of democratic governance, economic security and public LGBTIQ visibility as in Western countries, there is no guarantee that such visibility will be accepted uniformly within societies or across transnational regions, given the experiences of the West and the complexities evinced therein. At a very broad level of both civilizational 'values' and historical processes of change, we can perhaps assume that the acceptance of sexual diversity will 'progress' in similar sociological ways to the West, but the point is that the 'broad' picture is all too easily slotted into the discourse of Islamic otherness to modernity. When we know this political reality, we should perhaps attend to the more complex sociological picture of modernization that we know applies in the West, and resist any attempt to simplify that explanation when applying a modernization framework to Muslim societies and populations.

Understanding Muslim homophobia in the contexts of modernity and Islamophobia

> In order to criticize Muslims as backwards and as enemies of European culture, gay rights are now heralded as if they have been the foundation of European culture for centuries (cf. Wekker, 2009). This instrumentalization of gay rights puts progressives, anti-racists, feminists, and lesbian and gay activists in an impossible position: taking up the defence of lesbian and gay rights and public gayness comes to be associated with Islamophobia, while solidarity with Muslims against Islamophobia is represented, especially by the populist right, as trivializing or even supporting 'Muslim' homophobia. (Mepschen et al, 2010: 965)

It is no doubt tempting to take a reductionist modernization thesis as the basic framework within which we can explain the acceptance of homosexuality. Indeed, such a thesis underpins the civilizational discourses discussed in the previous chapter and this is precisely why sexual diversity can be used as a key marker of Islamic 'otherness' to the West. At a very simple level, the combination of economic development, democracy and secularization are understood both as the foundational basis for the social equality of LGBTIQ and as having reached a threshold of progress in the West that has inevitably produced the acceptance of sexual diversity. I am conscious, moreover, that the evidence I have presented on the extent of Muslim antipathy to homosexuality *can* be read as supporting this modernization and civilizational thesis and thus contribute to a broader construction of Islamophobia. My aim, however, has been both to acknowledge the extent of Muslim reluctance to accept homosexual rights and visibility, and to provide a more complex understanding of the modernization thesis in the process. In doing so, I suggest that we can begin to navigate our way out of the 'impossible' oppositional position described by Mepschen et al. above.

First, we must acknowledge that the sociological components of broad modernization arguments are much more complex than a crude civilizational dialectic proposes. Thus, the foundational elements of socio-economic wealth, democratic governance and secularization must be understood in their (often national or regional) context and analyses from Western societies suggest that there are important complexities and variations within each of these categories when accounting for attitudes to homosexuality, particularly in the consequences for gender and class divisions. At the very least, this requires a more considered assessment of the impact of the 'Islamic' variable as an independent determining explanation, and reminds us that religious Muslims are entirely *conventional* in their attitudes to homosexuality in comparison to other groups of high religiosity, both in the West and globally. There is a further issue here about whether large-scale surveys and more qualitative approaches can begin to conceptualize Muslim identity beyond a prescriptive religious default identity, as Meer argues is necessary in explaining contemporary Muslim political consciousness (Meer, 2010).

Nonetheless, at a very broad level, the modernization argument seems to be convincing and we should not dismiss it when thinking about how cultures might change. In this more complex sociological account of modernization, the 'solution' to Muslim antipathy to sexual diversity is still focused on 'progress' and most certainly the progress resulting from certain 'modernizing' processes, namely secularization of both governance/culture and individuals' beliefs within these communities and economic development in general and specifically in the independence of women. The limited available evidence from Muslim populations broadly chimes with specific components of this more complex argument;

men are less tolerant than women, higher levels of class and education produce more tolerance, broader social and gender equality seem to be important contextual factors, underpinned by social institutions. Thus we can perhaps focus on these factors with some confidence as underlying social changes that are required to produce more tolerant attitudes in Muslim majority and minority populations. Again, this picture is entirely conventional in terms of broad social 'progress' and resistance around issues of sexual diversity in the West, and so, at the very least, we should be careful to resist any deployment of such arguments exclusively within the contemporary orientalist Islamophobic discourse.[25]

I suggest, however, that even the more nuanced modernization thesis is problematic as a beginnings for a 'solution' to Muslim homophobia largely because of a conceptual teleological assumption that equates modernization processes with a particular outcome of modernity as a social formation. Specifically, the patterns and momentum of development in the West cannot be merely replicated in the East, as if the East merely needs to 'catch up' and this is particularly true in the area of gender and sexual formations. We cannot logically sustain a suggestion that sexual diversity will emerge in the same way in non-Western countries as it has in the West, largely because the discourse of LGBTIQ rights is currently being promoted within IGOs and within some Western countries' policies towards development, and because LGBTIQ visibility is now global through popular cultural technologies such as the internet and broadcast media. None of these conditions existed in the period of Western gay liberation and so we have to consider Muslim reactions to homosexuality in a contemporary historical context of 'modernization' that is markedly different from Western societies' recent 'progress' on this issue. If the modernization methodology is broadly to measure the outcomes of certain long-term processes, it fails to account for contemporary shifts in context that impact those processes. So, for example, the current activity at the UN on queer rights (see note 8) includes outlining the obligations of member states towards queer populations, even if many of these states have not yet 'progressed' sociologically to the modernized stages that Western societies reached *before* queer rights could emerge. What impact does this have on how modernization will now occur in these countries, many of which are Muslim? At the very least, the internal logic of the modernization argument is challenged by these recent political shifts because they change the context in which both emergence and reaction to homosexual politics occurs.

More specifically in our terms, we have seen the instrumentalization of gay rights within the Islamophobic civilizational discourse. We therefore have to consider the formation of Muslim homophobia *within* the context of Islamophobia, not simply explain it as a pre-existing component of either Islamic otherness to modernity or exclusively as a religious reflex. In such a context to modernity, can anyone seriously contemplate that all Muslim societies and Muslim populations have to do is simply 'catch up' with Western modernization in order to be accepting of sexual diversity? We have, instead, to face the fact that Muslim antipathy to homosexuality is a complex combination of factors, not all of which are developing in the same way as they did in the West, and that Muslim homophobia may be becoming further embedded within Muslim identities as a reaction to the contemporary 'exemplary' positioning of LGBTIQ rights as central to Western exceptionalism. Thus we have to explore further the role of sexual diversity politics within what Meer has described as the rise in Muslim consciousness that has resulted from the contemporary stigmatization of Muslims (Meer, 2010). This further exploration has three dimensions; elaborating Muslim formations of homophobia in more historical and political context *and* interrogating the conceptualization of sexuality that is being deployed in Western and internationalist LGBTIQ politics, often against Muslim cultures. In this sense, subsequent chapters focus on the politics of identity being deployed in Muslim communities and in LGBTIQ organizations as the terrain of opposition that has created the 'impossible' position described above. A final crucial dimension, however, is to refute the absolutist opposition between Muslims and sexual diversity by focusing on the traditions and contemporary formations of Muslim homo-eroticism and thus leading us onto a terrain that precludes mutual exclusivity in the identity politics of LGBTIQ and Muslims. As I have already discussed in Chapter 1, this subject is perhaps the most controversial and difficult for both 'Western' LGBTIQ politics and for Muslim cultures, but without some acknowledgement and understanding of Muslim homo-erotics, I argue that we cannot even begin to navigate our way through the oppositions of Muslim and LGBTIQ politics. The following chapters therefore use Muslim homo-erotic traditions and identities as the central theme in exploring the identity politics of Muslim reactions to homosexuality and Western deployments of sexual diversity.

4
Traditions and Transformations of Muslim Homo-eroticism

Introduction

The preceding two chapters have focused on the ways in which queer politics and Muslim identities are broadly drawn into the civilizational dialectic. Moving beyond this critique, the remaining chapters are focused on how to challenge these common sense political understandings, using the Muslim experience of homo-eroticism as the lever with which to prise open the apparent discourse of exclusivity of Western modernity and Islam and thus bring us onto a shared terrain of sexual diversity and Muslim cultures. Chapter 5 considers the contemporary manifestations of Muslim queer identity and the Chapter 6 relates these to political strategies. Preceding those, however, we need to consider the history of Muslim homo-eroticism during the period of modernity as a more accurate way of understanding the development of contemporary Muslim politics around sexuality and their relationship to Western queer politics. Detailing those historical traditions and their transformations in relationship to understandings of modernity is the basic aim of this chapter.

I begin with a review of the available historical analyses of Muslim same-sex eroticism. In this field, the majority of the contributions we have are from Arab regions and Southeast Asia and the broad picture is of the existence of homo-erotic behavior within the prevailing gender structures of many of these cultures in the period before modernity. Most writers agree that these sexual traditions have been affected by modernity, more specifically by what Roscoe has called the spread of 'homosexualization' (1997); what we can understand as the modern Western identity and knowledge frameworks of explaining homosexuality as a stigmatized core or essential identity through medical and legal technologies. This process of homosexualization is also, in many of these cases, part of the process of colonization,[1] both in the direct imposition of particular laws and scientific understandings of sexuality, and in the broader adoption of these understandings throughout culture, often within native elites as well the colonizing classes (Massad, 2008). We might then have expected to see the rejection of colonial era laws and sensibilities with the gradual liberation of colonized states in the twentieth century but, of course, that has absolutely not been the case in the realm of sexuality. There has been no return to the 'traditions' of wider sexual and gender diversity than those permitted by colonization (Lennox and Waites, 2013b, Human Rights Watch, 2013).

There are two broad explanations for the post-colonial regulation of homosexuality, which do not differ on the extent to which Muslim traditions have been transformed, but rather on whether homosexualization is an exclusively colonial imposition. Writers such as Massad suggest a continuity in recent times with colonial era regulation, arguing that the internationalization of LGBITQ politics simply extends the imposition of Western norms on non-Western cultures and that Muslim homophobia is therefore largely a rejection of Western versions of sexuality, and this rejection is merely another dimension of resisting Western imperialism. I deal with this critique of contemporary Western homosexualization in some detail because it goes to the heart of contemporary politics of queer and Muslim identities, forcing us to confront whether the two have become mutually exclusive because of the identification of the former with Western colonialism and contemporary neo-colonialism. I work through an answer to this question by focusing on the second broad explanation for the post-colonial regulation of homosexuality, which is that post-colonial states have benefited from using normative gender and sexuality as a marker of national identity, thus inevitably continuing the regulation of homosexualities and gender diversity more broadly, both through laws and wider cultural proscriptions. These arguments are, I suggest, more convincing explanations for the contemporary positioning of Muslim cultures against homosexuality because they recognize the reality of state-led homophobia and Muslim cultural agency. I therefore reject the elements of post-colonial analysis that suggest that contemporary Muslim homophobia is largely a reaction to external forces of neo-colonial homosexualization. However, I also argue that we must take some of Massad's insights seriously, particularly those around the ways in which the contemporary politics of rights can be drawn into the civilizational dialectic described in Chapter 2.

I therefore attempt to stake out a middle ground that combines the insights of both sets of explanations for the contemporary regulation of homosexualities by recognizing that historical colonization, current state homophobia and contemporary international (Western-led) politics are all components of the 'forces of homosexualization' that have transformed Muslim homo-eroticism into the contemporary versions of gender and sexual identity that position them against sexual diversity in general, and Western versions of homosexuality in particular. In doing so, I focus on the idea of 'connected histories' (Bhambra, 2007; Subrahmanyam, 1997) as a way of thinking through a 'middle ground' in terms of how we might understand the versions of modernity at play in the explanations of homosexualization and post-colonial regulation. In the preceding chapters, I have attempted to unravel the teleological assumptions of modernization in Western discourses of sexual diversity as Western exceptionalism, and I suggest that something similar needs to be applied to post-colonial analyses. Specifically, we need to be aware that some post-colonial analysis may replay the Eurocentrism of explanations of modernity by ceding the construction and regulation of modern homosexuality to the West. In contrast, I argue that the impact of homosexualization is not wholly Western but rather forms components in continuing regulation by non-Western cultures and states, based on the significance of homosexuality for maintaining normative gender regimes, including self-identifying LGBTIQ movements. Thus, we need a different, connected understanding of sexuality within modernity, one that is not prescriptive in terms of the teleology of either modernity or sexual liberation, nor proscriptive in terms of post-colonial understandings of contemporary sexual diversity.

Homo-eroticism in traditional Muslim cultures

Although it is somewhat of an overstatement to describe a first 'wave' of research on Muslim homo-eroticism, there are some works that emerged in the 1990s that have remained significant to this field, and with which the more recent research is still engaged.[2] This engagement occurs around two main related issues: cross-cultural differences and the exclusivity of Western gay identity, and the teleology of gay liberation based on Western identity. Murray and Roscoe's collection from 1997(a) remains an important one, moving beyond previous writings by journalists and tourists such as Schmitt and Sofer's *Sexuality and Eroticism Among Males in Moslem Societies* (1992). This early English language collection is largely based on personal reflections and experiences from tourists, temporary residents and journalists based in a range of Arab countries. Murray and Roscoe's various contributors engage in a more academic analysis of literatures and draw more specifically on the contemporary theoretical ideas in sexuality studies in the 1990s. The editors begin with the assertion that cross-cultural and historical research on homosexualities is still scant and particularly that 'Islamic homosexualities (and those of sub-Saharan Africa) have been almost completely overlooked' (1997b: 3). The central contention of their book is that identities for homosexuals did and do exist in Muslim societies, but they are more complex than the simple Western 'egalitarian' identity of present – the ontologically coherent individual public identity that has been previously described as an 'ethnic' homosexuality (Epstein, 1992).[3] In this sense:

> The thrust of this collection is to challenge the dominant, Eurocentric model of gay/lesbian history and the implicit, occasionally explicit, assertion in many social constructionist accounts that contemporary homosexuality is somehow incomparable to any other pattern (or that there are no other patterns). The implication is that nothing at all preceded modern homosexuality or that whatever homosexual behavior occurred earlier was too disorganized, spontaneous, and insignificant to compare with modern homosexuality. 'Pre-modern' societies are assumed to be more hostile toward same-sex relations or lacking the conditions necessary for social roles and identities incorporating homosexuality to develop. Despite their pessimistic post-humanist disavowals, social constructionist accounts still evoke a history of homosexuality as a progressive, even teleological, evolution from pre-modern repression, silence, and invisibility to modern visibility and social freedom. (Murray and Roscoe, 1997b: 5)

The collection includes this and other overview essays in Part 1, literary studies in Part 2, historical studies in Part 3, and anthropological studies in Part 4, presenting a wide range of historical evidence from literature, travel accounts, social commentators, that overall suggests a wide variance in how homosexuality existed and was understood. The studies are too numerous to detail here but they cover historical periods from antiquity to the emergence of Muslim cultures around the seventh and eighth centuries CE, as well as subsequent developments in the medieval period, with some slight emphasis on the nineteenth and contemporary twentieth centuries. Roscoe argues that ancient societies had status and gender variant forms of homosexuality, and that these appear to have been transmitted through time into emergent Islamic societies so that part of Muslim heritage is an enduring legacy of diversity from antiquity (Roscoe, 1997)[4] – a point that is also made by studies of India and wider Southeast Asia discussed below. A central idea that the various contributors to Murray and Roscoe put forward is that homosexual behavior existed in many different locations of Muslim cultures, from between the thirteenth and sixteenth centuries in Egypt, Arab medieval Spain, the Ottoman Empire from the thirteenth to nineteenth centuries, through to the nineteenth century Balkans. However, there is no evidence of the social identity of exclusive homosexuality that developed in the West from the nineteenth century. Rather, there is evidence – drawn from literature and historical accounts – that both status differentiated and gender variant homosexual conduct existed.

The former is identified in homo-social male cultures, such as the *Mamluk* (Mameluke) military elite who were a slave class, recruited specifically for military roles and removed from their families and places of origin to serve various Muslim Sultans in Egypt. A similar slave class of administrators was also used in Ottoman Turkey, removed from their families and forbidden from passing on wealth to these families with the aim of creating loyalty only to the ruling Sultan (1997a, 1997b).[5] In both cases, there is evidence of homosexual behavior, both within these groups who were acquired as children and lived separately from the general population, and also between specific individuals and people of higher status in associated royal courts, sometimes including the rulers themselves. The latter case of gender variant homosexuality is discussed in relation to both men and women, such as the Balkan sworn virgins of the nineteenth century, women who took on a male social role and thus could not marry (Dickemann, 1997); and the *Mustergil* role that women took on in southern Iraq in the mid-twentieth century, when they chose to live as men, enjoying the privileges of the male patriarchal culture and usually not marrying (Westphal-Hellbusch, 1997). Anthropological work identified the *Khanith* role in Oman in the 1970s, but the evidence points more to men taking on this 'third gender' and being available for sex in this role (Murray, 1997c), similar to reports discussed from Indonesia from the nineteenth to twentieth centuries, where men in travelling entertainment troupes played the social role of a female, both onstage and off, often including availability for sexual relations with other men (Murray, 1997d). These are brief examples of the range included in this collection and it is worth looking at these in detail, not least because the contributors and editors are careful to acknowledge the limits of available evidence and methodologies.

Nonetheless, drawing on this evidence, the editors make the point that there is a huge variety in Muslim societies and suggest that:

> ... the contrast between 'Western' and 'Islamic' homosexualities is not so much one of visibility versus invisibility or modern freedom versus traditional repression, but of containment versus elaboration, of a single pattern of homosexuality defined and delimited by institutions and discourses closely linked to the modern nation-state versus the variety, distribution, and longevity of same-sex patterns in Islamic societies. (Murray and Roscoe, 1997b: 6)

This elaboration is supported by the variety of historical literary studies included in the more recent collection by Babayan and Najmabadi (2008) which also focuses on a range of Muslim cultures, from Iberia in the mid sixteenth to seventeenth centuries, medieval Arab literatures and the *Mamluk* elites in Egypt in late medieval times. Again, we see that sexual activity between males is represented in historical literatures (there is very little evidence on female homo-eroticism as Murray points out in Chapter 5 of his collection, 1997e) but beyond this fact, we also see that there is an emphasis on the active and/or older male partner keeping his heterosexuality intact whilst the passive 'female' role is more subject to social stigma. The oft-cited *Mamluk* example stresses that the older warriors had access to the younger initiates, as did the higher status men, including the Sultans whom they defended. This differentiation of status is true also in the gender variant model, where the 'female' role adopted by some men identifies them as the passive sexual partner. When we consider the non-Arab Muslim world, these patterns of gender variance and status differentiation are repeated, although with cultural specificity. For example, in his review of the anthropological and historical work on gender and sexuality in Southeast Asia, Peletz demonstrates that many of these cultures had ritualized transgender roles for both men and women in religious ceremonies, often pre-existing Islam and thus having continuities with antiquity, but that many of these also continued under the variety of Muslim cultures that gradually took over in this region (2006). Same-sex behavior is documented in the *Bissu* transgender ritual specialists of Indonesia but not convincingly so in other such identities, such as the *Sida-Sida* in the Malay Peninsula.

Recent queer literary analysis from India also suggests the existence of same-sex identities in both Muslim and Hindu cultures, but again the contributors argue that the Western model of exclusive sexual orientation is not apparent for the most part (Vanita and Kidwai, 2000a). Rather, they describe a variety of references and terminologies used in the historical literature they have gathered together, making the point that the various cultural traditions within India recognized same-sex eroticism and sometimes fairly stable same-sex identities (Vanita, 2000: xxi).[6] This broad historical collection also demonstrates continuities between ancient and medieval literary traditions and between medieval Sanskritic and Muslim literature that appeared from the tenth century onwards (mainly in Perso-Urdu languages). Kidwai suggests that 'Homoerotically inclined men are continuously visible in Muslim medieval histories and are generally described without pejorative comment' (Kidwai, 2000: 107) and argues that the urban cosmopolitan and migratory nature of emergent Islamic centers and the expansion of printing technologies created both the homo-social spaces for homo-erotic encounters and the means through which to record and celebrate them in writing, such that 'Medieval poetry depicts romantic and erotic interaction between men across class and religious divides (2000: 108)[7]. Kidwai acknowledges that the strictly Islamic view on sexual diversity was severe but that the wide range of literary evidence suggests that this view did not prevail in everyday life.

What can we conclude from these historical studies? Given both the historical and geographical range covered by the studies in these collections (and the preceding volume by Schmitt and Sofer, 1992), it is difficult to talk in terms of a consistent Islamic sensibility around homosexuality and homo-eroticism. Indeed, the studies point to culturally specific variations of Islam and its precursors, and variation in how far a specifically Islamic religious orthodoxy impacted various cultures, thus producing a wide range of variations of gender and status differentiated forms of homosexual behavior and identities within these cultures. My purpose has not been to review this evidence in exhaustive detail, but to highlight the fact that it exists, and thus that we must resist the crude reductionist characterization of Islamic influence that appears to be a dominant contemporary discourse on both sides of the oppositional civilizational dialectic. The historical traditions of Muslim homo-eroticism further undermine the certainties of the modernization thesis discussed in the previous chapter, as a coherent explanation for Muslim homophobia by demonstrating that Islamic influence is neither uniformly dominant nor without traditions of acceptance or at least acknowledgement of sexual diversity. Of course, these literary and anthropological histories also give lie to the arguments put forward by Muslims that homosexuality is inimical to their 'traditional' cultures.

This evidence challenges the simplistic binary positioning of homosexuality as Western versus Eastern resistance to it, and perhaps supports Murray and Roscoe's point above; that it is more accurate to think of Western 'containment' versus Eastern 'elaborations' with both commonalities and divergences across these broad cultures in the recognition of same-sex identities and behaviors. In terms of divergence, the major point remains that the varieties of Muslim homo-eroticism provide evidence of homosexual behavior but also demonstrate clear cultural and historical differences in whether and how this is both socially significant and provides resources for sexual and gendered identity. It is therefore more accurate to think in terms of a specific version of Western public and 'ethnic' homosexuality versus a range of Muslim homo-erotic traditions, the vast majority of which do not follow the public version of homosexuality found in the modern West. Nonetheless, there are commonalities and the most consistent one is that the prevailing gender order provides the framework for much of the homo-eroticism discussed in Islamic cultures, both when representing sexual acts and in the stigma associated with those acts, if they are made public. Murray argues that the common practice in Islamic cultures is not to acknowledge publicly any issues of deviance from the norm but of course, the 'deviance' is from a heterosexual gendered order (Murray 1997f). The dominance of hetero-gender was, of course, the departure point for academic analysis of the 'deviance' of homosexuality in Western contexts (McIntosh, 1996 [1968]; Rahman and Jackson, 2010; Seidman, 1996) and has remained a consistent focus of sexuality studies. In common with the West, gender is a dominant framework of both understanding and regulation of sexual diversity in Eastern cultures and the historical evidence from Muslim cultures continues to be manifested in the survey and qualitative evidence of Muslim attitudes discussed in Chapter 3, broadly supporting one dimension in the modernization thesis; that traditionalist cultures tend to be patriarchal, and this consequently limits tolerance of both gender equality and sexual diversity. Whilst there are some historical similarities in recognizing fairly stable same-sex identities and behaviors in some cultures (Boellstorff, 2005a, 2005b, 2007; Sharlet, 2010), the overriding historical difference is that the modern Western essentialist identity for homosexuality is largely absent from Muslim cultures during the period of modernity. At the very least, this suggests that a Western teleology of gay liberation is culturally specific, based as it is on a culturally specific identity formation, regardless of the fact that the social significance of homosexuality in relation to gender hierarchies seems to be a culturally universal starting point for its stigmatization. This conclusion, based on these historical studies, raises some difficult questions for contemporary theories and politics, not least of which is how this divergence came to signify a 'civilizational' divide, and I turn to these issues below.

The transformation of Muslim homo-eroticism through the 'Gay International'

Roscoe suggests that modern times have brought about a consolidation of Western understandings of homosexuality such that Muslim ways of knowing and being sexual are under threat:

> Today 'homosexualization,' the social forces and historical events that produce homosexual identity, is spreading throughout the world. This, together with internal forces within Islamic societies – in particular, the conjunction of Islamic fundamentalism and the emergence of modern nation-states with all their pervasive means of social regulation – make the future of traditional forms of homosexuality in the Oikoumene region[8] uncertain for the first time in their long history. (Roscoe, 1997: 55)

Joseph Massad also reaches this conclusion in a 2002 article and subsequent book, *Desiring Arabs* (2008), although he arrives at this position through a critique of the work described above. Massad argues that much of the work on Muslim cultures is ahistorical, inaccurate, and consequently politically problematic. The first charge is a valid one in that many of the arguments made by those such as Schmitt and Sofer (1992) and Murray and Roscoe (1997) draw upon a wide historical range of material to discuss contemporary Arab and Muslim cultures or indeed lack any evidence on contemporary cultures (2002: 366). This also occurs in the more recent research, such as the collection by Babayan and Najmabadi (2008) which does not include a single essay on contemporary Muslim cultures, despite being aimed at instituting a field of study on 'Islamicate' sexualities. Massad is therefore correct to argue for a more precise historical 'archive' as he does in conclusion to his book (2008: 415), one that does include the nuances of social change in contemporary Muslim societies rather than the implication that 'time in the context of the Arab world and Islam is not an agent of change but rather the proof of its lack' (2002: 371).[9] For Massad, furthermore, the lack of clear historical knowledge contributes to the current dominance of exclusively 'Western' frameworks of sexual identity that are being deployed in the Arab world. This is an important point and relates back to the evidence presented in the previous chapter, or rather lack thereof, of how Muslim communities understand sexual diversity in their cultures, and forces us to question thus how far their reactions to 'homosexuality' are reactions to Western forms of identity politics, particularly in those surveys that seem to use only Western conceptions of homosexuality.

Whilst Massad seems at first to concur with the challenge to Western identity politics contained in the literature described above, his key argument is in fact critical of this research. Not only does he argue that these historical studies are inaccurate and ahistorical but, crucially, that they have been used politically to render Muslim cultures as 'other' to Western civilizations by LGBTIQ activist groups, often in collusion with Western governments and international organizations such as the UN. Massad therefore posits a hierarchical relationship between Western gay movements and Eastern cultures, one, indeed, of orientalism, because he claims that it is a Western sexual ontology (based on a hetero/homo binary) that is being incited, imported, and imposed on non-Western cultures (2007: 40).[10] He identifies the International Lesbian and Gay Association (ILGA) and International Gay and Lesbian Human Rights Commission (IGLHRC) as key players, particularly because these US-based organizations engaged with the increasing emphasis on human rights in development policies since the 1990s[11] but he includes all 'missionary tasks, the discourse that produces them, and the organizations that represent them' in his identification of a 'Gay International' (2008: 161). His key argument is that through its emphasis on the universality of sexual minority human rights, the 'Gay International' is inciting a Western discourse of gay identity which creates both state and cultural resistance in Muslim cultures, effectively both stabilizing same-sex desires into Western identities and consequently creating heteronormative responses from Arab states, resulting in further oppression rather than liberation. In essence, he argues that the politics of a public gay identity creates the problem:

> When the Gay International incites discourse on homosexuality in the non-Western world, it claims that the 'liberation' of those it defends lies in the balance. In espousing this liberation project, the Gay International is destroying social and sexual configurations of desire in the interest of reproducing a world in its own image, one wherein its sexual categories and desires are safe from being questioned. (Massad, 2002: 385)

This view has provoked a sharp debate within activist and academic circles between those agreeing with his critique and those rejecting aspects of it (Awwad, 2010; Ahmed 2011; Babayan and Najmabadi, 2008; Bracke, 2012; Habib, 2010a; Landry, 2011; Rahman, 2010; Traub, 2008) but his position has currency precisely because his argument goes to the heart of the questions raised at the beginning of this chapter about the teleology of gay liberation based on Western conceptualizations of sexual identity.[12]

I would argue that one can read the historical studies described above as concurrent with one of his major points about the difference in Eastern understandings of sexuality. There may well be epistemological and methodological issues with some of these studies, as Massad suggest, but regardless of how inaccurate he thinks the previous research is, he agrees that there have indeed been different cultural formations of sexual behaviors and identities in Muslim cultures. On that key point we can see some broad agreement and, indeed, evidence from other non-Western, non-Muslim cultures supports this point (Greenberg, 1988). It is worth reiterating that this insight makes it difficult to accurately talk in terms of a monolithic or consistent Islamic cultural formation or Muslim traditions of sexuality and indeed, as suggested both in the previous chapter and above, part of any resistance to the orientalist civilizational dialectic needs to acknowledge this fact. Nonetheless, if we can accept that there are historical cultural differences in the social construction and significance of sexuality, this would indicate that a Westernized version of gay liberation is indeed culturally specific, perhaps even orientalist. There are, however, two major problems with the subsequent argument Massad builds from this initial position.

First, the political critique of the 'Gay International' is overly determinist, associating NGO activity (particularly the ILGA) with a direct influence over and accommodation with national and international governmental institutions whereas more careful accounts demonstrate the fact that gay rights have not been evenly successful across different institutional arenas. For example, Sweibel argues that the EU has been more receptive to gay rights than the UN, partly because of the use of a fashionably current human rights discourse in a period when the EU was seeking to expand its competences and significance to cultural values, in contrast to a declining UN where human rights were not a coherent discourse (Sweibel, 2009).[13] The evidence reviewed on IGO activity in the previous chapter supports this conclusion, and gives empirical cause to be skeptical of a consistent trajectory of progress for the 'Gay International'. Within Europe, furthermore, despite EU-wide discourses and legislation on discrimination there is evidence that these state or transnational elite-led politics are not uniformly accepted within the cultural values of all populations (Gerhards, 2010;

Kollman, 2009). In the American context (which Massad identifies as a dominant one for LGBTIQ NGO activity), more detailed studies have shown that gay rights have been wholly uneven in their advance for a mix of cultural, institutional and political reasons.[14] Even Puar's polemic on the emergence of 'homonationalism' in the domestic US recognizes that this emergent discourse is contingent and only encompasses a limited type of contemporary queer identity (2007: xii). The recent announcement by US Secretary of State Clinton that gay rights would become mainstreamed in foreign policy objectives may seem to confirm the influence of the 'Gay International' in the American context, but this policy speech to the UN Human Rights Council in 2011 neither detailed implementation strategies, nor, of course, was it coupled with any domestic policy announcements to progress LGBTIQ rights in the USA.[15] Given that the Human Rights Council was the venue for the very first joint statement on LGBTIQ rights at the UN in March 2011 (see Chapter 3, note 8), we can speculate that the US is contributing to a strategy to iterate the importance of LGBTIQ rights at the UN, but we should remember that this Council remains the only supportive forum in the UN to date.

Lack of empirical success for the putative Gay International does not negate the fact that a discourse of international human rights for sexual diversity has emerged (Hamzic 2011, Waites, 2009). Massad argues that this discourse is actively interpellating erotic identities into a Western binary heterosexual matrix, and in this he follows an established body of work where the strategic use of rights discourses has been subject to critique for many years as potentially reifying sexual categories as essentialist universal 'truths' (Epstein, 1992; Evans 1993; Rahman, 2000). More recently, these essentializing tendencies have raised a concern for the potential cultural imperialism of such discourses, particularly whether Western versions of 'sexual orientation' are appropriate political levers in non-Western settings (Kollman and Waites, 2009; Sweibel, 2009). Waites, for example, provides a thorough critique of the essentialism and universality implied by the concept of 'sexual orientation' and the way its codification emphasizes a stable subjectivity over and above the potential fluidity of behavior, thus universalizing cultural differences into a Western understanding of the heterosexual matrix (Waites, 2009). Massad's work has no doubt influenced these concerns but they also address a question that is absent from his work, which is the second major problem with his analysis.

The bulk of the criticisms of the dangers of rights simultaneously recognize that the translation of anti-essentialist analyses of identity into political frameworks is difficult because there is an inevitable institutional momentum to talk in terms of human rights that are 'attached' to a specific identity group. As I have put it before: 'the convergence of structures of democracy and the material and social construction of sexuality produce an almost irresistible movement towards essentialist sexual and political discourses ... this in turn leaves us with little room for social equality: a genuinely equivalent organization, regulation and acceptance of different genders and sexualities' (Rahman, 2000: 197). In the more recent context of the internationalization of sexual orientation, Waites argues that:

> ... the crucial analytic issue to grasp is that, irrespective of authorial intent, when introduced into mainstream human rights discourse, these concepts become subject to interpretation in the context of broader gender and sexuality discourses operating in global governance and a fragile, emergent global civil society. This is the context in which it is necessary to develop a strategy for engaging with these concepts, appraising costs and benefits for political movements. (2009: 152–153).

Massad really has no contribution to this central institutional dilemma of a practical strategy that both critiques the universality of Western ontological frameworks, and reformulates them through this critique. Indeed, he simply rejects gays rights and identities as Western imperialist discourses that are 'destroying' Arab cultural formations of sexuality. Leaving aside the lack of detail he provides for what these Arab formations are,[16] his own description of the forceful impact of Western homosexualization surely demands an engagement with its formations and discourses, rather than simply rejecting them. This lack of engagement, I suggest, is a symptom of his underpinning conceptualization of modernity, a framework that both narrows his understanding of the 'forces' of homosexualization, and replays cultural exclusivity between Western and Eastern social constructions of sexuality.

Modernity misunderstood? Colonialism, post-colonial cultures and the regulation of the sexual

Positions such as Massad's may provide a useful critique of Western gay movements' involvement in these political discourses of Islamic 'otherness' but they do not ultimately contribute to deconstructing that discourse because their analytical frame identifies modern sexual diversity as wholly Western and thus reaffirms that its presence is indeed a marker of Western dominance and colonialism. The broader frame is, of course, post-colonial critique, particularly its epistemological challenge to Western forms of knowledge and their use to render non-Western countries and peoples subordinate during modernity, exemplified by Said's paradigm shifting critique of 'Orientalism' as a discourse of Western superiority during modernity (1978). Bhambra elaborates on the Eurocentrism of specifically sociological knowledge thus: 'colonialism ... was intrinsic to the contemporary scene in which dominant forms of inquiry were formed and yet the colonial is rendered unseen. These forms of inquiry elaborated universal criteria and presumed themselves to be universally relevant and yet ... were constructed on the basis of marginalizing and silencing other experiences and voices ... postcolonial scholarship challenges the universals of modernity and modernization as these are commonly represented' (2007: 21–22). Massad's critique sits squarely in this tradition, but it would seem to me that his argument, in his determination to vilify the neo-orientalist 'Gay International', relies on a mistaken conceptualization of the coherence and exclusivity of modernity and the formation of cultures within the 'modern' world, one that potentially replays the cultural exclusivity that has become central to positing Islam and Muslim culture as 'other' to the West and the former as simply subordinate to the power of the latter.

It is important, therefore, to unpack the understandings of sexuality within such a framework of modernity and its colonial and neo-colonial aspects if we are to work towards disembedding sexual diversity from the contemporary orientalist and/or Islamophobic discourse. This is a particularly urgent issue because we are caught up in a world in which 'gay international' discourses are being deployed within the Islamophobia discourse, but also because there is contemporary evidence that sexual diversity political movements are becoming more public in Muslim majority countries and minority communities. Thus, as Awwad puts it (commenting on the *Queen Boat* arrests in Cairo that Massad uses as a key example), we are caught in a dilemma: 'A postcolonial predicament emerges for human rights work: intervention is problematic because it adopts a universalizing posture and non-intervention overlooks the plight of persecuted same-sex practitioners and renders the state unaccountable for its violations' (2010: 319). Similarly, in her introduction to her recent edited collection, Habib focuses on Massad as exemplifying the culturally specific arguments that Western homosexuality does not have relevance for those in the Arab world and she rejects this, arguing that:

> The critiques of culturally insensitive approaches to sexual practices in the Arab world have overlooked their own insensitivity to the very real struggles of homosexual people in the Arab world (regardless of

whether such a term is universally identified with, these individuals are in the least aware of their inherent difference and exclusion from the socially sanctified sexual currencies of marriage and children). (Habib, 2010a: xviii)

Habib is basing this position on the struggles for the advance of rights, and I sympathize with the assertion that some do see themselves in this way, or at least are trying to reach for a recognition of their difference from prevailing gender hierarchies and identities since these are recurrent themes in the contemporary research on queer Muslims (discussed in greater detail in Chapter 5). Awwad and Habib therefore direct our attention to a predicament of which one side is precisely about the contemporary experiences of Muslim sexual diversity in the contexts of the increasingly internationalist emergence of LGBTIQ rights discourses and the resistance to those by their own cultures and governments. The question thus becomes whether we can we work through this predicament without reinscribing the neo-colonialism of Western gay identity. Massad seems to suggest not, but his argument about contemporary neo-colonialism relies on two important factors. First, that a Western binary of hetero/homo is being imported into cultures where this understanding does not exist. However, we must remember that this matrix is fundamentally an essentialist framework of sexuality *and* gender and that the power of essentialist thinking is not simply expressed through political identities (such as gay and lesbian). We should, therefore, consider the wider sociological basis of essentialist frameworks, leading us to explore their purchase on many different cultures, rather being exclusively identified with a Eurocentric worldview. Second, Massad posits a mutual exclusivity between colonial/neo-colonial and colonized cultures that is, of course, part of the orthodox understanding of the power dynamic at work in colonialism. We should consider, however, whether this is comprehensively accurate in the realm of the sexual, both historically and in contemporary times given that the regulation of genders and sexualities is not exclusive to the West. Underpinning both issues is a theoretical presumption about both the momentum and 'ownership' of modernity; expanding from the West outwards because it is understood as originating in the West, and gay rights thus become an exemplar of this understanding of the momentum of modernity – a position that those such as Massad share with those modernization theorists discussed in the previous chapter. As I argued in conclusion to the previous chapter, modernization theories are logically flawed when contemplating the contemporary conditions in which Muslim cultures are experiencing the politics of gay rights and my concern is that post-colonial critiques of sexual diversity politics may contain similar flaws.

Of course, we know from both the literature discussed earlier and from studies of other cultures that the epistemology of modern Western sexual identity is historically specific. The diversity of sexual behaviors was connected to pre-Islamic influences, localized and not uniformly transformed by the advent of Islam. Sexuality was not seen as identity in the modern Western sense and, therefore, we can argue that historically, there is no doubt that imperialism plays a significant role in transforming traditional Muslim homo-eroticism. For example, Murray suggests that there is a historical relationship between the regulation of public homosexuality in Muslim cultures and imperialism in that some of the regulation is due to the impact of Christian colonialism that sought to use 'Eastern' sexual depravity to justify Western moral superiority (1997d: 15, 1997f), something that Peletz also suggests was present in colonial Southeast Asia (2006) and has been documented in India (Vanita and Kidwai, 2000b: 191). The impact of this was twofold: first, as Massad illustrates in his analysis of Arab literatures, there was an epistemological shift in understandings of sexual behavior into sexual identities. These understandings, moreover, were overwhelmingly brought into discourse as objects of regulation and his analysis provides detailed expositions of how this framework of modern homosexuality and its underpinning taxonomies of both hetero and homo desires came to be both incorporated and resisted by Arab intellectuals during the colonial era (2007). The second important point is that the emergence of modern Western notions of homosexual identity were deployed in the colonial relationship as part of transformations in gender in the 'home' colonizing countries. The arrival of imperial discourses on homosexuality therefore serve to construct the 'home' nations as morally superior through the framework of gender hierarchies and sexual moralities that were being consolidated during the imperial and industrial eras in these Western nations and then used as part of the 'civilizing' discourse of imperialism (Lennox and Waites, 2013a). This occurred as well in settler colonialism, as Morgenson and others have pointed out (Blackwood, 2000; Morgenson, 2010). This is not, however, to argue that sexuality is merely a reflex of colonial power but rather that is a key component of the array of 'civilizing' discourses and practices of imperial dominance (McClintock, 1995; Stoler, 2010).

As McClintock suggests in her engagement of Said's work, there is a problem with post-colonial analysis that uses sexuality simply as a metaphor for aspects of colonialism: 'Sexuality as a trope for other power relations was certainly an abiding aspect of imperial power ... But seeing sexuality only as a metaphor runs the risk of eliding *gender* as a constitutive dynamic of imperial and anti-imperial power' (McLintock, 1995: 14). Whilst she acknowledges the foundational nature of Said's work on male imperialism, she raises a concern about whether we can understand the impact of colonialism *and* post-colonial states without taking gender structures into account. This is a problem that I think Massad shares with his mentor because he remains focused on sexual identity and the hetero/homo binary without relating the structural existence of these to gender formations. This is not to criticize the integrity of his empirical focus on same-sex eroticism but rather to suggest that his theoretical characterization of the processes of homosexualization in Arab culture is limited in its range by focusing on the Gay International, the AIDS pandemic and the rise of Islamism. He might retort that gendered frameworks as the basis for sexual identity are precisely a Western epistemology and so are included within his critique, but other studies suggest a more complicated historical and contemporary picture, particularly in post-imperial cultures which link gender more explicitly with sexuality.

As Abdulhadi argues, this historical emergence of homophobia in relation to colonialism does not simply disappear in post-colonial times, but rather the post-colonial era furthered this regulation with the deployment of more rigid gender and sexual moralities as part of national liberation strategies (2010). Focusing on liberation movements in both Algeria and Palestine, she suggests that the colonial era 'Victorian' morality of strict gender and sexual divisions survived as a regulatory discourse in nationalist political movements and ideologies, which then became more enshrined in response to the challenge of Islamism, part of which was the identification of ruling elites within Arab nations with 'decadent' Western moralities (2010: 473–474). Similar patterns are cited in the Indian context where the British-imposed anti-sodomy law of 1861 was retained by independent India and defended by political elites and public discourses as part of Indian culture (Vanita and Kidwai, 2000b), a debate that continues even though the High Court effectively repealed the law in 2009.[17] Peletz's research on wider Southeast Asia (2006) confirms the proposition that Western imperialism may have begun the process of narrowing acceptable gendered and sexual behaviors, and constructing specific identities through this, but that this continues in the post-colonial era, particularly when nations are either reclaiming a 'traditional' culture (as in Burma), or promoting 'Asian values' in their route to modernization (as in the case of Malaysia). The Malaysian example also provides stark evidence of the way in which political power uses homophobia in the saga of the imprisonment of the deputy Prime Minister, Anwar Ibrahim, on charges of sodomy when he challenged the policies of the long-standing incumbent Prime Minister, Mahathir Mohamad (Shah, 2013; Williams, 2010). Williams suggests that this political incident also led to an increasing regulation of homosexuality by the government, both internally and in international forums such as the UN.[18] Blackwood's detailed research on homo-eroticism amongst women in Indonesia similarly provides evidence that the regulation of homosexuality in post-colonial eras has continuities with colonial times, although in this example there is a movement from social regulation of normative gender in Dutch colonial and Indonesian post-colonial eras (rather than legal prohibition) towards more legal proscription in a time of political upheaval after the fall of the Suharto regime:

> Under this new discourse Indonesian *lesbi*[19] and *gay* may no longer be viewed as bad examples of men and women but as individuals whose sexual desires are a threat to the stability of the nation. These proposed revisions represent a transformation from a civil society in which human consensual relationships are governed by moral norms expressed in notions of normative gender to one regulated much more heavily by criminal law and state surveillance of individual behaviour. However, the intense debates about the proposed revisions indicate that these transformations are still unfolding, their direction uncertain as competing discourses of morality, modernity, individualism and sexual rights struggle for dominance.
>
> Offord and Cantrell (2001: 245) suggest that as 'homosexuality becomes more visible (in Indonesia) there will be a legal and political response' regarding the concept of homosexual rights. Yet homosexuality has been visible at least in the media since the early 1980s. For Indonesia, it is not the emergence of a newly visible, activist *lesbi* and *gay* movement that has led to the shifting discourse on sexuality, but the development of a moral panic associated with the tremendous political and social changes occurring with the demise of the Suharto regime. Amid shifting alliances certain religious and political factions have been able to redirect international pressure for same-sex marriage and sexual rights toward a debate on the morality of the citizenry, whose growing sense of individualism and free choice threatens to undermine the stability of the state. In their efforts to redefine a normatively gendered citizenry, certain factions have sought to prop up heterosexual marriage by attempting to criminalise a wide range of sexual practices. (Blackwood, 2007: 304)

Along with Massad, Blackwood acknowledges the impact that international LGBTIQ human rights pressures can have on states who then use this discourse to regulate further their own populations but, crucially, she provides the local context in which this emerges. Similarly, Awwad's analysis of the *Queen Boat* affair in Cairo provides a more complex rendering of the Egyptian state's repression than is found in Massad's work, illustrating the ways in which sexual license was identified with the British colonial era (particularly in its legal tolerance of prostitution servicing the colonizers), producing a movement towards regulation and more conservative morality in the post-colonial state which found keener expression in the state's attempt to resist the rise of conservative Islamism (Awwad, 2010).

The complex historical interaction of colonialism and post-colonialism has produced a regulation of sexuality that is not simply the imposition of a Western morality and epistemology, but a complex deployment of gendered and sexual discourses as part of civilizational, national and ethnic identity from both sides of the colonial divide.[20] Even if we begin with the proposition that Western epistemologies have dominated national cultures of gender and the sexual since colonial times, and this is now globally dominant in the contemporary era, that still cannot fully explain the investment in these epistemologies by national cultures that are seeking to distinguish themselves from Western neo-imperialism. Such a recognition seems absent from Massad's perspective to the extent that he suggests that it is the 'Gay International's' incitement to discourse that produces homophobic reactions, rather than explaining why a contemporary state might draw power through stigmatizing homosexuality as 'Western', even though he acknowledges that this process does occur. We must accept that the Western forces of homosexualization indicated by Roscoe and described partially by Massad are not wholly 'owned' by the West, even if they are seen as originating there. Thus, we need to consider the wider basis for the transformations of traditional Muslim homo-eroticism than simply a political 'incitement to discourse'.

Connected histories: the wider sociological basis of homosexualization during modernity

In her rethinking of sociological theories of modernity in the context of post-colonial challenges, Bhambra argues that conceptualizations of modernity have largely ignored the impact that colonial endeavors had on shaping modern institutions, governance, and political thought *within* the colonizing nations of Europe (Bhambra, 2007). She argues that a more accurate understanding of modernity requires a recognition of the historical connections in cultures and the cultural specificity in the social thought that emerged to explain such formations but located them as wholly 'Western'. I propose that we can use this perspective to rethink how we conceptualize modern sexuality. First, as demonstrated above, we know that regimes of sexual identity that were constructed by colonizing powers were simultaneously being enshrined in their home nations as a basis for reordering bourgeois gender divisions and then using these relationships as one aspect of legitimizing colonialism (Lennox and Waites, 2013a; McClintock, 1995; Peletz, 2006; Stoler, 2010; Vanita and Kidwai, 2000a). Moreover, in post-colonial times, the continued and sometimes expanded regulation of homosexuality suggests a continuing connection in how sexuality can be conceptualized by a ruling national elite (whether exclusively as a government or more widely in elite public culture) to promote its own governing legitimacy. That empirical fact alone suggests that we cannot simply see modern understandings of sexuality as wholly Western, even if the technologies that brought them to bear are understood as emanating from the West. Second, however, Bhambra also suggests that the assumption that modernity emerged in the West and is now being followed by other regions is a mistaken understanding; modernity and its consequences have always been globally interconnected. Her argument is thus a critique of both classical sociological theory and some post-colonial theories, particularly the idea of multiple modernities, precisely because the latter replays the prioritization of the West when it suggests that non-Western countries are *following* modernization patterns (2007: 69).[21] The internationalization of LGBTIQ rights and identities, seen either positively or critically, is often located within such understandings of modernization, either as a universal process or as multiple routes to modernization and indeed such assumptions underpin many of the arguments put forward about Muslim antipathy to homosexuality critiqued in Chapter 3. My concern is that arguments such as Massad's share this mistaken assumption of the direction and 'ownership' of modernity by reducing sexuality to a reflex of Western modernization. Whilst it would be unfair to characterize Massad's thesis as explicitly framed by an assumption of this divergence in modernity, he nonetheless assumes a cultural exclusivity between West and East which implies significant difference in social formations of sexuality as part of modernity which can be read as multiple modernities of the sexual.

This is neither to deny that the emergence of the modern homosexual identity may be located in the regulatory modernization discourses of the West, nor to dismiss the historical evidence that shows how these emergent understandings were part of colonial methods of 'othering' different cultures. Rather it is to raise the question of whether the impact of the modern 'incitement to discourse' has had coherent or exclusive consequences, either in the countries of origin or those that they colonized. Not only do there remain significant same-sex behaviors in the West that are not identified as 'homosexual' (such as men who have sex with men) but the survey evidence cited in the previous chapter also shows that the 'liberated' gay identity is not consistently accepted across the West. The coherence of Western versions of gender and sexuality is also undermined by the shift from stigma of the homosexual identity to the gradual (and very late) emergence of a positive 'gay' social identity in the modern West. Whilst we can debate whether this is simply a 'reverse' discourse as Foucault argued, and we can accept that contemporary gay identity is indeed represented as an 'ethnic' essentialist category, its very existence marks a break with the regulatory gendered discourses of imperialist modernity. Whilst I agree with Massad that the current political formations of gay politics are problematic when projected internationally, I do not think that we can explain them exclusively as a consequence of neo-colonialism because the significance of gay identity cannot be reduced to its politics, but rather politics – specifically liberal democratic individualist rights strategies – is one component of the way in which gay identity has become constructed. There is a wider basis to the emergence of homosexual identity that includes bureaucratization and social control; urbanization and the creation of homo-social leisure spaces; the reorganization of gender divisions and ideologies based on wage-labor/domestic binaries; the impact of legally free wage labor in industrial societies on notions of individuality and the medicalization of sexual identity. Most historians of modern sexuality discuss these themes in various combination, but most agree on the relevance of all of these sociological aspects (D'Emilio, 1993; Greenberg, 1988; Weeks, 1989). In more contemporary times, the role of market capitalism in creating and sustaining LGBTIQ subcultures has increased (Evans, 1993) but not only in the West as Jackson points out in his analysis of the emergence of gay capitals in Asia, where he argues that 'comparing the histories of Western and non-Western gay capitals reveals a range of structural commonalities largely independent of historical cultural differences. The material similarities among gay capitals in culturally distinct societies constitute a matrix from which similar queer cultures have emerged by local market-based processes of sex-cultural differentiation' (2009: 370). As with the spread of capitalism, can anyone really contend that the wider sociological basis for homosexualization is somehow 'owned' by the West? Can we seriously contemplate that the modern sources of social control, regulation and socio-economic ordering are exclusively Western when we know that contemporary states have many, if not all, of these aspects at their disposal as illustrated in the examples of post-colonial era analysis above? As Weiss and Bosia put it, there is an emergent global homophobia that is driven by particular states who are able to use the regulation of sexual identity as a technology of their own national and cultural legitimacy (2013a), something evidenced in the specific examples from Egypt, India, Indonesia and Malaysia cited above.

I explore the contemporary evidence in support of this argument in the following chapter and I do not want to pre-empt that more detailed discussion. Rather, my aim here is to suggest that the relationship between traditions of Muslim homo-eroticism and their transformations cannot be seen in a linear way that assumes certain momentums to modernity and, more specifically, colonialism and post-colonialism as dialectical movements in the realm of sexual regulation. In doing so, I am trying to clear some conceptual ground by drawing on Bhambra's post-colonial critique of sociological ideas of modernity. She is arguing that understandings of modernization contain Eurocentric value judgments, because modernization becomes abstracted as a set of theoretical principles and concepts without recognizing that it is *partial*, particularly through its almost total elision of colonialism as a period that was central to the development of Western modernity and therefore the ideas that came to explain it are necessarily flawed. What I am suggesting is that we extend this appreciation of connection around modernity to the formation of sexuality into contemporary times, rejecting a simple polarity in sexual cultures that is initially derived from a desire to render visible the continuing colonial nature of international relationships, but in doing so repeats a mutual exclusivity that potentially *reinstates* a Eurocentric world-view by de-emphasizing local and/or national cultures of sexuality. I argue that LGBTIQ politics and identities in contemporary times are empirically part of an interconnected modernity, deriving indeed from connected, often colonial, histories. As such, I am following Bhambra's call to rethink our theories of modernity in a way that is as free as possible of value judgments, that focuses on 'connected histories' – an idea she borrows from the historian Subrahmanyam (2005a, 2005b) – which she elaborates thus:

> Simply pluralizing the civilizational approach to include the experiences and histories of other civilizations does no more than lay those experiences and histories alongside European ones. In contrast, as Subrahmanyam (1997) argues, what is needed is to understand socio-historic processes in terms of them being global, conjunctural phenomena with different, and connected, sources and roots.
> ... I argue that there is an urgent need to address these *interconnections* as opposed to reifying the entities that are supposed to be connected, all the while keeping in mind 'that what we are dealing with are not separate and comparable, but connected histories' (Subrahmanyam, 1997: 748) (Bhambra, 2007: 76)

Homosexualization beyond westernization and the politics of Muslim identity

The evidence on Muslim homo-erotic traditions makes the discourse of homosexuality as Western modernity untenable and it also challenges Muslim politics to recognize these traditions in local and national contexts. Of course, what the historical evidence does suggest is that there have been a variety of 'elaborations' of same-sex desire in many Muslim cultures, but that the modern Western version of homosexuality is not common to these cultures. Does that take us back to the reflex of Western exceptionalism exemplified through modern Western homosexuality? I have suggested not, largely because the transformations of traditional homo-eroticism have not been exclusively 'owned' by the West, even if there is undeniable evidence that the colonizing impulse to 'civilize' certainly drove initial transformations of sexuality into medico-legal discourses that were simultaneously emerging in the 'home' imperial cultures. However, rather than seeing a return to 'traditional' forms of sexual diversity in post-colonial independence, we have seen the continued use of colonial era regulations and/or the imposition of new forms of regulation to control sexual diversity, often in the name of national or civilizational (Asian and/or Islamic) values and with the purpose of upholding the power of the state.

Thus, contemporary Muslim antipathy to homosexuality may well be partly a reaction to Western homosexuality as another dimension of contemporary neo-colonialism, but it is also part and parcel of the regulation of gender hierarchies and identities in national, sometimes regional context. It is, I have suggested, better to think of modern sexual regimes as part of the connected histories of colonialism *and* post-colonial state development throughout the cultural and institutional realms. Western modernization through colonization may have produced the contemporary understanding of homosexuality as a 'type' of person, but that understanding has not been disowned by post-colonial states and cultures. Moreover, with the increasing use of sexual diversity within the Islamophobic discourse, we have not seen political claims from Muslim communities and states that their own traditions of homo-eroticism should be recovered or take precedence, but rather we have seen an outright rejection of homosexuality, howsoever it is manifested, either internationally or within specific Muslim cultures.

Is one way forward to attempt to recover the legitimacy of Muslim homo-erotic traditions, as implied by the title of the Human Rights Watch report on colonial regulation, 'This Alien Legacy' (2013)? While that may be a necessary component of challenging the discourse of opposition between Muslim cultures and homosexuality, I do not think that is solely sufficient, given that the 'forces of homosexualization' have not been exclusive to the West in recent modernity. Whilst there have evidently been historical differences in Muslim ways of knowing and being sexual, I am not convinced that in contemporary times it makes sense to talk in terms of separate and distinct cultures that can be returned to or 'rediscovered'. If the emergence of homosexualization is part of a connected history of sexual modernity, then we must consider how those forces continue in current eras, and so we must explore contemporary, connected modernity in the sexual. Massad's questioning of Western identity politics as the only political strategy for sexual diversity remains valid but I suggest that we cannot provide an alternative until we know more about the impact of globalized gay liberation to understand what identities are being formed and experienced by those who inhabit Muslim cultures, and on this question, the truly empirical one, there is only emergent evidence. What there is suggests that whilst the political strategies of sexual 'liberation' may have originated in the West, that to reduce the meanings of gay identity to a similar Western origin would be to replay the mistaken assumption that modernity is an exclusively Western phenomenon. These further considerations of contemporary contexts therefore form the basis of the following chapter.

5
Queer Muslims in the Context of Contemporary Globalized LGBTIQ Identity

Introduction

In the previous chapters, I have challenged understandings of LGBTIQ politics as both an inevitable consequence of modernization, and as a neo-colonial imposition of homosexualization from the West. In doing so, I have suggested that both positions have partial understandings of modernity underpinning their view on LGBTIQ politics. Having argued instead that contemporary contexts are more complex than either of these models of modernity allow for, I turn in this chapter to a more detailed consideration of the sociological formation of contemporary LGBTIQ identities in order to illuminate this complexity in modernity. In this sense, my review of current evidence on queer Muslim identities is aimed at exploring the extent of their 'connected histories' with both the contemporary manifestation of traditions of Muslim homoeroticism and current globalized queer formations.

There is a danger, however, in simply thinking of 'connections' as unproblematically global, in that such a perspective potentially underplays the power imbalances between the West and non-West, both between nations and cultures and between minority and majority populations. I begin, therefore, with a picture of the current formation and politics of LGBTIQ identities in the West and their relationship to non-Western countries. This is important if we are to understand contemporary Muslim queer identities in a framework of contemporary connected histories that is both globalized and seen as Western. Thus, whilst it is important to understand these connections in the evidence on contemporary Muslim queer experience presented below, we must first assess the shape of these formations in the West to properly account for their power in non-Western contexts in shaping understandings of sexual identities and political strategies. I suggest that there remain some problematic sociological assumptions in contemporary understandings of the globalization of sexual diversity, and argue that these optimistic views need to be tempered with a recognition that sociological and political contexts for queer Muslims are different in some significant ways. Contemporary times may seem to offer an unconditionally positive view of LGBTIQ rights and identities in Western countries and although I have critiqued this assumption in previous chapters, it nonetheless remains an important context within which contemporary politics is undertaken. This political reality is therefore an important context for queer Muslims, in terms of rights within the West and how these have become the basis of Western-led international strategies, and in terms of the public culture that queer Muslims inhabit, either as minority or majority populations.

Having established these important contexts for 'connections', I provide an overview of extant research on queer Muslim identities, both in Muslim majority countries and in Muslim minority populations in the West in two sections that are both focused on contemporary connected histories. I suggest that this research illuminates that Western discourses of LGBTIQ identity and politics provide only one set of resources in a complex intersection of factors in how queer Muslims are experiencing the negotiation of their sexual identities. Exploring these intersections further, I go on to develop a framework of Muslim queers as intersectional subject locations, drawing on intersectionality theory but extending its general approach to include socio-political contexts of intersection. In conclusion, I discuss the implications such an intersectional understanding of queer Muslims has for our conceptualization of sexual modernity, suggesting that we need to move towards a more intersectional sensibility when considering the relationship between contemporary sexual formations and modernity.

The world 'they' have won

> We are living ... in the midst of a long, unfinished but profound revolution that has transformed the possibilities of living sexual diversity and creating intimate lives ... I believe the long revolution to have been overwhelmingly beneficial to the vast majority of people in the West, and increasingly to people living in the global South whose lives are also being transformed dramatically – and I say that while acknowledging the major problems that remain: fears, anxieties, prejudices, the play of power, and the power of

privilege, discrimination and exploitation, desires stimulated and hopes deferred. It often feels that two steps forward are followed by one step backward. But the momentum is positive, and largely due to one essential feature of this new world: grass-roots agency is central to the direction we are moving in. Increasingly the contemporary world is a world we are making for ourselves, part of the long process of the democratization of everyday life. (Weeks, 2007: ix–x)

In his 2007 book *The World We Have Won*, the social historian Weeks is engaged in assessing the transformations for LGBTIQ politics and identity achieved over the course of his career. Although he resists the characterization,[1] his assessment is ultimately an optimistic one, identifying four key shifts in the long transition from the 1960s to the present: democratization and the informalization of personal relationships (effectively breaking the functional equation of sex with reproduction, marriage with sex, and parenting with marriage); an increased sense of sexual agency; rendering the boundaries of public/private more visible and permeable (so, for example, sexual violence and pornography become, following Mills, public issues rather than private troubles); and finally, the increasing culture of risk anxiety (most explicitly identified with HIV). Moreover, despite his acknowledgement of the complications and non-linear changes implied in all of these central features, he concludes that 'the underlying trends show a consistent story: of liberalization, secularization and growing agency' (2007: xii). I have deliberately chosen such an optimistic view because it rightly asserts that changes have occurred in the cultural stigma and public recognition of sexuality. As I discussed in Chapter 1, I have to agree with him that there is actually experienced day-to-day change at the level of individuals, social interactions and dominant cultures. A recent illustrative example from Canada was the disciplinary action taken against a baseball player in a Toronto team because he used a homophobic message on his sports gear.[2] Here we are witnessing a public culture in which homophobia has become unacceptable to the extent that it is no longer tolerated in organized sport; a key arena of hegemonic masculinity in modern times that has been constructed to both 'annihilate' femininity (Whannel, 2002: 45) and rigidly police homo-eroticism within its homo-social environment (Pronger, 1990: 9). In the midst of ever more sophisticated theoretical analyses of culture and sexuality, we should not lose sight of the experiences that indicate a new sense of freedom, respect, agency in contrast to previous eras of stigma. The central questions for our purposes are to what extent these changes are sociologically specific to the West, what their overall momentum is, and what their consequences are in terms of the context for queer Muslims globally and in the West.

Weeks' take on the first two issues is neither the 'modernization as progress' thesis critiqued in Chapter 3, nor the 'modernization as westernization' post-colonial critique discussed in the previous chapter. Rather, he identifies the contemporary era of globalization and reflexivity as key features in making possible the democratization that he positions as central to sexual communities' agency in forging this new world of public sexual diversity. This reflexivity, both local and global, is something he characterizes as 'connections':

> Connected lives are reflective and reflexive lives; that is, lives lived in growing self-consciousness of who we are, where we come from and what we may become ... For connected lives are also lives lived reciprocally, with Others who shape what we are in the ties that not only bind but bond, and make us human. Connected lives are lives that link the global and the local, bridging distances and linking questions of sexuality and intimacy to issues of rights and responsibilities, to social justice. (2007: x–xi)

Of course, this seems at first to converge with my argument that we should understand sexuality as part of the wider connected histories of modernity because he is suggesting that the agency of sexual identities derives in large part from various processes of coming together and building public identities, intervening in public debates and challenging dominant norms by rendering visible the social and relational nature of sexual stigma, increasingly on a global scale. There are, however, a number of problems with Weeks' view that need to be addressed before we can flesh out a more precise understanding of 'connections' that is, as much as it can be, sensitive to the power differentials between the West and its Muslim others. Weeks sees liberalization of political and social life as displacing traditionalist values, particularly religion, as the key to providing increased sexual agency. This view is the orthodox modernization argument discussed in Chapter 3, but he tries not to fall into the trap of assuming inevitable or automatic progress, either historically or in its essentialist (or Freudian) characterization of sexual freedom after sexual repression and in this, he remains consistently Foucauldian and seems to avoid a modernization analysis. He does, however, consistently focus on Britain (and the West more generally at some points) in order to build his arguments. In extending his analysis to the potential for change around the world, he therefore builds on a modernization thesis with the addition of globalization in the late modern era. The key elements of globalization are then identified as the democratization of personal life and reflexivity of self and culture and he effectively states that these features are being extended to the global South, presumably primarily through his version of 'connected lives'. This framework of social change needs some unpacking, both in terms of its relevance to the West, and its generalizability to the non-West.

Whilst he identifies the key 'underlying trends' of 'liberalization, secularization and growing agency', his more detailed explanations for social change in the West focus on what he describes as 'unfinished revolutions'. This is where he is both empirically comprehensive and analytically vague, articulating a large number of unfinished 'revolutions' that have contributed to the contemporary visibility and legitimacy of sexual diversity but, by his own admission, not prioritizing them in any causal framework.[3] His specific focus is on the following: gender, transformation of intimacy; pluralization of families; broadening of reproductive rights; coming out of homosexuality; recognition of sexual diversity; explosion of sexual discourses; proliferation of sexual stories; recognition of sexual violence and abuse; expansion of intimate/sexual citizenship; intransigence of gendered differences; continued institutionalization of heterosexuality; fear of difference, and the continued circulation of power around race and ethnicity, class, age; commercialization of the erotic; threat of sexual disease; rise of fundamentalisms, and the reality of culture wars. Certainly this is a comprehensive list, but not one that clearly describes a causal logic or is categorized clearly within his four key shifts of the 'long transition'.

The characterization of the conditions for 'agency' is therefore very broad, both in relationship to the West and when being extended to subjects in non-Western cultures, either as minorities in the West or in other countries. In large part, I would argue that this is because Weeks relies on a one-sided view of agency as a positive quality of individual subjects, exemplified in the detraditionalization thesis developed by Giddens in his work on self-identity in late modernity (1990, 1991). Therein, Giddens describes the qualitative threshold of detraditionalization reached in late modernity, whereby its inherent tendencies to destroy traditional social bonds results in the increasing emphasis on individuality, creating both an anxious reflexive self that must constantly make its own identity, but also thus the possibilities for new identities and agency. Indeed, Giddens cites the emergence of lesbian and gay identities as evidence of these growing possibilities for reflexive agency in late modernity and Weeks clearly endorses this view (2007: 132). As Elliot demonstrates in his review of contemporary theories of the self in late modernity, a range of theorists have converged on the terrain of detraditionalization, concurring with Giddens that social bonds are indeed dissolving into, in Bauman's words, a potentially 'liquid modernity' (2000, 2005). Most of these theorists emphasize the potentially negative consequences of such new modes of subjectivity, whether or not they explicitly endorse the Foucauldian pessimism of the self as regulatory technology. Giddens' view is, therefore, almost singular in its optimism. As Elliot has argued, '... there is a difficulty with the almost excessive emphasis that Giddens places on the tacit knowledge and self-understanding of social agents – excessive since it threatens to break the link with issues of social power and political domination that Giddens recognizes elsewhere in writings' (2001: 41).

Weeks' view of both sexual agency in the West and its potential for being the basis of global connections is similarly overplayed, particularly by underplaying the socio-economic changes in late Western modernity as the basis for a more individualized and consumerist citizenship, something that others have demonstrated has been central to the public emergence of queer identities and, in Weeks' terms, the agency of different subjects' ability to partake of these queer scenes (Evans, 1993, Hennessy, 2000). Moreover, this is nowhere near any kind of intersectional analysis and thus most obviously misses out issues of how ethnicity and class structure sexual identities and the ability to negotiate new, legitimate intimacies, something that is self-evidently pertinent in any discussion of Muslim sexual diversity. McDermot (2011) criticizes his analysis in relation to class and educational choices that young LGBTIQ people make in the UK, demonstrating that their desire to choose a location that is queer friendly is structured through class and thus, as she puts it, it's a world only 'some' have won. Jackson (2011) also points out that heterosexuality is structured according to class and that these normative class expectations also affect what is normative about LGBTIQ – hence the valorization of same-sex marriage is partly based on the class structuring of normative gender. Similarly, we will discuss evidence below that demonstrates how ethnic identity structures both individual agency and cultural identity in accessing the queer 'world'. Within the West and even with Britain, there is a real danger that Weeks is talking only about a world of sexual diversity that is not accessible to all, precisely because the quality of agency that he positions as central to both the development of and participation in this world is limited by structural factors that constitute sexual subjectivity, rather than merely circulate 'around' sexuality.

Perhaps the implications of this broad materialist basis for the possibility of sexual liberation is not explicitly explored in his analysis because he is genuinely attempting to avoid a Western-centric explanation:

> The privileges enjoyed by Western gays provide models and ideals that LGBT people in other parts of the world may envy or aspire to – though it also has to be acknowledged that most of their legal rights are very recent, and that these gains have in part been built on material comfort. Of the nineteen countries with some recognition of same-sex relational rights or 'love rights' in 2003, all were ranked in the top twenty-four OECD countries for GDP per capita (Wintermute 2005: 218). But the Western gay is not seated at the top of an evolutionary tree, the only model of development, and notions of what it is to be sexually different are likely to be radically modified as the 'perverse dynamic' at the heart of so many cultures (Sinfield 2005: 144) confronts the imperatives of global connectedness. (2007: 217–218)

I'm not sure, however, that he really develops a model for social change that is not implicitly based on Western experience, given that his identification of the agency he argues is so central is based on Western experiences of late modernity, both structurally and in terms of the conditions for reflexive agency. Whilst I argued in Chapter 3 that the teleological assumptions of a modernization outcome to sexual diversity could not be sustained in contemporary political contexts, I also acknowledged that many modernizing processes do seem to broadly indicate 'progress' around the acceptance of LGBTIQ. Many of the key sociological processes, moreover, are connected to 'wealthy' societies: the social independence of women, class and educational levels, relatively egalitarian wealth distribution within societies (creating the shift in orientation from 'survival' to 'self-expression'). In ignoring these empirical contexts, or more specifically, by not interrogating the equation of rich, democratic capitalist societies as the only basis for 'love rights', I think Weeks actually reinstates an assumption of sexual diversity as Western exceptionalism. Specifically, my concern is that there is a revised modernization thesis that underpins such views of the changes in sexual diversity but one that now relies on 'reflexivity' and 'globalization' to characterize LGBTIQ rights and identities as part of an expansionist, self-aware, global culture which, in fact, reiterates rather than displaces the previous narrative of progress extending from the West as non-Western societies 'develop'. It's the bits of the world we have won, and therefore – inevitably so for those who cannot inhabit the full agency of the 'Western' identity – the bits of the world that *they* have won; those successful, detraditionalized, probably white, probably male, definitely metropolitan, reflexive selves for whom it may be accurate to say that *their* lives illustrate an '... inevitable reality: that the world we have won has made possible ways of life that represent an advance not a decline in human relationships, and that have broken through the coils of power to enhance individual autonomy, freedom of choice and more egalitarian patterns of relationships'. (2007: 7).

Let's leave aside the somewhat startling claim (for a self-identified Foucauldian) that some subjectivities are lived outside of power,[4] and think for a moment about whether we can understand the contemporary context of LGBTIQ politics and identities as one that is part of a global connectedness without reinstating the dominance of a wide range of Western momentums. The assumption of an 'inevitable reality' seems to me to quite clearly reinstate a progress narrative, based on the Western experience of late modern, neo-liberal, capitalist detraditionalization that has also made some new forms of agency and identity possible. However, I am not keen to simply reject Weeks' take on 'connected' modernization because, as I have been arguing throughout, the contemporary global conditions for sexual diversity politics are *different,* but my focus was on the fact that they are inevitably different from those experienced in the West, precisely because of the growing globalized connectedness that exists in current media technologies and political and cultural discourses that have promoted the idea of both queer identity and, in the same period, the idea of a problematic Islamic identity and resultant Islamophobia. Weeks, it seems to me, underplays the complications of such connectedness because when he talks about globalization, he is reduced to a slightly reformulated modernization thesis narrative of expansionist progress, based on a purely optimistic account of conditions for reflexive selves and detraditionalization as underlying features, which only really permits a benign view of a globalized gay culture. Such a view begins with the assumption that progress is an inevitable part of modernization – now entering its latest reflexive stage of globalization – rather than acknowledging that the 'inevitable reality' he describes is based on Western experience. The conditions of liberation he describes therein cannot apply to queer Muslims because, as I am sure he recognizes, they are not likely to be able to live as subjects who have 'broken through the coils of power' in contemporary Western or global contexts.

The world that Weeks describes *does* exist (even if only for some), but it provides only some components in the connectedness that he is trying to reach for: a context where some countries and some subjectivities in the West have experienced significant social change and new formations and some aspects of those are being translated into international cultures. In trying to both understand the actual formation of 'connections' across East and West and in assessing the impact of Western identity politics, we need to acknowledge the successes of LGBTIQ politics in their political and sociological context, rather than uncritically reinstating a progress narrative of modernization that somehow implies the sexual liberation of a pre-social and pre-political identity group of subjects has occurred in the West and now simply needs to be extended to others around the world. We must therefore understand these formations of Western LGBTIQ social identities and consequent politics as a likely resource in the negotiation of queer Muslim identity and reactions to it, whilst simultaneously trying to resist the assumptions of a reformulated evolutionary modernization thesis based on the existence of bits of the world some have won.

Connected contemporary histories: queer Muslims in Muslim majority cultures

As argued in the historical overview in the previous chapter, it is simply too broad a generalization to talk of a consistent Islamic influence on the formation and significance of homosexuality and homo-eroticism. National and regional historical traditions seem to matter more than a clear-cut Muslim organization of gender identities and behaviors but there does seem to be relatively consistent evidence of homo-eroticism, something which challenges the contemporary Muslim denial of homosexuality. The current climate of the oppositional discourse of homosexuality, modernity and the West versus Islam provides very little space, however, to consider those queer Muslims whose existence belies such claims. The research discussed below challenges this assumption by focusing attention on those who are both Muslim and gay; those who demonstrate the intersection of apparently exclusive cultures. The extant research is, however, very limited in numbers of studies, which individually are often too small scale to provide much certainty. This limitation can perhaps be interpreted as a consequence of the epistemology and politics of the oppositional discourse whereby nobody thinks to consider homo-eroticism within Muslim cultures and populations because we already think that it doesn't exist, or that it is too 'sensitive' a topic. As discussed in Chapter 1, I think that my own exploration of these issues illustrates my complicity with the latter frame of mind. Nonetheless, some evidence does exist on contemporary identities, and an overriding theme within these accounts is the issue of connections between Eastern and Western cultures, both that 'Eastern' cultures *are* being influenced by Western ones, but that local manifestations of a 'gay international' discourse are not adopted wholesale and without reformation to localized context.

While Habib's collection from 2010 is similar to both Murray and Roscoe (1997) and Babayan and Najmabadi (2008) in its historical and literary emphasis, it also contains some evidence on contemporary Muslim cultures and the experiences of those who identify as homosexual within these. Khan (2010) reprises themes from his contribution on 'Not so Gay Life in Pakistan' to Murray and Roscoe's collection, which was one of only three chapters in that earlier volume on contemporary gay Muslim life (1997a). Khan's autobiographical work was an important initial contribution to illuminating gay Muslims, particularly through his book *Sex, Longing and Not Belonging* (1997b) and in these more recent personal reflections he sees some hope for increasing freedoms for and acceptance of gay Muslims through secularization of Muslim societies but argues that, despite the increase in support groups such as *Al-Fatiha*, the post-9/11 climate makes it more likely that Muslim communities will remain outside Western citizenship and that many LGBTIQ Muslims may thus have to prioritize their Muslim community over their sexual identities. Whilst Khan therefore talks in terms of a progress narrative towards secularization he does also recognize that contemporary Islamophobia fundamentally alters the likely course of Muslim secularization. In a recent account of lesbian life in Pakistan, the couple who are the research subjects mention the complexities of living a lesbian life in a culture where there is no vocabulary for such identities, whilst acknowledging that modernizing influences are gradually shifting the possibilities of a previous, gender-segregated culture where homo-eroticism flourished towards a more regulated binary world of sexual identities (Gandhi, 2012).

Kramer discusses evidence of the advance of Western ideological identities in online chat rooms with Arabs, where he argues that contact with Westerners and Western concepts of distinct homosexuality seem to have an influence on how Muslims are constructing their own identities (2010), supporting Massad's contention that Western dichotomies of sexual identity are influencing the Arab world. Kramer also argues that this emergent trend is more evident in the younger members of his sample[5] but suggests that the individualization central to Western concepts of homosexuality will be difficult to pursue in Arab cultures. Luongo's very small sample of four Iraqis during the American occupation replays this Western influence, particularly through the accessibility of the internet, which was restricted under Saddam's regime but his subjects also describe how the closeted but available gay social spaces that existed in Baghdad prior to the war have now become targets of the new Iraqi militias, as has public homosexuality (2010). Long (2009) and Afary (2009) discuss the political context in which homosexuality is deployed by the Iranian state as a sign of westernization, but their evidence is not based on the lived experience of LGBTIQ in Iran, aside from some limited anecdotal accounts. Mahdavi's recent ethnographic research throws more light on the lived experience of young people in the Islamic Republic, arguing that a sexual revolution has occurred since around 2000, resulting in 'a *change*, in the way in which communities think, act, or talk about sex' (2012: 36). Mahdavi's participants see the shift in discussing sexuality in terms of a broader social movement of change that challenges the restrictions of Islamic law under the Iranian regime, and absolutely driven by younger people, who comprise an increasing majority of the population (2008, 2012). Whilst her research is focused more on the changes in young heterosexual culture and discourse, there is some evidence that homosexual organizing was also part of this shift, and that that dialectical discourse of homosexuality and Islam was a self-conscious part of such organizing:

> 'Maybe we used to see being gay as a Western thing, but it seemed that being gay was seen as being Western by the regime too, and it was a threat to them, so we decided, yes, let's go for a sexual and social movement that is Western, sexual and the regime hates! Yes, let's do that!' (Mahdavi, 2012: 37)

Western conceptualizations, of both politics and identities are, therefore, an important resource for local and national developments of queer identities but they are not necessarily a blueprint for how sexual diversity will develop in non-Western cultures. In her detailed ethnographic research on Indonesia, Blackwood's work on lesbians demonstrates that they incorporate Western discourses into local and national ones to make sense of their identities and create communities that are influenced by but adapt Western gay identity discourses in the creation of locally distinct identities (2005a, 2005b, 2010). Thus, *tomboi* and *lesbi* are identity categories claimed by the women Blackwood interviews but she makes the point that, whilst they have been appropriated from the West, they are not direct equivalents in identity terms, with 'lesbi' being more socially understood as a deviant category, and thus avoided in public by some of her subjects in preference to 'tomboi', which denotes more of a gendered identification of a masculine woman. *Lesbi* were more understood as a gendered identity that was still feminine and it seems that they were often in relationships with the more masculine *Tombois*, whose 'girlfriends see themselves as normative women who happen to be lesbi at this point because their boyfriends are female bodied' (2005a: 226). Blackwood argues that the normative expectations of gender are the main boundaries and resources that govern how same-sex identities are created, rather than a focus on homosexuality as a specific identity and, moreover, that in the Indonesian context, the post-colonial state has focused on a heteronormative conceptualization of citizenship as part of its nationalism. What she calls transnational queer discourses do circulate, however, mostly through exposure and participation in European, North American and Australian cultures and politics by metropolitan-based English speaking men and women who began same-sex support networks in Indonesia in the 1980s. Again, she suggests that whilst this Western 'queer knowledge' is used as a resource for modeling activism and in creating a sense of shared identity, the specific identity formations and politics are translated and adapted and therefore experienced differently by Indonesian homosexual men and women, not only in a national context, but on a regional, class and gender basis. These intersections of social structures affect the day-to-day basis of movement and public identity, and the feminine *lesbi* are therefore often dependent on the more masculine *tomboi* who have more license to move around and travel, and their experience of feminized male *warias*[6]:

> Lesbi subjectivities in Padang, however, are neither traditional nor backward but a product of modern national and transnational processes. As the stories in this article reveal, lesbi in Padang reflect the dominant modern gender binary in defining their own lives. But the flow of state and Islamic discourses is interrupted by queer discourses that circulate indirectly through the movement of tombois and their connections with waria communities. These knowledges have not interpolated lesbi into a homogeneous national or international lesbian identity but rather have the effect of creating a sense of shared community and solidarity among lesbi, waria, and gay in Indonesia, as individuals of like mind. Research on transnational sexualities cannot overlook the importance of particular localities. The realities

of everyday lesbi life for those in Padang show the unevenness of transnational processes as well as the power and impact of particular forms of gendered subjectivities produced by state and Islamic ideologies. Attention to the ways these individuals are situated, the meanings of their particular relationships, and the particular local, national, and global processes that intersect in Padang enable a finer grained reading of sexualities and genders. This view of one locality helps to disrupt the expectations of Western queer discourse and its modern sexual identities. (2005a: 238–239)

I have concentrated on Blackwood's research in some detail because it illustrates two general and related points that are relevant beyond Indonesia. First, normative gender frameworks in the wider society are still the dominant reference point for understanding sexual identity and if these are 'traditionalist', as in the Indonesian case, then non-heterosexual identity is still a source of stigma. This much seems to lead us back to the teleological modernization thesis of 'progress' but, in fact, the second conclusion from Blackwood's work demonstrates that the contemporary influence of Western queer knowledge is not accelerating Muslim cultures into a path that mimics Western gay liberation, but being adapted for its local circumstances, both in terms of politics and concepts of identity. Wong's research with women in Malaysia also supports both of these points: she describes the Islamist political campaigns in recent Malaysian history that have brought the specifically Malaysian social identity of *Pengkids* into wide public consciousness as a threat to traditional Malaysian heterosexual values because it denotes masculine females involved in erotic relationships with women (2012). She also demonstrates the very localized historical emergence of this term since the 1970s in Kuala Lumpur's alternative music and entertainment scenes,[7] and how it came to be used to self-identify by masculine lesbians, often in distinction to the previous cultural term of 'tomboy'.

Boellstorff's extensive anthropological studies on transvestites and gay men in Indonesia supports this framing of localized lived experiences of transnational sexualities both in the cultural traditions of transvestite *warias* and the emergence of gay subject positions (2007: 196). His detailed ethnographic work leads him to argue that there are three common, overly positive, misperceptions about gay men in southeast Asia; ...'their socioeconomic status, the form and intensity of their connections to Western gay men, and the degree to which they are accepted in their Southeast Asian societies' and that the evidence suggests in fact that 'due to the fractured way to date by which most gay men in Southeast Asia have encountered Western notions of gay subjectivity, most are middle class or below, not directly linked to Western gay movements, and not accepted or even recognized by their societies' (2007: 198–199). His work thus challenges the teleological model of expansionist globalization of sexuality, and instead he directs our attention to the strategies that 'gay' Muslim men use to inhabit the 'incommensurability' of being gay and Indonesian and Muslim as part of their everyday life. His anthropological research concurs with Blackwood's in demonstrating that heteronormativity continues to render it difficult to be publicly gay in this Muslim culture, with strategies varying between marrying women and living as privately gay, to some subjects who hoped never to marry, often by reconciling homo-eroticism as part of God's creation of individuality and being able to participate in localized networks of private gay communities (2005a, 2005b, 2007). Recent research on same-sex behavior amongst men in Turkey also suggests that Western versions of gay identity are becoming more common, although they remain a minority and indeed coexist with the more common gender variant understanding of homosex in Turkish culture (Bereket and Adam, 2006; 2008). Cardoso points out that the modern exclusive sense of gay identity is more common in the urban center of Istanbul rather than rural spaces (2009) but that active/passive identification coexists with this more recent sense of gay identity, concurring with Bereket and Adam's research. Bereket and Adam do suggest that the more westernized understanding of exclusive 'gay' identity is more identified with a narrative of selfhood and a more flexible accommodation with Islam than the traditional gender variant form of homosexuality – with the latter not deployed as a public identity in contrast to the civil activism of LGBTIQ organizations and individuals who adopt a more explicit *'gey'* identity. As they conclude:

> Based on interviewee responses, it is clear that there is a diversity of viewpoints concerning the degree to which Turkish men see themselves as part of a 'global gay identity'. Indigenous modes of seeing oneself have not been replaced or lost their validity with the emergence of the gay identities, rather they continue to co-exist with gay identities that at times resemble European and North American counterparts but may also be adapted into syncretic *gey* identities. Such co-existence provides a broader spectrum of alternatives for men. One form of identity is no less authentic than the other; there is no totalizing discourse around same-sex bonding in Turkish society. (2006: 146)

These brief and limited examples continue the suggestion from historical studies that we must recognize a different ontological construction from the West when we think about Muslim queer identities and gay liberation. This is not, moreover, one that is exclusively Eastern or, indeed, consistent across Muslim cultures, but rather the ontology of contemporary homosexual identities are being formed in intersection with the increasingly globalized discourse of Western gay political identity and their own localized histories of gender identity frameworks and regulation and, crucially for our concerns, the contemporary reactions of Muslim cultures to both traditional and Western forms of homosexuality in the context of a globalized Islamophobia and/or civilizational positioning.

Connected contemporary histories: queer Muslims in the West

Research on LGBTIQ Muslims living in the West is even more recent than the scholarship on Muslim cultures and homosexuality,[8] and the tension between homosexuality as a 'Western' identity and Muslim cultural traditions is a central issue in this research. For example, American-Iranian Khalida Saed discusses her mother's reaction when she came out: 'The most compelling argument she came up with was that I was far too Americanized and that my sexuality was an offspring of the American values I had internalized. This last argument may or may not have a ring of truth to it. I'm not sure I would have had the balls to discuss my sexuality at all, or even consider it, if my American side hadn't told me I had the right' (2005: 86). This theme of the perceived 'westernness' of a homosexual identity is mirrored in other research, ranging from my similarly auto/biographical narrative in the opening chapter to this book, and the contributions from Badruddin Khan discussed earlier (1997a, 1997b, 2010). Other research on lesbians in the USA (Al-Sayyad, 2010) and both lesbians and gay men in the UK (Siraj, 2006, 2009; Yip, 2004, 2005, 2007, 2008a, 2008b) confirms this as a central theme. The dialectical opposition of Muslim cultures and homosexuality thus has a direct effect on the day-to-day experiences of being queer and Muslim in complex ways, as demonstrated in the evidence reviewed in the previous section on Muslim majority cultures. The negative aspects of this dialectic, however, are a more consistent theme in the very limited research evidence on queer Muslims in the West. This is evidenced in Abraham's research in Australia that indicates that a queer Muslim identity is not only improbable but also potentially unintelligible to both Muslims and 'Westerners' (2009, 2010) and, more damagingly, to 'Western' queer communities: 'So whereas for conservative Muslims a *queer* Muslim becomes the unviable subject, for some in the queer community, a queer *Muslim* is an impossible – or at least dubious – subject' (2009: 88–89). Both religious/ethnic Muslim cultures *and* Western/gay cultures are therefore implicated in deploying an assumption of mutual exclusivity.

Broader themes also emerge from other small-scale studies done to date. One of the first, focused on six activists in an *Al-Fatiha* support group,[9] comes up with the following issues from their respondents: religion; East-West cultural comparisons including gay identity, marriage expectations, coming out; 'color' dynamics (a term used to discuss ethnicity in the USA) (Minwalla et al., 2005). Subsequent studies on *Al-Fatiha* (Rouhani, 2007) and the other commentaries cited above confirm and refine these themes, giving us a grasp of four overriding issues. The first – the perception of public homosexual identity as 'Western' – has been discussed above. This relates to the second theme, however, which is that of the negative, or perceived possibility of negative reactions from their ethnic communities to queer Muslims declaring a public homosexual identity, often translating into severe psychological pressures for the individuals concerned (Jaspal, 2012). This may provide further evidence for those who argue that the Western version of homosexuality is irrelevant for Muslims, but that conclusion does not accurately represent the whole issue. Rather, the research shows that Western versions of gay identity are indeed used as resources by LGBTIQ Muslims in the West (as they are in Muslim majority countries), but they are adapting it to fit their circumstances. As Al-Sayyad argues from her small-scale research on lesbians in North America:

> While family rejection may be used to demonstrate the incompatibility of Arab culture and Islam with homosexuality, many complex factors are left out in this oversimplification. It is true that many participants discussed their families' and parents' negative reactions to or rejections of their sexual identification, but it is also important to consider that all of the participants interviewed maintained close relationships with their families. The strength of familial ties was overwhelmingly evident for the group of women I interviewed and whose narratives I analyzed. Despite this, many queer Muslim women living in the diaspora did feel pressure from their families to adhere to normative gender roles and, most notably, to marry a suitable man, as most of them are not 'out' in the mainstream American sense. (2010: 380)

Despite the heteronormativity in Muslim communities, many queer Muslims do not reject their ethnic or kinship networks outright, partly it seems because of the need to remain close to an ethnic community in the face of wider racism (Abraham, 2009, 2010) and perhaps increasingly because of Western cultural exclusions of Muslims (Khan, 2010). In this sense, gay identity is not the totalizing identity that many have experienced and chosen in the West, since it has to be negotiated in intersection with other significant identities. It may also be partly because of the racism encountered within gay communities who are mostly white and share with Muslim communities the assumption of incompatibility of Muslim identity with an out gay identity, what Abraham neatly describes as 'Hegemonic Queer Islamophobia' (2010).[10]

A third and perhaps more hopeful issue is the attempt to rationalize or reinterpret Islamic texts to accommodate homosexuality from queer Muslim individuals, largely dependent on their individual strategies to reinterpret religious texts.[11] This is consistently evident in the research done by Yip in the UK, which remains the largest contribution to this emergent area of study. His various articles detail strategies for managing the contradictions and conflicts of lived experience with a consistent theme in the data on 'queering religious texts' (2007, 2008b), something that is apparent in other work (Siraj, 2006, 2008). Moreover, this theme speaks to a wider issue, that of the absence of stable and visible communities, leading individuals to attempt reinterpretive strategies in their own way and within whatever limited Muslim gay communities they can find. However, the existence of some support groups is important and regularly mentioned in this research are *Al-Fatiha*, which is web based but has some local organizers across North America; *Salaam*, based in Toronto; and the *Safra* and *Naz* projects in the UK, although it seems that the British ones are more permanent than their North American counterparts.[12]

What can we glean from this flowering of research in relation to the questions of lived experience, identities and politics? The main contributor, Yip, acknowledges the need for an intersectional approach (2009, 2010), drawing upon Abraham's idea of 'critical hybridity'. Despite this recognition, he seems in fact to take a fairly 'Western' approach, arguing that belonging for queer Muslims is easier in secular Western society than in Muslim communities and making the point that it seems to be the secularization of Western societies that has been the impetus to the expression of diverse sexualities. Abraham would contest this, I think, providing a more political reading of the 'compartmentalization' of identities identified in Yip's work and arguing that both 'hegemonic

Muslim Homophobia' and 'hegemonic queer Islamophobia' are present and are both contested by queer Muslims (2009). Moreover, he draws upon ideas of 'homonormativity' to suggest that the current discourse of gay human rights is part of a liberal and bourgeois settlement that does not fundamentally contest homophobia, or heteronormativity, echoing other arguments discussed above that are skeptical about the universality and essentialism of the rights discourse. I sympathize with his political position but I have suggested an alternative theoretical understanding. In Abraham's work, he uses the term 'critical hybridity' to describe the intersectional location of his subjects, but refers to them as queer in the everyday sense. What I have suggested is that these LGBTIQ identities are properly understood as theoretically 'queer intersectional identities' because they represent 'impossible' or 'unviable' subjects (2010). The disruption of identity comes in challenging the ontological coherence of the dominant identity narratives ('gay' and 'Muslim') which exclude queer Muslims as 'impossible'. Muslims can be understood theoretically as *queer* subjects who are negotiating their ontological deferment from 'coherent' dominant identities, not able to easily live within specified categories and engaged in constant negotiations of their lived experiences at the intersections of identity. Ritchie's recent fieldwork in Israel/Palestine demonstrates this intersectional 'incoherence' in full measure, given that:

> ... queer Palestinian activists have refused to emulate Western and Israeli activists' politics of visibility which takes its terms from the lexicon of neoliberalism and articulates its demands in a way that justifies state violence against racial others in exchange for recognition of a victimized class of domesticated queers. In that refusal, queer Palestinians can imagine a kind of activism that does not avoid politics in favor of normalization but articulates a vision of a society transformed by a fundamental restructuring of power. (2010: 570)

From connected histories to queer Muslims as modern intersectional subjects

Rather than taking the Western empirical version of gay liberation as teleological, as Yip does, I think we can use an intersectional perspective to help us make sense of the lived experiences of queer Muslims as illuminating a different *telos*; one that is neither exclusively Eastern or Western, but rather one that is formed at the intersection of Western and Eastern cultures, negotiating the dialectic of Islam and modern homosexuality. The very limited evidence on identities discussed hitherto turns our attention to the sociological complications of lived experience, and particularly the ways in which queer Muslims are inhabiting hierarchies of oppression that intersect through ethnicity, religion, gender regimes, class and geography. First and foremost, we can understand that to be queer and Muslim is therefore a deconstruction of the dominant identity category of each and thus fulfils the common academic definition of intersectionality as a challenge to monolithic understandings of oppressed identity. As Davis puts in her assessment of the success of intersectionality as a feminist concept: 'Feminist theorists inspired by postmodern theoretical perspectives viewed intersectionality as a welcome helpmeet in their project of deconstructing the binary oppositions and universalism inherent in the modernist paradigms of Western philosophy and science ... Intersectionality fits neatly into the postmodern project of conceptualizing multiple and shifting identities' (Davis, 2008: 71). At this very simple level, thinking about queer Muslims as intersectional identities permits us to begin to interrogate the ways in which they exist *within* dominant categories of both queer and Muslim, raising challenges for both queer and Muslim politics of identity and providing the initial lever to crack open the monoculturalism on which the discourse of Islam versus homosexuality is based. This presents a challenge to both Muslim communities to recognize the diversity in their historical and contemporary cultures, but also to Western gay communities to recognize the same diversity in their own 'ethnic' identity. Of course, this recognition will be uncomfortable and institutionally problematic in terms of LGBTIQ rights strategies, particularly because the lived experiences of queer Muslims indicate difficulties in moving towards public ethnic homosexuality. However, these differences in lived experience might, at the very least, provide more impetus to support more groups such as the *Naz* project and *Al-Fatiha*, and also remind us that those who cannot publicly access rights are nonetheless part of our 'community'.

Intersectionality, moreover, is about more than deconstruction. The 'novel twist' that Davis argues is central to intersectionality's success as a concept, is that its methodology is focused on standpoint theory, giving a credence to the experience of those located at intersectional social locations (Hill Collins, 2000: vii). This is a significant analytical and political distinction from post-structuralist theories because while it similarly challenges the politics of dominant knowledge construction evident in post-modernist approaches, it does this through its emphasis on the authenticity of the experience and knowledge of those caught between major locations of identity, rather than pursuing the ultimate deconstruction of identity that is theoretically implied in much of post-structuralist analysis. Whilst there is a constellation of concepts that attempt to think through the kind of 'intersections' that queer Muslims represent – such as 'hybridity' (Abraham, 2009, 2010) and 'assemblage' (Puar, 2007), to name but two[13] – my attachment to intersectionality is partly because it makes sense of the lived experience of those located at the crossover between dominant categories, rather than implying that they are somehow one step on the path to dissolving identity categories altogether. Queer Muslims as intersectionality do have various social experiences of identity and communities, and a properly intersectional perspective asks us to attend to this standpoint rather than simply to engage in a theoretical exercise of complicating or deconstructing dominant categories.[14] Thus, Mahdavi's (2012) description of how queers in Iran use the resources of global gay identity confirms Korycki and Nasirzadeh's analysis of shifts in the state's use of homophobia in Iran (2013), aligning international gay discourses with 'liberation' in that case, whilst the experiences of others (particularly in the West) provoke a consideration of how Western discourses are exclusionary and potentially Islamophobic. There are legitimate and credible lived experiences that are different depending on the socio-political intersection at which they are formed and so I suggest that an intersectional sensibility offers the most useful approach in attempting to work through these complications.

Furthermore, I argue that we can think of queer Muslims both as conventionally queer in the sense of inhabiting identities of sexual diversity, and theoretically queer. In this sense, I am drawing on queer theory's analytical focus on deconstructing dominant ontological productions of coherent subject categories of gender and sexuality and suggesting that this deconstructionist affinity between intersectionality and post-modernism that Davis identifies (2008) can be combined with intersectionality's emphasis on lived, standpoint experience. Thus, I have argued previously that:

> The 'impossibility' of gay Muslims is exactly their power in resistance; in researching their lived experience we should be engaged in the intersectional illumination of a marginalized standpoint, but with a keen sense in which this lived experience is disruptive to established identity categories. The disruption of identity comes in challenging the ontological coherence of these dominant identity narratives, which exclude gay Muslims as 'impossible' and ... the

uncertainties of ontological coherence are also a major focus of queer analytics ... Thus, gay Muslims can be understood as *queer* subjects who are negotiating their ontological deferment from 'coherent' dominant identities, not able to easily live within specified categories and engaged in constant negotiations of their lived experiences at the intersections of identity. (Rahman, 2010: 952–953)

Whilst research from the standpoint of queer Muslims will inevitably challenge monolithic versions of identity, a thoroughly intersectional perspective on identity also requires an appreciation of how these identities are the instantiation of social structures (Rahman, 2009), and particularly those structures of oppression, or what Hill Collins described as the 'matrix of domination' (2000: 18). Taking a fully intersectional perspective begins with the standpoint of queer Muslims but also demands that we analyze how various vectors of experience are constituted by social and political hierarchies. This focus on hierarchies of oppression helps us to retain an understanding that there are power differentials at work. As Abraham's research on queer Muslims illustrates, there is an issue of 'impossibility' in understanding Muslim queers and much of the other research covered in this chapter speaks both to this perceived 'westernness' of a queer identity and concurrent homophobia of Muslim identity. The former is part and parcel of the discourse of Western exceptionalism described throughout this study, reminding us that the current embrace of queer politics through intermittent 'homonationalist' impulses is part of reasserting Western superiority. Add to this the contemporary reality that many Muslim majority states and minority communities use homophobia to define the integrity of their own identities (Blackwood, 2007; Korycki and Nasirzadeh, 2013; Shah, 2013) – ignoring both colonial inheritances of regulation and homo-erotic traditions in their own cultures – and we have a complex, intersectional picture of the modernity that queer Muslims inhabit, along various vectors of oppression that include both Muslim homophobia and Islamophobia. We cannot explain this experience without referring to the wider cultural dialectic of Islam versus homosexuality and the ways in which that assumes a modernization momentum to social structures that have permitted sexual diversity in the West and made them unlikely in the 'traditional' East. This political discourse is therefore an important structural context to the intersectionality of queer Muslim experience, both in terms of their own identifications and the ways in which they experience Muslim homophobia and Western Islamophobia. It may be that proposing a fully intersectional approach to queer Muslim identities is a relatively simple methodological claim – asking that we attend to the experiential, sociological and political contexts of how the 'intersection' is constructed. Even at this simple level of methodology, however, there are epistemological consequences that challenge the oppositional discourse of Islam versus homosexuality.

Towards an intersectional modernity?

Whilst I am engaged in an attempt to emphasize the potentialities of contemporary global sexual culture as part of a complex, connected history of modernity, I have argued that Weeks' view of 'connections' fails to acknowledge the full range of how sexual subjectivity and related agency is socially constructed in intersecting, enabling and regulatory ways and, therefore, that he implicitly interpellates a universalist version of LGBTIQ identities based on the latest stage of Western modernization – something that he attempts to characterize as having passed a threshold of globalized formation but which, in his own arguments, is based on the evidence of advanced capitalist detraditionalization in the West. The limited evidence on lived experience does suggest a connection between Western identity and contemporary adaptations by Muslim LGBTIQ subjects. Rather than see this either as the Western imperialism of a 'gay international' or the benign globalized diffusion of Western sexual politics, however, I argue that we should think of this connection as an intersection of historical, cultural and political formations that continues to be the complex context for the political significance of homosexuality, varying by national context and dependent on gender formations within those contexts.

The first point to make from such a perspective is that we cannot talk in terms of a monolithic Islamic or Muslim culture, either within the West or globally and indeed, contemporary research on the similarities and differences in queer Muslim experience reinforces this point. Furthermore, the evidence suggests that the Western version of a public and ontologically essential gay identity is not the only version of homosexuality that exists, and, at the very least, must be recognized as an incomplete basis for political actions. Evidence on the lived experience of queer Muslims thus pierces the exclusive culturalism deployed by both East and West, both by deconstructing the exclusion of queer from Muslim and Muslim from queer and thus rendering those exclusive cultures as interconnected and interdependent rather than as static points in a civilizational opposition. How we see and know modernity, and the sexual within that modernity, therefore changes. Illuminating the relevant sociological vectors of intersectionality complicates the modernization paradigm, fundamentally destabilizing the prioritization of Western exceptionalism that is the origin and consequence of these unconnected, exclusive visions of modernity as owned by the West that underscores the political justifications of both Islamophobia and Muslim homophobia. Muslim queers as intersectionality are thus an empirical and epistemological beginning to disrupting the assumed Western superiority in sexual diversity; a beginning brings into focus important contemporary political questions around LGBTIQ politics that will only be astutely addressed by pursuing further standpoint research on the experiences of queer Muslims.

A major question is what forms of homo-eroticism and homosexual identities are developing in non-Western cultures. Whilst there is vast evidence on sexuality in relation to HIV/AIDS, we have less research on sexual diversity more generally, particularly in Muslim cultures, either globally or within minority populations. This is not to dismiss the established bodies of research from a wide variety of disciplines on various cultures around the world, but it is to stake a claim for *more*. Even the limited range of research we have available, however, draws us towards certain political conclusions. We should recognize that those of us in the West (even us queer Muslims) cannot decide which strategies are 'relevant' or politically acceptable but rather we should approach this fact with an understanding that a 'Western' discourse of identity and politics may be a useful discursive and institutional starting point from which to articulate and shape a version of equality around sexual diversity. In Western contexts, we need further research to understand how multiculturalism might conflict with values of sexual diversity, how Muslim communities react to homosexuality within their ethnic groups and how much this reaction is driven by reactions to Islamophobia, and whether Western queer political identities and rights strategies can accommodate religious and/or ethnic difference. The evidence as yet supports no definite conclusions on these issues but this fact alone suggests the need for more consistent and comprehensive research on LGBTIQ Muslims. Any approach to such research, I have suggested, needs to adopt a thoroughly intersectional perspective.

I expand on these political questions in the following chapters but let me consider a final implication of the intersectionality of queer Muslims. Does the logic of this approach or sensibility inevitably lead us towards an intersectional understanding of modernity? In a gloriously imperious statement, Butler asserts: 'I do not traffic in theories of modernity because the concept strikes me as too large, they are, in my view, for the most part too general and sketchy to be useful, and people from different disciplines mean very different things by them' (2008: 5). I have argued, however, that we must understand modernity both as a particular (conceited) discursive formation that structures the understanding of Islam versus homosexuality – in agreement with Butler's position on the discursive deployment of modernity[15] – but also that modernity has specific sociological formations that are structuring the possibilities of identities, politics and experience for queer Muslims. Butler's disdain for the trade in theories of modernity is understandable, given the ways in which these become academic dogma, but I cannot see how we can avoid making some claims about important sociological factors if we are to displace the sexual sociological modernization thesis in which the various expressions of orientalism and Western exceptionalism are embedded. My intention has not been to suggest that we need a 'new' model of modernity but rather that the intersectional analysis of queer Muslims demands a more intersectional sensibility when discussing contemporary modernity, but I recognize that this may not be a sustainable position. I therefore attempt to clarify this position in relation to the political implications of my analysis in the following chapter but I promise no resolution to this overarching question, but rather, like the discussion of political implications in the final chapter, I map out some beginnings.

6
The Politics of Identity and the Ends of Liberation

Introduction

Since I have argued that the evidence on Muslim sexual diversity points us towards a more intersectional understanding of modernity, I begin with a reiteration of my central theme throughout this study but with a more direct characterization of it as an illustration of intersectionality. Thus, my core argument that specific understandings of modernity underpin the discourses of opposition between Muslim cultures and sexual diversity is reframed as a process of triangulation. Specifically, I characterize Western exceptionalism as the primary political idea that is triangulated through the process of 'homocolonialism' that institutes the opposition of Muslim cultures and sexuality politics by deploying LGBTIQ rights and visibility to punish non-Western cultures, and conversely reassert the supremacy of the 'home' Western nations and civilization. I describe the intersecting formations of both the positioning and the processes of triangulation as the broad beginning for political interventions. I suggest that an intersectional sensibility contributes to the disruption of the narratives of modernity that underpin the triangulation of Western exceptionalism through queer politics, and thus throughout the remainder of the chapter, I go on to think through what 'disruptions' are possible in rethinking our assumptions about sexual diversity and Muslim cultures.

The review on Muslim sexual diversity indicates that such identities illustrate the need to break down monolithic versions of both Muslim and queer identity and so I consider the implications of this deconstruction for both Muslim and Western politics of identity and for the logic of 'modernization' as a route to sexual liberation. First, I suggest that we rethink the assumptions behind Western politics of sexuality, both in terms of its current construction as 'identity' politics linked to human rights, and its assumption of the outcomes of sexual liberation. I discuss the problems with identity politics as 'homocolonialist' presumptions based on Western forms of political and sociological subjectification and thus suggest that we need to disrupt some of these technologies and assumptions. I argue that we must start to consider the differential outcomes of 'equality' that are possible in contemporary socio-political contexts, focusing more on equality as a set of discursive and institutional resources rather than as a teleological, pre-formed universal outcome based on Western sociological and political formations. In this sense, I suggest that we think about 'possible' sexual selves and how they can shape equality using available political resources. The second major disruption we can achieve through an intersectional analysis of the triangulation of Western exceptionalism is to understand the ways in which Islamophobia and homophobia reinforce each other. I therefore raise the question of whether we can have 'liberation' from one of these hierarchies without liberation from the other. Whilst our first disruption of the process of triangulation might be to point out that Muslim homophobia reinforces Islamophobia, we also need to think through how the reverse is true and thus whether queer and Muslim politics can begin to discuss how this happens and how to disrupt this process.

In conclusion, I argue that the analysis presented throughout the chapter can be used to begin a movement towards a terrain of dialogue between queer and Muslim politics. I suggest, however, that the routes to this dialogue are different for each and in particular we have to recognize that in many contemporary political contexts, queer politics has a privileged position over Muslim politics and that this means that there will be important differences in practical political strategies between how these groups arrive at dialogue. This chapter therefore sets the stage for my final concluding chapter on how we might begin to translate these arguments into a practical politics.

The triangulation of Western exceptionalism: homocolonialism, Muslim homophobia and monoculturalism

The discourse of Islam versus homosexuality *as* modernity described at the beginning of this study structures contemporary political reactions and strategies and, as such, can only give us cause for a pessimistic prognosis for the relationship between Muslim cultures and sexual diversity politics. If homosexual politics and identity continues to be seen as a marker – or increasingly, *the* marker – of Western modernity's progress, then Muslim reactions against it are inevitably going to confirm Muslim traditionalism which in turn confirms Muslim incompatibility with modernity, either within the enclaves of Muslim diasporas in the West, or the majority cultures worlwide. What I think is important to consider as a starting point for an analytical challenge is that the current discourse not only structures our understandings of Muslim homophobia and queer politics within a frame of modernity but also that this ultimately reinforces a sense of Western exceptionalism. Indeed, the prioritization of the West is triangulated through the contemporary deployment of sexual politics in the international realm and its home 'homonationalist' manifestations. This triangulation is at first a definitional conceptual positioning; sexual politics are located in the relations *between* West and East, both internationally and within Western nations. This serves to provoke and then define Eastern cultures as against modernity, confirming that queer identities and rights are possible *only* in the West. Moreover, the 'inside/out' uncertain acceptance of gay rights in Western societies makes them particularly suited to being positioned in the space between the West and East,[1] defining an accelerated modernity within the West itself. Thus, queer rights both confirm that Western social and political formations are *definitive* of modernity in general (it is only in Western modernity that they are even possible) and illustrative of its most progressive manifestation in specific civilizational examples where they exist. In this sense, queer rights are positioned at the apex of Western exceptionalism, not simply located within the space of the West, hence my characterization of triangulation rather than a simple dialectic. The examples discussed in Chapter 2 testify to this in full measure, and we have seen further deployments of queer rights within the international realm as criteria for 'progress', both by governments and NGOs[2] and I think there is some danger that the recent statement on Sexual Orientation and Gender Identity (SOGI) rights by the UN could be both deployed and resisted within the frame of this triangulation.[3]

There are effectively three spaces of this triangulation and we have already seen sophisticated accounts of the rise of 'homonormativity' (Duggan, 2002), 'homonationalism' (Puar, 2007) and the 'gay international' (Massad, 2007) as various descriptions of the international and internal deployment of sexual politics within these various spaces. What I think we can add to these accounts of cultural discourses is an intersectional analysis that appreciates the *process* of triangulation of

Western exceptionalism through sexuality. I have argued throughout that this deployment of sexuality is not simply about sexual exceptionalism (Puar, 2007: 3–11) but rather sexual exceptionalism is conjured as the marker of civilizational exceptionalism. This point is implied in Puar's argument, but her focus remains on homonationalist discourses of sexuality rather than the underpinning formation of modernity.[4] I think here that Massad's work adds a distinct explanation of the second space of the international realm because he recognizes that this projection from the West is designed to construct particular formations in the 'East' based on the assumed superiority of Western civilization. Although I have criticized the empirical basis of his analysis of the 'gay international' (see Chapter 4), I think he is absolutely correct to identify the colonizing potential of the internationalization of LGBTIQ rights discourses. However, he does not pay much attention to the ways in which this internationalization also constructs 'home' identities in a particular way – although he acknowledges that it is a dimension of the sexual universalism he critiques – and this is where Puar's recognition that the tactical construction of homonormative nationalist identities excludes many queer 'others' can be woven into his analysis. Whilst I am not suggesting that these analyses are completely convergent given their different subject matter and theoretical approaches, I think we can use their major insights to think about the processes of triangulation of Western exceptionalism.

It seems to me that we can combine their ideas to understand the current process as a homocolonialist one since it is the deployment of homonormative nationalism within a dialectic of respectability/otherness in a classic colonializing mode, directed at 'traditional' Muslim cultures as homophobic, non-Western 'others' that need to be civilized or modernized but also constructing 'home' Western normative queer identities. This is not, therefore, simply a static or one-way process whereby the West projects its exceptional sexual diversity outwards, but rather a process of triangulation through homocolonialism: sexual diversity – as the 'shell' for Western exceptionalism – is deployed in the space of international/internal relations and operates dialectically and definitionally towards the 'traditional' space of the East but also towards the originating space of the West. We are provided here with a reassurance of our Western civilizational superiority through the presence of increasingly homonormative versions of homosexuality (such as gay marriage) which are contrasted with their absence in Eastern multicultural communities and Muslim communities worldwide. Moreover, these characterizations have to rely on a monolithic version of culture: monoculturalism operates in defining the space of the East and the West, purporting a uniform, static and civilizationally broad culture to both East and West. Thus, only a certain type of homonormative/homonationalist queer becomes used to represent the West as superior, creating 'others' at home *and* abroad through a classic dialectic colonial technology. Any deployment of queer politics must therefore acknowledge this homocolonialist potential and in our specific focus here on Muslim cultures, this homocolonialism can be understood as a key component of how the process of triangulation of Western exceptionalism operates.

An inevitable insight from disrupting the processes of triangulation through an intersectional analysis is to understand the matrix of oppressions of homophobia and Islamophobia as connected through sociopolitical formations. Homocolonialism provokes Muslim homophobia, which becomes part of the process of triangulation, reinforcing Islamophobia because the resistance to sexual diversity is taken as fundamentally indicative of Muslim 'otherness': Islamophobia is therefore being interpellated in some circumstances through sexual diversity politics. This analysis therefore provokes questions about the politics of Western queer identity, particularly whether the hard won rights and identities in the West can be reconstructed to resist their deployment within a homocolonialist dialectic that contributes in part to reinforcing orientalist Islamophobia. A beginning to this reconstruction would be to recognize the disruption that an intersectional perspective permits; queer Muslims as intersectionality challenge the monolithic, monocultural versions of queer Western identity politics and, moreover, the positioning of queer politics within the process of triangulation renders visible the intersecting political discourses at work. Above all, this has implications for our ideas of queer liberation and queer equality because a recognition of the intersectionality of both identities and processes of modernity disrupts those narratives of progress and particularly of outcomes of equality or liberation that underpin the queer political project.

There are, similarly, important questions for Muslim politics of identity arising from this analysis, specifically whether the politics of Muslim homophobia can be recognized within this dialectic. Neither Puar nor Massad attend in any detail to the wider reasons and formations of Muslim homophobia that were discussed in Chapters 3 and 4[5] but this resistance exists, however, and perhaps a beginning to providing a challenge to it is to explain it as part of this process of triangulation. Muslim homophobia reinforces this process because it becomes part of the triangulation; resistance to queer rights may be constructed as resistance to neo-colonialist impositions, but this premise relies on the acceptance of sexual diversity as the vanguard of Western modernity, leading us back to the original prioritization of Western exceptionalism. A conceptualization of triangulation permits us to locate Muslim resistance within the homocolonialist dialectic and also thus to explain it within the discourse of Islam versus homosexuality *as* modernity. Given this process, can we conclude anything else other than Muslim homophobia ultimately reinforces Western exceptionalism, because it accepts the premise of homocolonialism?

Again, an intersectional sensibility towards both Muslim identities and the conceptualization of Western modernity has the beginnings of a challenge to this triangulation. Muslim resistance to queer Muslim identity depends on rendering invisible traditions of Muslim homoeroticism and contemporary manifestations of sexual diversity. In this sense, Muslim homophobia depends on asserting monocultural versions, either in national terms or in broad civilizational forms, much in the same way that the dialectics of homocolonialism renders Western culture as a monolithic space that welcomes sexual diversity. Thus, homocolonialism and homophobic resistance are both premised on monolithic cultural assumptions of the West and the East but with a definite hierarchy of Western culture as superior, evidenced by its promotion of sexuality in the relations between these as its credential of advanced civilization. A Muslim retort might be that homosexuality is indeed a Western formation, and that resistance to it is therefore culturally integral to Muslim cultures. But that argument is based on a monocultural version of Muslim cultural identity and gender frameworks; the monoculturalism that is part and parcel of the process of triangulation that interpellates Islamophobia, and so the political question becomes what the costs are in Muslim cultures accepting their own monoculturalism.

Every iteration of the triangulated discourse of Islam versus sexual diversity, at every distinct stage or space, compounds its logic, reinforcing it in a vortextual manner because each stage of triangulation reinforces the others.[6] The process of triangulation described above begins and ends with the exceptionalism of Western cultures which is effectively the ownership of modernity by the West.[7] In contrast, I have argued that both sexual modernization arguments, and those that attempt to resist the imposition of Western sexualities, inevitably reinforce this idea of Western exceptionalism by accepting the provenance of contemporary sexual politics as exclusively Western. We therefore need a more accurate conceptualization of modernity and its relationship to contemporary sexual diversity and, as a beginning point, I have borrowed the idea of 'connected histories' in the previous two chapters. Given both its introduction by Subrahmanyam (1997) and its subsequent use by Bhambra (2007) to challenge Eurocentric historical accounts of modernity, it may seem of limited use for our contemporary concerns, but Bhambra's project is precisely about how the 'present' politics of knowledge constructs history in a particular way and how the contemporary present emergence of post-colonial theory and contemporary manifestation of globalization permit a reconsideration of the historiography of modernity.[8] The invisibilization of Muslim traditions of homo-eroticism (by both East and West) has been one obvious reason to think through the connected, colonial histories of sexuality, but I am also reversing the logic, if you will, by arguing that the historical connections of modernity detailed by Bhambra and Subrahmanyam also force a recognition that the present continues to be an intersecting, complex, conjectural 'modern'. In the realm of the sexual, moreover, the evidence reviewed in the previous chapters points us clearly in the direction of historical and contemporary connections, what I have termed 'queer as intersectionality' in the latter case. I argue that an intersectional understanding of modernity takes us closer to a sensibility of connected histories and the connected present that I think is necessary to challenge the model of modernity that underpins the triangulation of Western exceptionalism through sexual politics.

In a sense, this use of an intersectional perspective is about moving from the realm of discourse towards the realm of social and political practices. Whilst the strength of the various critiques of homocolonialism lie in identifying the discursive ways in which identities are being folded into a process of Western superiority, evidence on lived experience points towards intersectionality as a keener sensibility in understanding the contemporary sexual modern. This is neither original nor controversial when considering that queer Muslims disrupt dominant identity categories but I am suggesting that intersectionality demands an appreciation of the full range of the sociological and the political, and thus, by logical extension, we are talking about an intersectional modernity. I am resistant to claiming that this is a new 'model' of modernity (I think that is a debate for another time) but rather I am emphasizing the epistemologically disruptive productivity of an intersectional sensibility. This I think permits us to disrupt modernization processes as linear and teleological, but not to reject specific processes in themselves as potentially important to a queer Muslim 'liberation' – so civil society group organization, law-based societies and institutions that permit them, civil society openness to information, reformulations of Muslim identity as open to gender and sexual diversity, all remain as important institutional and sociological factors as outlined in Chapters 3 and 5. The key is that approaching the contemporary world as a formation of connected intersectional processes enables us to resist locating these as exclusively 'owned' by the West. Modernity has always been a global, interconnected phenomenon and the historical colonialism of the West demonstrates that in relation to sexuality in full measure. In contemporary times, moreover, these processes continue but now in a different form which is nonetheless constructed through particular but intersecting hierarchies of oppression that produce particular, intersectional standpoints of experience of being queer and Muslim.

The political presumptions of homocolonialism: 'coming out' and the essential context of political identity

Western gay liberation has depended on a fundamental initial act; as Altman put it, 'The essence of gay liberation is that it enables us to come out'. (1993 [1971]: 237). This reminds us that the whole political venture of sexual diversity and its identity politics is based on this premise and, moreover, the recent achievement of citizenship rights is fundamentally dependent on both the public claims and public recognition of sexual identity. The Western model therefore requires subjects who identify as gay and are able and willing to self-organize around this identity. As Adam et al. argued in their analysis of comparative LGBTIQ movements (1999), institutional spaces are required for both group association and subsequent political demands and this organizational point seems entirely logical in a practical sense and the absence of such forums in Muslim cultures is part of the difficulties of rendering Muslim homoeroticism visible. The conflation of this point with democratic political structures was critiqued in Chapter 2, however, so we should bear in mind that the principles of democracy alone do not inevitably provoke sexual diversity movements: they have developed as an *unintended* consequence of the civil and political structure that modern capitalist societies gradually evolved for the practice of commerce and protection of property. Moreover, feminist and queer movements have contested and widened this limited liberal inheritance, contributing to a fundamental shift in what we think of as 'equality' and social justice, building on a transformation begun by organized labor and its claim for redistributive social justice well beyond liberal democracy's version of governance

(Phillips, 1993). What I want to focus on here is the related requirement of political identity, organized first through self-identification as homosexual and then as public identification. In the narrative equation of Western modernity with secularism, democracy and equality discussed in Chapter 2, the existence of public political identity is taken for granted as a representation of a stable, natural identity – that of the 'homosexual' or, in common terms, the 'lesbian and gay'.

Altman initially hoped for the eventual dissolution of the binary gender framework to make the category of homosexuality irrelevant (towards potential bisexuality in his understanding from the 1970s). That version of gender and sexual diversity has clearly not been the consequence of coming out, either sociologically or politically. Similarly, Weeks acknowledges that whilst gay liberation began as a revolutionary force to end sexual categorization, its sociological reality became about asserting a specific form of self-identity, and an essentialist one at that (2007: 81–85). What we have is a world of public culture that celebrates being 'born this way'[9] and promotes relationship rights on the basis of identifiable, stable sexual identities. The material basis of this world of sexual citizenship has been described in detail by others who demonstrate that decriminalization led to community organization for both politics and for sexual lifestyle behavior and consumption (Evans, 1993; Hennessey, 2000). The period of gay liberation in the West is also the period in which the 'Golden Age' of social democracy (Callinicos, 2007) gave way to consumer societies and the withdrawal of the state from much public provision, uniformly characterized as producing ever increasing emphasis on individualist social and political forms. One consequence of this individualization and marketization has been the emergence of what Duggan has called 'homonormativity' (2002) whereby equal citizenship strategies have mirrored and reinforced the institutions of material heterosexual privilege and created new moral divisions of respectability amongst homosexuals – a line of argument extended to nationalist incorporations of homosexual identity in Puar's thesis (2007) and in both cases, located as a consequence of the neoliberal economic and governance hegemony that emerged after the fiscal crises of the 1970s (Hall, 1983, 1988). Indeed, this is the more critical take on the detraditionalization momentum that underscores both Giddens' and Weeks' arguments on the emergence of positive opportunities for new forms of agency. Thus, the sociological basis of gay liberation has included both detraditionalization of gender divisions and their institutions but also the shift towards an individualist culture, overwhelmingly experienced through lifestyle consumption organized through essentialist understandings of the reflexive project of the self – what I have previously described as 'reflexive essentialism' (Rahman and Jackson, 2010). The claims for citizenship and the varying extent of LGBTIQ normalization – at national and international levels – is therefore fundamentally based on essentialist ideas of identity which have not been challenged by the process of coming out, but rather confirmed by the sociological forms of identity that have resulted from that initial 'moment' of liberation. Political subjectivity is constructed within and from these sociological resources, rather than simply being a reflex of 'universal' principles. Moreover, it *contributes* to these sociological forms of identity; visible, public politics becomes another resource in identity formation.

I have argued before that the political structures of liberal democracy must be understood as contributing to these sociological constructions of sexual identity, rather than simply as technologies that are deployed *after* identity is formed (Rahman, 2000). There has been a convergence between essentialist understandings of sexuality and liberal democratic strategies of equality, based on individual rights as a basis for social equality. My initial critique of the limits of liberal rights strategies was written before the recent advances in LGBTIQ rights across many countries in the West, and I acknowledge that such progress may seem to undermine my caution, but the predictions about incorporating liberal formal rights without troubling the social construction of essentialist gender is, I would suggest, borne out by the emergence of homonormative forms of gay identity. In the realm of sexual identity the lobbying for human rights has been based on a minority or ethnic group model that fundamentally reassures the majoritarian nature of heterosexuality precisely because it is based on essentialist understandings of gender and sexuality. What may also be happening, however, is that these incremental formal changes are contributing to a slower, more socially diverse process of detraditionalization of heterosexual privilege, in concert with the many other changes around gender that Weeks correctly identifies as part of the 'long transition'. Nonetheless, I would argue that the description of convergence between liberal democratic technologies and essentialist understandings of sexuality remains an accurate picture of how LGBTIQ rights are being pursued and framed both nationally and internationally. As the recent statement on Sexual Orientation and Gender Identity from the UN puts it, we are 'born' that way[10] and, because of that essential fact, we can have rights. Thus, the individualism central to liberal rights strategies reinforces the individualism of essentialist understandings of sexuality, so that our politics compounds rather than deconstructs the dominant construction of gender that creates the oppression in the first place.

This is not to deny that rights discourses and strategies based on identity politics have been successful in many contexts. The most striking example, I think, is the affirmation of queer lives achieved through the widespread resistance to homophobic characterizations of HIV/AIDS as a gay 'plague'. There are innumerable accounts to mention here, but let me use an exuberant example to demonstrate the logic of affirmative identity politics. The gay American artist Keith Haring produced a number of AIDS education and awareness posters during the first wave of the epidemic in the 1980s, including one titled 'National Coming Out Day' in 1988 for the National Gay Rights Advocates (easily accessible on the web or see the exhibition catalogue[11] by Doring, 2011). The image shows a typical Haring human figure literally high-kicking their way out of a closet door, affirming that the public declaration of identity is necessary for activism around AIDS policies. Identity politics does work in many contexts because it provides the basis to both represent experiences of oppression and for collective political participation. Moreover, we have seen the legislative and cultural impacts of queer identity politics reach a critical threshold in the last 10 years or so, mostly in Western countries but also in some from the global South (Itaborahy and Zhu, 2013; Pew, 2013). However, such strategies, successful as they appear to be, create a dilemma for queer 'liberation'.

Whilst political identity and political structures would seem to be irreducible components in any story of increasing reflexive conditions for sexual liberation, they are not attended to in any detail in Weeks' history of change, either in Britain or the West more generally. Rather, following Giddens, Weeks emphasizes the democratization of personal lives and relationships that is made possible through detraditionalization of Western societies. He does, however, focus on the internationalization of human rights discourses as the current dominant strategy for LGBTIQ and he endorses these, arguing that they are crucial in putting issues of sexuality on the agenda to promote global queer liberation, whilst recognizing that they are in danger of reifying a particular version of the 'necessary fiction' of stable, essentialist, sexual identities – the dilemma that so exercises Massad and which is identified as unavoidable by Awaad if we are to intervene in protecting the rights of those who identify as queer (2009).[12] I suggest, however, that this dilemma is not simply relevant to the current internationalization of sexual rights, but underpins the formation of political strategies in the West and has, therefore, fundamentally contributed to the ways in which gay liberation has emerged in the West.

The 'dilemma of difference' has been long identified as a central tension in identity politics, elaborated most succinctly by Young in her democratic theories, focused on difference-based groups within specific, usually national, polities in the West (Young, 1989, 1990). In brief, the argument goes that attempting to achieve the recognition that oppression is socially based rather than a reflection of 'natural' divisions involves organizing as a group to make political claims to address social inequalities, but that very act of organizing can seem to endorse the fact that groups are 'naturally' different, thus potentially reinforcing the very discourses that construct oppression in the first place.[13] What I suggest that we are potentially seeing in the internationalization of LGBTIQ rights is this dilemma of difference played out across cultures but with a Western version of essentialist natural sexual divisions as the one being deployed and then reinforced in the global connectedness that Weeks describes. For example, whilst we cannot dispute the five recommendations for member states to fulfill their obligations to LGBTIQ populations in the recent UN report on SOGI rights, its reliance on the concepts of sexual 'orientation' and gender 'identity' are hostages to homocolonialism given that they are based on Western essentialist versions of queer politics.[14]

The reinforcement of essentialism is therefore a central problem in this dilemma of internationalization because the interpellation of essentialist monoculturalist versions of sexuality is occurring *both* in protagonist Western cultures and resistant Eastern cultures. For example, the recent campaign for marriage equality in the USA is similarly open to a homocolonialist deployment because it has sought equality with heterosexuals, confirming the dominant framework of heteronormativity and seeking a place for a natural minority within that, thus reifying (homonormative) essentialist versions of sexual identity within the West. The trajectory of social change around sexuality in the West has been conditioned by political and social structures that have reinforced essentialist understandings of sexuality and these provide a difficult context for illuminating Muslim homo-eroticism. Muslim communities and politics may frame the resistance to queer politics as a resistance to Western neo-colonialism, but in this they are drawing upon a monocultural essentialist version of their own sexual cultures ('homosexuality does not exist in our cultures'), and confirming the same for Western cultures ('homosexuality is a Western disease'). Western and Western derived international rights strategies are therefore not only a potentially colonizing project that validates Western dominance by projecting a certain version of sexuality at home and abroad, but because this version of rights so clearly reinforces an essentialist understanding of gender and sexuality, it permits a 'reverse discourse' resistance to queer rights that accepts essentialist sexual cultures but identifies them with distinct civilizational and monolithic, essentialist cultures between East and West. We should therefore be aware of the fact that the context of current human rights strategies – both in national and international contexts – is not only based on Western constructions of gender and sexuality, but also then on Western experiences of coming out and its consequences, and that these culturally specific essentialist formations are potentially reinforced by the very political technologies and strategies that purport to provide universal routes to sexual liberation but actually contribute to the triangulation of Western exceptionalism and the reification of distinct sexual cultures.

Beyond homocolonialism: the ends of liberation and equality as resource

At the end of his classic text of Western gay liberation in the 1970s, *Homosexual Oppression and Liberation,* Dennis Altman suggests that:

> We are, I believe, moving toward a far greater acceptance of human sexuality and with that toward both a decrease in the stigma attached to unorthodox sex and a corresponding increase in overt bisexuality. To see the total withering away of the distinction between homo- and heterosexual is to be utopian. I suspect, however, it will come before the withering away of the state and may indeed be a necessary prelude to that ...
>
> One hopes that the answer lies in the creation of a new human for whom such distinctions are no longer necessary for the establishment of identity. The creation of this new human demands the acceptance of new definitions of man- and womanhood, as are being urged by gay and women's liberation ... and the homosexual as we know him or her may indeed disappear. (Altman, 1993 [1971]: 246–247)

Some 30 years later, he revisits the question of liberation in his exploration of *Global Sex:*

> ... I would argue that a meaningful sexual politics in a globalizing world must involve both the inequities of the larger socioeconomic order, and those implicated in the broader structures of sex and gender, which are constantly being remade through the very processes of globalization ...

> ... In the end, ideas of human rights, social justice, acceptance of diversity, and the empowerment of those who are marginalized and deprived are universal goals which remain important no matter the particular culture. Moreover, they will require both strengthened global order *and* effective national governments ...
>
> ... The sexual politics which burst upon western countries in the late 1960s spoke a vague language of internationalism, but its preoccupations were largely with the immediate and the nation-state. Three decades later the world is very different. Much of what we fought for then has been at least partially achieved in the west, but equally the triumph of liberal capitalism to a degree unforeseen by either its boosters or its detractors has created new challenges and new sorts of oppression. Those of us who are part of the privileged elite whose lives are being enriched by the processes of globalization must never forget just how precarious and dangerous the world is for most people. (Altman, 2001: 163–164)

Altman acknowledges the differences in context and focus between the first wave of gay liberation in the West and the contemporary internationalization of queer politics around the world. He recognizes that we are not dealing with linear or expansionary models of 'freedom' here, both by putting the gains of the West in their broad sociological context, particularly the socio-economic basis to the emergence of queer identities and political mobilization and the absence of such conditions in much of the world, and also by reminding us of the parochialism of liberation movements. He does not revisit the question of whether new versions of masculinity and femininity have been made possible by Western gay and women's liberation, instead accepting – as most contemporary writers do – that the ethnic essentialist version of gay identity is now the dominant political and cultural formation and that it has achieved partial success in acquiring citizenship. Despite his astute analysis of the various similarities and differences between cultures in the era of contemporary globalization, Altman nonetheless argues for a continued universalism in sexual politics, framing it now as a combination of 'human rights, social justice, diversity and empowerment of the marginalized'. Whilst he is careful to locate gay liberation within its own national contexts and suggest the differences its manifestations will thus take in different cultures, he is therefore suggesting that the political idea of liberation *from* sexual regulation and oppression is still relevant. I agree with this suggestion because I think it is still important to recognize that we are talking about something that is cross-culturally common when we talk of LGBTIQ oppression.[15] For the moment, we can think of the common sense understanding of this 'freedom' as liberation from homophobia, and however problematic that term may be, it has become common currency to denote stigma, discrimination and oppression of non-heterosexual identities resulting from the social oppression of gender organization that structures and justifies that regulation; what Seidman calls heterosexual dominance (2004), or what queer theory has described as heteronormativity. Whilst it is important to reiterate that the commonality in queer politics should not default into thinking about common sexual identities across cultures, let's accept the broad definition of common homophobia and the need for liberation from that for the moment and explore what implications the preceding intersectional analysis has for that idea of gay liberation.

The obvious first point to make is that queer Muslims as an intersectional identity exist at an intersection of homophobia and Islamophobia. If we are exploring the liberation of those located as such groupings (different as they are in various diasporic and Muslim majority contexts), we have to think about whether we can have freedom from one without the other. If we accept the political premise of the triangulation of Western exceptionalism through sexual diversity politics, then we are only permitted to imagine the defeat of homophobia in Western civilizations, and Islamophobia not only remains, but is reinforced through this purported defeat, deployed as it is in the homocolonialist triangulation. The evidence on the lived experience of queer Muslims suggests that such an outcome will not lead to a full liberation for them and my auto/biography in Chapter 1 concurs with the research from Chapter 5. We must also query whether Muslim attempts to challenge Islamophobia without acknowledging and challenging both wider cultural and specifically Muslim homophobia will benefit those Muslims who are queer or simply cede their identities to the West, defined by their queerness rather than their Muslim cultures. Even if many Western queers and Muslims do not care about queer Muslims, I would suggest that a fully intersectional analysis that included the socio-political contexts for standpoint experience indicates that the vectors of oppression denoted by homophobia and Islamophobia are not completely discrete.

This is not to claim that either homophobia or Islamophobia are manifested most acutely at the site of queer Muslims. Whilst these vectors of oppression intersect at the site of queer Muslims, they do not originate there. Whilst it is Muslim homophobia that is provoked and deployed in this particular circuit of triangulation, homophobia exists both internally in the space of the West, and, crucially, at a global transnational level (Weiss and Bosia, 2013b). Moreover, the same can be said for Islamophobia, a concept which is now being used to describe myriad forms of racialization of Muslims anchored in an overall opposition of West and East.[16] Tracing the intersection of Islamophobia/homophobia is therefore *also* to acknowledge that these oppressions are broader than the homocolonialist triangulation, and thus potentially to locate both Muslim homophobia and Islamophobia within larger global and political spirals of each. At the very least, this extended intersectional appreciation can lead us towards another challenge to the vortex by permitting a critique of Muslim homophobia within the context of these wider spirals, specifically national deployments by specific Muslim majority states as part of their statecraft and legitimization processes, and as part of global homophobic movements that include Western religious groupings (Bosia, 2013; Kaoma, 2013; Korycki and Nasirzadeh, 2013; Weiss, 2013). This appreciation acknowledges Muslim homophobia, but challenges the triangulated positioning by interrogating its intersectional formation, rather than reductively explaining Muslim homophobia as the reflex of a universal Muslim culture. Furthermore, it can lead us to appreciate that the politics of sexual diversity is folded into Islamophobic discourses and force us to render that visible, both to challenge its use as a criterion of modernity that contributes to orientalist Islamophobia and, moreover, to raise the question of whether spirals of Islamophobia actually reinforce circuits of homophobia because they contribute to affirming both the positioning and the processes of homocolonialist triangulation.

An intersectional perspective therefore retains an idea of some 'universals' of oppression, although it complicates their manifestation through their intersection and thus provides the disruptive opening of a queer intersectional perspective. However, even if we can begin with the acknowledgement of the oppressions we are trying to liberate ourselves from, we also have to consider the assumptions about where that momentum of liberation is taking us both in terms of process and in terms of whether there is an assumed teleological outcome to liberation. I have criticized the Western political processes and strategies at work in the previous section but I would argue that assumptions of political outcomes also need to be disrupted. The political goal of equality becomes much more complex an issue once universal identity and experience and the related assumed universal experience of being queer or Muslim become problematized through an intersectional sociological perspective. If we accept an intersectional analysis, it illuminates the distinct ontological possibilities of queer Muslim subjecthood, experientially, sociologically and politically. These possibilities and experiences are not, however, completely exclusive to the subjectivity of queer Muslims, but rather there are distinctions to their standpoint along certain shared or general vectors of oppression, primarily here homophobia and Islamophobia. The implications for equality outcomes need to be thought through on this basis of *both* distinct and shared oppression. First, it is in the distinction that we must realize that universal strategies and outcomes of equality are not universal, but based on partial ontology, defined by dominant categories of Muslim or queer and thus dominant experiences of oppression. Intersectionality demands a qualitatively different understanding of dominant, unitary categories and therefore implies potentially differentiated policies as process in remedying inequalities and perhaps, ultimately, the implication of differential outcomes in terms of what constitutes 'equality'. I am not suggesting that we challenge the authenticity of dominant identity categories as the basis for claims of oppression or equality, but rather that we understand that the ways in which identities are intersectional *also* indicate that equality claims are not simply universal but refer to different lived oppressions and hoped-for 'equal' ontological conditions. Of course, the distinct experience of queer Muslim oppression is constituted in part through shared ontological experience of key vectors of oppression and so these remain constitutive and important in an intersectional analytic, rather than being deconstructed away. So it remains important to think about challenging Islamophobia and homophobia as distinct forms of oppression, but with the added insight that these intersect through the triangulation process described above. A politics of queer Muslim liberation should contribute to challenging both Islamophobia and homophobia as individual vectors, but also in drawing out their intersections. For queer Muslims, can we really have liberation from one without the other?

This is difficult terrain in the sense that we are complicating assumed universal outcomes of equality but I have already argued that Western forms of liberal democratic queer politics have defaulted into an assumption of liberation as the emergence of 'true' selves into the public realm, rather than acknowledging the truth of possible selves in sociological context. I have suggested that we need to think about the forms of subjectification, the possible selves if you like, that are available as resources for identities in different contexts, rather than to assume a teleological outcome of 'equality' that is universally possible in each society. Again, this can only be the beginnings of an understanding of what equality might look like, accepting that the discourse of equality framed within the complex of human rights is a dominant contemporary political formation. But can we begin to think about equality as a means to an end, without claiming any certainty, or implicitly assuming what the 'end' will look like? Can we begin to think of equality politics as one resource, amongst many, that must be understood in this wider intersectional context, so that it is not a defined outcome, but rather a resource for shaping lived experience in sociological and political context?

Arriving at the terrain of dialogue and recognizing queer as privilege

The analysis presented in this chapter is an attempt to lead us towards a more productive terrain of political engagement around sexual diversity and Muslim cultures than we have at present. As such, it speaks broadly to two issues. The first is that we have to create routes towards a political space where there can be dialogue around these issues, rather than to reinstate the mutually exclusive positioning of the triangulated process described throughout this chapter. Moreover, this does not have to assume a terrain of consistently shared 'values' and hence agreement, but rather arrival at the inevitably uncertain space where politics is debated and worked through, albeit within some commonly agreed parameters, what Parekh describes as any society's operative public values (2006: 267). In the case of multicultural Western societies, this space already exists for both groups in different shapes but underscored with a common principle of diversity and minority rights. Internationally, there is less certainty that there are common values, particularly because Islamic human rights discourse, as well as regional Asian ones, dispute the basis of individual relationships to the state and to wider culture, contesting the Western liberal bias in much human rights policies (Parekh, 2006; Woodiwiss, 2012) and, of course, because there are differences in the understanding of what sexual 'orientation' means. Thus, whilst the intersectional analysis of the connections between Islamophobia and homophobia and their contribution to asserting a sense of Western exceptionalism can serve as beginning points for the disruption of the current discourse of opposition, I do not think we should assume that this 'disruption' will lead to a 'solution' that is assumed to result in common values around sexuality. Rather, we should think of this disruptive technique as a way of developing and conducting politics that resists these oppositional characterizations. Muslim homophobia and Islamophobia might and probably will remain, but if we can break the equation between the two, we are working towards the beginnings of challenging both and creating a political space for queer Muslims that exists only tenuously, intermittently at present.

The second issue is to recognize that the ways in which queer politics is identified with Western exceptionalism have produced certain privileges for queer groups over Muslim cultures and communities. In this sense, creating a route to a terrain of dialogue has different requirements for queer politics and Muslim politics, largely because the former appears nearer to the general expectation of citizenship than the latter, even if that citizenship is a limited liberal one. Puar has correctly identified some aspects of this privilege as the embrace of homonationalism, capturing the advances in formal citizenship and public visibility that are normalizing homonormative queer identities to some extent, in stark contrast to the stigmatization of racialized others (2007). I have argued, moreover, that we must also recognize that liberal political structures have in part produced the subjectification of queer liberation in ways that effectively reassert Western exceptionalism through Western essentialism. Querying the Western outcome of citizenship as the only assumed one to LGBTIQ public identities and social liberation is therefore necessary, but supremely difficult, since this form of politics has delivered genuinely experienced 'freedom' for many in the West. I am not suggesting, however, that we let go of that privilege, but rather that we start to think about what different forms of equality as lived experience might look like for queer Muslims around the world and in Western nations, without assuming the Western 'blueprint' for liberation. That is a pretty difficult task because the default mindset in LGBTIQ politics remains focused on oppression and homophobia, but I think that we have to recognize that the processes of triangulation described in this chapter position us on the 'inside' in some important ways, both internationally and nationally. The real political question therefore becomes whether we retain those privileges and continue to fight homophobia in the West and globally without reinforcing homocolonialism. To put it another way, is it possible to have a genuinely inclusive homonationalism without homocolonialism?

In light of both queer privilege and the need to create a terrain of dialogue, I move on to practical strategies for politics in the concluding chapter, attempting to translate the insights of the preceding analyses for practical politics. This is less a genuine conclusion, but rather, in keeping with my emphasis on not predicting the shape of equality, a series of beginnings.

7
Beginnings

Introduction

A project such as this has no conclusion, given that it can only be a beginning to navigating the opposition of Muslim cultures and homosexuality. To paraphrase that unrepentant colonialist Winston Churchill[1] – this concluding chapter is therefore neither the end, nor the beginning of the end, but merely the end of the beginning; an attempt to think through the practical implications of the preceding arguments for the continued pursuit of sexual diversity politics without contributing to either Islamophobia or Muslim homophobia. I accept that there is much cause for pessimism in the sense that the sociological and political formations of contemporary sexualities and Muslim identities make it highly unlikely that we can find an easy 'solution' to the oppositional understandings of homosexuality and Muslim cultures. Nonetheless, we need some beginnings, some navigation points for a way forward that, at the very least, delivers some better experience of being queer and Muslim, and may perhaps deliver more when we consider the implications for the politics of identity and belonging for Muslim groups and for Western queer groups.

Moving to specifics that derive from the broader political critique in the previous chapter, I think through what political strategies become relevant or appropriate to navigate through the oppositional bequest of homosexuality as Western modernity. Here I retain the sense that we are attempting to move towards a politics of 'liberation' that is the ultimate goal of the politics of sexual diversity whilst keeping the intersectional skepticism of a universal route or strategy of liberation. I discuss political strategies in relation to both international politics and the politics of multiculturalism within Western societies and in relation to the politics of both Muslim and queer cultures and identities. This practical exploration is, in many ways, the most difficult discussion to have, given that it demands a reflexive interrogation of political strategies and equality outcomes from both Muslim communities and Western queer ones, requiring a pivot towards understanding equality resources, as suggested in the previous chapter. I suggest that thinking about the actual *shaping* of equality in specific contexts may help us to begin the process of identifying useful and effective strategies that undermine the damaging dialectic of Islam versus homosexuality from both sides of the divide. Above all, what we are dealing with in contemporary LGBTIQ Muslim politics is emphatically *not* the diffusion of *Western* outcomes of equality and routes to that particular liberation, but historically distinct circumstances that require a precise intersectional appreciation of how the sexual is being constructed in contemporary modernity.[2] In this sense, we are trying to achieve 'progress' without knowing its outcome and that is the difficult but necessary beginning to a reformulation of the politics of both queer and Muslim identity. As Said argued in his analysis of literary beginnings in the novel, they reflect intention whereby 'an intention, therefore, is a notion that includes everything that later develops out of it, no matter how eccentric the development or inconsistent the result. I do not mean, on the other hand, that *intention* is a more precise equivalent of *totality*' (1985: 12). By claiming this conclusion as only 'beginnings', I both acknowledge that this project has had a definite purposeful intention but that, inevitably, there are no definite outcomes to it. It remains a contribution to much wider themes and debates and the uncertainty, the eccentricity and inconsistencies of potential outcomes is something that we have no choice but to embrace.

The homocolonialist 'test' for internationalized Western queer politics and consciousness

Muslims are certainly being 'tested' when it comes to the politics of sexual diversity. This is both literal in the examples we have seen of immigration procedures[3] and, as we saw in Chapter 2, at the wider level of political culture, including both Western states and some feminist and queer groups (Haritaworn, 2012). One might well wonder what queer politics is doing messing with official 'testing', given the various miseries medical/psychological and state testing has imposed on us historically, but if we are to embrace this tactic, let's adopt a somewhat different stance focused on what I will call the 'homocolonialist' test. Let's think about whether in our political concepts, political strategies and tactics, and assumptions of their outcomes, we are reinstating or reiterating the triangulation of Western superiority, either in its positioning of cultures or in its processes, or whether we can begin to disrupt this formation.

This is not to denounce or abandon the advantages that Western forms of society have in terms of progressing sexual liberation, but it is to ask whether the assumptions of exporting or diffusing that model can really deliver effective sexual freedom within Muslim minority populations or majority cultures when the logic of modernization itself is based wholly on Western experience. As I suggested in Chapter 3, even if we take modernization as a universally imitable process that will lead to a universal modernity, the logic of how LGBTIQ politics has developed within this process would require that we abandon any imposition or expectation of queer human rights and instead focus on making Muslim countries and populations richer and making sure that wealth is distributed widely enough to create powerful propertied groups who require the rule of law to protect their interests, unintentionally provoking a culture of legal equality and equal opportunity that should eventually lead to new social movements focused around gender and sexuality. Of course, shifting the paradigm of gay activism towards engineering a linear modernity of liberation is a fantasy and the reality is that we are living in a world in which we are increasingly demanding both queer rights both as transnational criteria for 'civilization', and the willing acceptance of those rights as the price of supporting multiculturalism. Given that reality, we need to test our assumptions about how we proceed. In this context, what would the homocolonialist test focus on? What does a disruption to the triangulated positioning of cultures and queer rights, and the processes that sustain this actually look like? I aim here to offer some beginnings for political intervention, not with any prescriptive or totalizing intention, but rather to begin the process of translating my analysis into practical strategies, incomplete as that translation will inevitably be.

First, an accurate understanding of modernization politics would ask us not to impose queer rights on populations not yet 'modernized' enough to sustain them, but the political inversion of this logic abounds endlessly. 'Pinkwashing' is the most cynical expression of this assumption of sexuality as Western exceptionalism and thus a key process in the triangulation described above.[4] There are already numerous public and academic challenges to this strategy, but to disrupt it as part of the processes of triangulation, I think we also have to argue against any form of pinktesting whereby queer rights are used to define the positionality of monolithic civilizational formations. The reiterations of Muslim antipathy to homosexuality are a common Western public and political reflex and simply reassert a monolithic and static version of Muslim cultures, and this kind of unthinking assertion needs to stop if we are to begin to prise open the oppositional discourse. More broadly, recent indications from some Western governments that they may use assessments of LGBTIQ rights to attach conditions to general development aid is hugely problematic because it potentially reinstates the triangulation of homocolonialism, with non-Western populations and cultures resisting the imposition of queer rights as part of their resistance to neo-colonialism, and repressive state actors in particular deriving legitimacy from such a response.[5] We have to ask in such situations, whether actual reductions in general aid monies, or the accession of states to these demands around queer issues (usually 'tested' by formal rights) actually has any chance of enhancing equality resources for local queer groups or will simply position them as a 'problem' for the general population. Moreover, I am not aware of any actual situation in which either an IGO or a rich Western government has actually imposed any form of sanctions because of queer rights, leading us back to the suspicion that such pinktesting rhetoric may well be there to serve Western vanity over and above the lived equality of queers.[6]

Of course, in some situations where the proposals are literally murderous, we should articulate against these as forcefully as possible, as in the Ugandan example (Kaoma, 2013) but this can be done as a question of human rights without relating these to aid. In other situations, as Baudh's small-scale interviews in South Asia attest, what we might think of as the base line right of decriminalization is not uniformly seen as either necessary or welcome for the lived experience of queers, with some fearing the backlash such campaigns cause more than the formal 'freedom' such rights entail (2013). Thus, the local consequences of this kind of aid conditionality may be an increase in the stigmatization and state harassment of queers rather than some assumed 'trigger' to an expansion of public visibility and freedom. As Lind argues, there are both transnational dialogues between activists and scholars and social justice movements in the global South where the work of both queering development and cautioning against Western impositions of political concepts and strategies is ongoing (2010a) and it seems to me that this is where Western attention and money should be focused, without conditions apart from the overriding one that we do not reinstate the triangulation of Western exceptionalism through our own 'conditions' of what queer equality must look like. We know that development aid has enabled sexual rights activism in many contexts, often deployed in the framework of sexual health related to HIV/AIDS, but then used to develop resources and identity groups and engage in political activism (Lind, 2010; Moore, 2012). This kind of targeted enabling aid enhances equality resources; discursive pinktesting rhetoric does not.

Of course, the issue of development is a huge topic and I rely here on the expertise of others who are much more knowledgeable about the actualities of development politics and activism,[7] but I am arguing a general point; that we must defer to local, national priorities from queer groups as our beginning for what we might conceive of as our Western 'aid' to sexual subjectivities outside the West, drawing on horizontal alliances and genuinely transnational dialogue (Parker and Aggleton, 2012). This argument is not meant to be an agenda for the paralysis of transnational activism, but one that enables a more tactical sensibility; where the use of discourses of queer rights and/or international pressure on these is enabling for local populations, we should absolutely use them but the complications of queer transnational politics need further careful elaboration if we are not to revert to the parochialism of the initial queer wave of liberation, expressed now through homocolonialism. Pluralizing a concern for queer lives beyond 'rights' towards the material resources of equality in their local contexts is a shift that needs to become mainstream in any manifestation of international queer politics.

In terms of rights rather than aid policies, internationalization has had its benefits with the developing architecture of LGBTIQ rights woven into human rights serving as a resource for many local movements (Lind, 2010a; Lennox and Waites, 2013b; Waites, 2009). However, many of these movements have also demonstrated the contradictions of dealing with universal expressions in local or national contexts (Lind, 2010a), illustrating again the internationalization of the dilemma of difference described in the previous chapter. The challenges that local groups have in dealing with this dilemma demand that we query whether we are also addressing what lies beneath that highest, universal expression of abstract rights and whether we are providing a full architecture to lived experiences of equality. There is an established body of scholarship that queries this issue, focused primarily on two themes; that of the full range of resources needed to flesh out the conditions of human rights, and that of the limitations of the concepts being codified through international law. The former relates to the discussion above and reiterates the need to develop a Southern-led strategy of international queer politics, as Lennox and Waites argue for (2013b) and one, moreover, that takes account of the intersectionalities of sexual subjectivity with, at the very least, class, culture and gender, and the political structures available (Altman, 2001; Boellstorff, 2012; Lind, 2010a). In their analysis of LGBTIQ movements in the Commonwealth, for example, Lennox and Waites point to the national specificities of how movements have developed as far more important than international discourses or rights structures, even where the latter have been used as resources in the local context. Whilst being careful to limit the generalizability of their comparative analysis, they identify some broad common processes, primarily the building of alliances beyond exclusively LGBTIQ groups, and a concurrent legitimization of human rights within regional, rather than international, contexts (Lennox and Waites, 2013b). If we are to continue promoting an international framework of rights, perhaps we can refocus efforts to engage more directly with regional, pan-Islamic, Asian and African rights bodies, which uniformly ignore questions of sexuality at present as demonstrated in Chapter 3, perhaps using activism at the UN as a lever, but not necessarily a blueprint for outcomes.

This regionalization may help to refine the universalism in contemporary international human rights discourse, which is the second major issue at stake. For example, there is some danger that the recent description of obligations of member states towards LGBTIQ from the UN could be woven into the homocolonialist process and positioning on both sides of the divide, replaying the organized resistance of the OIC and Vatican, amongst others (Sweibel, 2009). Such resistance could induce more repression by both continuing the transnational level of alliances between homophobic groups (Weiss and Bosia, 2013b) and encouraging more resistance to change at the national level. The UN document is resolutely 'universalist' in its description of obligations as human rights, but also in its conceptualization of sexual diversity.[8] The one footnote that mentions the problems with its key concepts argues that they can be used to recognize culturally diverse expressions of sexuality and gender, something that we know is too often not the case. As argued in the previous chapter, the essentialism of these concepts is too often read as a specifically Western essentialism, immediately allowing these issues to be woven into the processes of resistance. Moreover, the primary obligation to protect 'LGBT' from violence includes recognizing claims for asylum. Again, whilst I support this obligation, it immediately replays the global divide thesis, and without some kind of concurrent process whereby the fundamental concepts of these 'soft', unenforceable laws are open to cultural specificity, they remain a hostage to homocolonialist processes. As Kollman demonstrates in her analysis of same-sex union policies in the EU, the 'soft' laws of EU anti-discrimination had varying effects, always filtered through domestic processes, including the 'hard' law of national regulations (2009). Despite the fact that many non-Western nations have led the recent activism within the organization, UN statements have encountered resistance in local contexts, and we must move towards some kind of international debate about the concepts of sexual diversity, and how they may be effectively woven into regional human rights, *within* but *beneath* the more universal expressions available at present, if such rights are to be a genuine resource for equality rather than being hostage to resistance that characterizes them as an expression of Western values.

We do have to accept that we need some form of codification when we are attempting to produce policies or formal laws; that is simply the nature of formal written, abstract policy-making and is also necessary to enable advocacy within institutions. Nonetheless, as Budhiraja et al. have suggested, this can cause huge mistranslations across cultures in crucial points of activism, particularly in the current dominant 'alphabet soup' approach, that involves adding more and more 'identities' to the category of (non-normative) sexual orientation (2010). They suggest an approach that is framed in terms of sexual rights and gender justice, pointing to the IGLHRC's adoption of this term as enabling a broader and more localized strategy of both advocating for and addressing abuses of queer rights within human rights and/or local legal frameworks and, moreover, one that moves towards creating a 'common context' for political activism (borrowing from Mohanty) rather than reducing activism to identity politics. What I think is particularly interesting here is the ability to think about principles of human dignity within this framework, rather than focusing on rights attached to identities. Again, this is a complex issue, but given the huge diversity in cultural forms of sexual and gendered subjectivity, any codification that is expansive rather than reductionist deserves further exploration, both as a means of enabling effective advocacy and also in terms of bringing more national actors into the transnational discussion and debate over the internationalization of queer rights. Impossible and potentially horrifying as it may seem, can we move towards encouraging a response from member states to the concepts and principles in play? There is as yet no common ground between Muslim IGOs' emphasis on Islamic human rights and those of the UN in the area of sexuality but there is some commonality when it comes to gender and of human dignity.

Can we then, reformulate concepts to include the possibility of cultural diversity in sexuality and relate it to gender rights? Is human dignity a shared value here, that might be open to productive contestations? We may immediately resist the notion of cultural diversity as a means of retaining hetero-nationalist repression of diverse sexualities but we should remember that this version of essential cultural difference is part of the triangulated positioning of opposition. Any conceptual progress that begins to disrupt that positioning at least opens up a space for dialogue and all we have with our concepts of sexuality right now is disagreement without dialogue. Can new ways of framing sexual diversity, rather than orientation, permit more space for groups to create Muslim homo-erotic archives and contemporary Muslim homo-erotic identities as part of the contestation over culturally specific sexuality in Muslim communities? At the very least, can we begin to incorporate statements of principle that acknowledge cultural sexual diversity rather than use universal terms, even if in the codification of policy we then have to move to some (reformulated) universal concepts?

Moreover, these strategies of reformulation are less open to redeployments of a regressive monoculturalism if there are concurrent strategies at work, such as the refusal of pinktesting policies conducted in the name of and/or under the legitimacy of queer organizations. This refusal is both practical (they simply reiterate the triangulated process of opposition) but also politically necessary – a challenge to that process opens up space to begin recognizing that sexual diversity will be developing in different ways, and may even open up the space to recognize culturally specific archives and their contemporary manifestations. Could we, for example, imagine campaigns that resist pinktesting by identifying queer politics as being against Islamophobia? A 'Queer Day against Islamophobia' as part of the annual political calendar? Or Pride days devoted primarily to such specific causes, to raise consciousness and build alliances? These interventions, moreover, do not silence our ability to critique Muslim homophobia, but rather they encourage us to resist describing it outside of a wider context of Islamophobia and thus, I would argue, allow us more credibility to confront specific instances of Muslim antipathy to sexual diversity and provide more credible indications of an openness to cultural debate about human rights.

Homocolonialism in multiculturalism

Pinktesting within the multicultural politics in the West is also something that needs to be abandoned, as it will inevitably reinstate the homocolonialist triangulation processes of homophobia and Islamophobia. The cynical use of queer rights by anti-immigrant groups and by national governments is something we should, collectively, argue against. Until such time as *all* residents and immigrants are routinely tested for homophobia and other forms of discrimination (and presumably then deported?) we cannot tell ourselves that lobbying to have queer rights included within immigration or multicultural 'tests' is anything other than discrimination against minority cultural groups, and most markedly against Muslims. Many of these societies in the West have achieved democratically and/or constitutionally agreed queer rights and that base line does not have to be abandoned and nor should it be. So we can and should demand that queer rights and visibility are included in any descriptions of the 'values' and society that governments use in immigration literature. But we have to accept that it is OK for particular groups not to share in believing that homosexuality is 'acceptable' to them, as long as they are not allowed to practice that belief in a discriminatory way in a country that already has those protections (Phillips, 2007). That is the price of diversity and a price that all groups that value diversity should be willing to pay if we are to remain consistent about the principles of diversity (Modood, 2013); we can disagree but we can't discriminate. This issue is, however, particularly tense for queer groups when confronted with the religious basis of Muslim antipathy, often conjuring the historic and contemporary battles with established Christian religions within the West. The fact that rising Muslim political consciousness is a factor in multiculturalism may seem to create an impasse, but we know that this political consciousness is broader than religion (Meer, 2010). Instead of characterizing all Muslims as uniformly religious, we should explore the possibilities of dialogue across issues of diversity and protection from discrimination that the evidence from Chapter 3 suggests is increasingly important to Muslim immigrant communities in the West.

In order to achieve such dialogue, however, we cannot simply talk to 'secular' Muslim organizations. Queer politics needs to rethink the understandable reflex towards unconditional secularism. Whilst there is a long history of religious queer groups in many countries of the West who have attempted activism within their religion (Rayside and Wilcox, 201; Valentine et al., 2010), mainstream queer advocacy has not dealt with these intersections within the queer community, understandably focusing on secular anti-discrimination and citizenship politics. The base line of secularism as a fundamental principle in public presence and the application of rights is important and should be retained where it exists, but I am suggesting here that the unthinking extension of that principle to all the technologies and practices of multiculturalism is a problem that needs to be explored. Not only does this potentially prevent the development of queer Muslim religious discourses within queer and Muslim politics (something which the evidence from Chapter 5 suggests is a significant resource for queer Muslims) but it lowers the likelihood of debate and change within Muslim communities on issues of sexuality and gender because it *weakens* multiculturalism and thus the practices of diversity and dialogue that it should entail. I am drawing here on Modood's argument that if religion is a primary identification of a particular group (usually but not exclusively ethnically based), then a robust multiculturalism must include religious identification as much as it does gender, sexuality or race, indicating a moderate rather than ideological secularism (2013: 72–79). If queer politics is increasingly aligned to ideological secularism, as in the examples of pinktesting, all we are doing is reinstating a process of triangulation whereby our politics contributes to Islamophobia and, inevitably, homophobia as part of the resistance to that oppression. Instead, by accommodating religion, we have the potential to create more spaces and experiences of dialogue, whilst recognizing that this will not lead to full agreement.[9]

I am sure that some queer groups and individuals will view this position with horror, but we already have *shared* experiences of oppression and exclusion and we surely cannot wish those on other groups, nor should we tolerate them when they happen to the 'other'. We would not tolerate, for example, soccer federations banning queer youth from participation in organized sports because they did not fit an appropriately masculine or feminine normative identity, but this assumption of 'normativity' was applied to Sikhs in Quebec recently. The provincial federation banned turbans from the pitch, with one official announcing that 'they' could always play in their back yards if they needed to wear their turbans.[10] The ban was overturned by Fédération Internationale de Football Association (FIFA) with uncommon speed, but the discourse of the privatized existence of difference that permitted its articulation in the first place is something that operates consistently in Islamophobia *and* homophobia. Similarly, does banning the hijab do anything more than encourage a defensive retrenchment of Muslim identity, and close off participation for Muslim women and girls in various aspects of public life, without encouraging an internal debate about the patriarchal legitimization of the garment? In any retrenchment of oppositional politics as a response to Islamophobia, we can be certain that this will reinforce homophobia. Islamophobia and homophobia reinforce each other in particular political discourses, and thus challenging one will also contribute to challenging the other.

Whilst many theorists of multiculturalism locate queer politics outside of the core, ethnically-based groups which have driven multiculturalism in *practice*, I am not sure it is correct to extend this to a theoretical distinction when both Muslims and queer groups are oppressed by the dominant society, and seek, in some form, 'liberation' from that oppression. As Parekh argues, there are certainly important differences in the kinds of challenges such issues present to the organization of the majority society (2006: 2–4) but in terms of challenging a dominant 'monoculturalism' in favor of specific diversity, there are political similarities. In contrast to Okin (1998), I would suggest that multiculturalism is not in principle a problem for women or LGBTIQ, but rather that the principles of diversity it entails are precisely the same conditions that queer politics has both shaped and benefitted from. Rights of non-discrimination are a fundamental part of the expansion of liberal equality towards social justice that feminism, gay liberation and ethnic politics have all helped to shape, and these should not be negotiable in the context of religious or cultural recognition.[11] Thus, there will be disagreement within the accepted boundaries of diversity but this is part of the process of recognizing varieties of cultural diversity. In terms of my specific concerns, accommodating the religious basis of Muslim identity will aid in challenging Islamophobia and thus potentially, Muslim homophobia, and it will also create more space for queer Muslims who refute the assumptions of mutual exclusivity that close off the visibility of common, rather than simply shared, oppression in multiculturalism.

Some practical, if not yet hopeful, illustrations of this kind of strategy exist. For example, Jivraj and de Jong analyze Dutch state funding of queer religious groups as part of encouraging the integration of religion within Dutch multiculturalism (2011). They demonstrate that the majority of groups who took advantage of this strategy were Christian rather than Muslim, and that part of the issue seemed to be the assumption that one would encourage the public visibility and 'speaking out' of queer Muslims along the same basis of 'liberation' as understood from the Dutch experience – funding the emergence of 'true selves' in my terms, if you will. In contrast, El Tayeb demonstrates more success at public intervention and visibility by a queer of color collective in the Netherlands, *Strange Fruit*, particularly around challenging the invisibility and unintelligibility of queer Muslims (2012). One state funded strategy and one not, and perhaps this autonomy is the key to effective strategies, but it will depend on the national and local context. Rather than a prescription, I think this example demonstrates that there are possibilities within multiculturalist practice that include a queer politics that disrupts the oppositional positioning of ethnic and queer. Strategies that encourage or support the autonomous development of queer Muslims – from both sides of the divide – and the routes to a dialogue that development might produce, are important strategies for Western queer groups and Western state multiculturalism to support. If these groups then emerge from mainstream Muslim communities, so much the better, but if they do not, we should not demand that mainstream Muslim groups have to develop them.

In both international politics and domestic Western politics, beneath the architecture of universal rights, can we accept that we should be working for a variety of 'possible' selves of sexual and Muslim subjectification? The beginnings I have mapped above are just that, beginnings to navigating our way through the established oppositional triangulation of Muslim cultures and sexual diversity. I have argued that specific expectations of outcomes are part and parcel of the assumption of Western superiority in this triangulation but, nonetheless, there are two broad outcomes that I think remain important and can replace our assumptions of a linear outcome to queer liberation. First, our aims can be directed to achieving and/or enhancing 'equality' as a framework of resources and a key part of a 'homocolonialist' test is whether we are likely to do that through our politics. In particular in the current political climate, I think we should refuse rhetorical and actual pink-testing, both because it is a cynical use of queer rights in the service of Islamophobia, and its consequences for queer Muslims are ambiguous and cannot be guaranteed to achieve what the queer communities affected might want. We know from the history of Western queer politics that sexual issues are a lightning conductor for moral anxieties and state legitimacy (Weeks, 1996) and thus have always entailed a 'playing with fire' (Phelan, 1997). Unless we can be certain from the groups affected that this form of conditionality will enhance their resources in achieving equality (and most of this will be absolutely locally, nationally based), Western queer politics is playing with a fire we cannot control.

The second outcome that runs throughout this critique is about positioning, primarily whether we can we break down the positioning of oppositional and mutual exclusivity that exists in the triangulation process. I have suggested the beginnings of interventions above, but the assumption that runs beneath them is that a terrain of dialogue is possible between Muslim and queer cultures. I turn now to how homocolonialism needs to be challenged within the former if we are to reach a space of dialogue and debate.

Embracing Western exceptionalism through homocolonialism: challenges for Muslim consciousness and politics

Muslim resistance to sexual diversity politics is just as much a part of the triangulation of Western exceptionalism as is Western homocolonialism because it accepts the formation of homosexualities as exclusively Western, possible only in the accelerated forms of modernity that are 'owned' by the West. Since both this positioning and the processes that it entails compound Islamophobia, the question becomes whether Muslim politics and consciousness can benefit from challenging this triangulation. There are, moreover, various strategies possible to such a challenge, from the gradual elimination of Muslim homophobia through to the continued expression of Muslim homophobia as part of a specifically religious identity that nonetheless accepts diversity in gender and sexuality. The latter is the more realistic path at present, so I will deal with that first although I will also argue that the two extremes of these possible outcomes are related.

The argument against pinktesting is partly premised on the fact that we cannot and should not force beliefs on any group, but also partly on the evidence that religiosity amongst Muslims is no more a motivation to homophobia than in other religious groups, either within the West or internationally. This may not be a welcome reality, but it is an accurate one. Hence, within the multicultural politics of the West, there is no reason that Muslim politics cannot continue to argue against the cultural/religious acceptability of sexual diversity but from within the boundaries of secular frameworks of rights and public policy. The only shift we might wish to see is an acknowledgement from Muslim groups that sexual diversity is part of the spectrum of diversity that includes ethnic and religious pluralism, and thus it has as proper a place in public politics as Muslim consciousness. Too often Muslim groups are silent on this issue, or vocal only in opposition to sexual rights, often in alliance with other religious groupings. Both the silence and the articulation of opposition in extreme ways has its consequences; when there are no Muslim voices articulating against discrimination and violence directed towards LGBTIQ communities, it is simple enough for those who wish to do so to use this position to compound Islamophobia. Can we imagine a Muslim position against homophobia that retains the right to disagree with the acceptability of homosexuality? In that this position would be much like the Vatican's, queer activists may disdain it, but accepting religious rights to disapprove of particular acts *within* the framework of a public politics that protects queers against discrimination is a reasonable outcome in multiculturalism and includes an obligation from Muslim politics to acknowledge the need to balance their cultural rights with the rights of others. Academic analysis of Muslim politics overwhelmingly repeats this invisibilization or mentions queer rights only as a source of conflict with Muslim politics. Perhaps this is a symptom of the fact that we do not really have a clear conceptual framework of the routes to resolution within multiculturalism between ethnic groups and those organized around sexual diversity (and I include my own previous work on *Sexuality and Democracy* here, 2000). Absence, rather than presence, is the defining feature of sexuality within the established literature on multiculturalism (Modood, 2013, Parekh, 2006; Phillips, 2007) and this conceptual gap needs to be addressed to counter those analyses that posit *only* conflict between Muslim groups and sexual diversity politics (Beckett and Macey, 2001; Okin, 1998) and, in this sense, provide no framework for Muslim or queer groups to coexist within multiculturalism.

In terms of Muslim majority cultures, I have suggested above the ways in which concepts of sexual orientation and their deployment internationally need to be rethought to encourage the participation of Muslim countries in a debate about the ways in which sexuality can form part of human rights. The Muslim route to such a debate is, however, presented with the obstacle of governments that are heavily invested in a hetero-nationalism legitimized through Islam. As the examples in Chapter 5 demonstrate, many Muslim governments benefit from the triangulation processes described previously, because it serves their own legitimacy to *embrace* homocolonialism, precisely so that it can become a vector of resistance to Western neo-colonialism. In these circumstances, the development of queer Muslim organizations will rely heavily on the transnational dialogues and strategies discussed in the previous section, but the development of a *general* Muslim consciousness around sexual diversity seems highly improbable and without that culturally specific change, it seems unlikely that queer Muslim visibility can become possible. Nonetheless, as Safi argues in his description of a progressive Muslim project, it is time for Muslims to criticize and argue against oppression by the West *and* by their own governments and those who benefit from the entrenchment of ideological religious traditions (2003). I can see no real practical resource for a movement towards including sexual diversity within Muslim political consciousness unless there is an engagement with the developing international discourse of queer human rights from Muslim nations, and this I think is highly unlikely unless there is a possibility that cultural differences can be taken seriously as part of the process of reformulation of rights discussed above.

This last point immediately takes us into the realm of broader social and political change, and this, ultimately, will be the necessary background for the more hopeful outcome that Muslim homophobia will diminish, rather than simply be contained within legal structures of diversity and human rights. There are three broad issues at play in this question of social change that relate to both minority communities and majority cultures, focused around spiritual reformations, pluralism within Muslim communities and thought, particularly around gender and sexuality, and the overriding issue of 'progress'. First, there is an emergent strand of religious reinterpretation around issues of sexuality, something that the evidence on lived experience demonstrates is important to many queer Muslims. Kugle's work is the most sustained rethinking of the role of sexuality within Muslim spiritualism and he illustrates the many ambiguities that inform scriptural and legal reasoning often used to justify Islamic condemnation of homosexuality (2010). Both he and other queer Muslims[12] are creating a body of scholarship that has already been a resource for Muslim queer organizations and this is a welcome development, but we have seen how attempting to encourage such organizations through state funding in the West has not been that successful. Given the limited nature of the examples of this strategy, it should not be dismissed out of hand, but perhaps we can argue more for autonomous queer Muslim scholarship and debate, through funding of queer religious conferences, for example, rather than hoping to magically bring into public being queer Muslim groups through public funding. It would of course, be extremely positive for this resource if Muslim communities were supportive of this emergence, but that seems unlikely, both empirically and because, beyond these attempts to develop a resource for queer Muslim spirituality, this scholarship speaks to broader concerns about the static traditionalism of religion in Muslim life and, in particular, recognizing the historical and cultural context in which Islamic traditions and canons have developed.

This is a contentious issue in any organized religion and it no doubt will remain so in Islam, particularly when there are widespread calls from Western political voices for a 'reformation' in Islam that seems only to be a call for 'modernization' based on Western experience

(Safi, 2003: 15–17). However, we must confront the ideological basis of the deployment of religion to serve what I have called a 'monoculturalism' in Muslim civilization, and more specifically, a hetero-nationalism that legitimizes particular governments or community organizations. This is not to concede to the demands for an Islamic 'reformation' in Western terms, or to encourage secularism through stealth, but to work towards an open tradition of Muslim spirituality that is not hostage to broader civilizational dialectics on either side of the divide, not least because this triangulation reinforces Islamophobia and thus oppresses many Muslims.

Letting go of an ideological version of Islam is difficult enough when it is seen as a defense against Western Islamophobia, but it also raises the question of diversity within Islamic thought, traditions of practice and, more broadly, within Muslim communities. Safi frames this issue as pluralism and that chimes with many of the institutional and social factors that seem important in developing a queer visibility and politics discussed in the previous chapters. The institutions and civic traditions of Western liberal capitalist societies may have unintentionally provided the impetus and space for queer emergence, rather than contained the principle of sexual liberation from their inception, but that does not dismiss the fact that plural, open forms of societies seem empirically to be the most productive for all forms of diversity. Again, many others have discussed the potential recovering of plural traditions within Muslim histories, but I want to focus on the one key issue of pluralism and diversity that relates most directly to sexuality and that, of course, is the acceptance of gender equality. This is a more hopeful area of Muslim engagement, largely because there is a strong tradition of Muslim feminist thought and an increasing number of political and civil groups that focus on gender equality (Bullock, 2005; Haddad, 1991; Simmons, 2003). We have seen, however, how the issue of gender equality is easily woven into oppositional dialectics, most brutally in the justifications of war and the scrutiny of Muslim immigrant populations (Phillips and Saharso, 2008; Razack, 2008) whereby its positioning is used to invoke both Islamophobia and Muslim ideological resistance. Nonetheless, the regulation of sexual and gender diversity is universally related to the maintenance of gender normativity, however culturally differentiated that normativity may be, and so this question of pluralism as gender equality fundamentally underpins any changes we might hope to see in Muslim sexualities. As with sexual diversity politics, Muslims must continue to engage with this issue ourselves if we are not to be subject to more uses of gender justice as a colonizing tactic.

I do not think that gender justice in Muslim communities will inevitably provoke the acceptance of sexual diversity (since gender justice can emerge with a heteronormative bias as it did in the West) but I do think that the discussions and debates around femininity and masculinity that gender justice should provoke will open up a space for related debate around sexuality. Of course, the privileges of patriarchy, enjoyed by hegemonic Muslim masculinities, will be an obstacle here. I am keenly aware that I have not talked about masculinity in any consistent way, despite the fact that we know from years of research into homosexualities and particularly homophobias, that dominant constructions of heteronormative masculinity are a major context for both. This formation is repeated in the evidence on Muslim homophobia presented in Chapter 3. The truth is that different versions of Muslim masculinities and femininities must emerge if there is going to be social change around gender and also homosexualities. Again, there is an emergent literature on this issue (Ouzgane, 2006) but we need much more, particularly to astutely understand whether a hegemonic Muslim masculinity exists, and the specific ways in which Muslim masculinities depend on gender and sexual hierarchies. As with our understanding of the intersectionality of queer Muslims, we need to know more about the intersecting existence of Muslim masculinities.

So are all these issues about 'progress' in Muslim politics, consciousness and gender regimes? At some blunt level the answer would be affirmative, but I have argued throughout that we cannot unthinkingly assume this progress has been laid out for us by Western societies. Rather, the 'progress' that a progressive Muslim consciousness seeks is not teleological, or at the very least not based on Western teleology (Safi, 2003). Let me conclude with a suggestion that might seem like hubris, but may be one possible outcome of the challenges that sexual diversity brings to Muslim consciousness and politics. What if the challenges of queer Muslim visibility and belonging could contribute to developing a progressive sense of Muslim *pride*, rather than a defensive assertion of Muslim culture? What if the rediscovery of the sexual archive, and the creation of new archives, could contribute to a pride in Muslim traditions of diversity? What if, moreover, the Muslim struggle with gender equality and sexual diversity produced versions of masculinity, femininity and social justice *beyond* Western bequests?

Thus, the challenge of sexual diversity may indicate a broader issue in Muslim consciousness, that it is time to think of different possibilities from within a confident, progressive Muslim identity, rather than to invest in the triangulation of Western exceptionalism by oppressing gender and sexual diversity.

The past and future imperfect, tense

Since I have concluded this study with a chapter of 'beginnings', it would be impertinent to pronounce any conclusion in this final section. Instead, I offer here some final thoughts about what might follow. For some time now, I have been considering contributing to the 'It Gets Better' site that hosts videos to encourage LGBTIQ youth.[13] I have not been able to do so, however, largely because I am too uncertain how I could frame a 'hopeful' path for others out there who share my ethnicity or cultural background. My story, outlined partly in Chapter 1, has not been one of 'progress' in Muslim cultures or indeed pride in that heritage and existence, but rather one that epitomizes the abandonment of Muslim culture for the liberation of Western queer culture. Whilst the auto/biographical tremor that rumbles throughout the book is in part an attempt to perform a reflexive 'audit of the self' (Stanley, 2000) that challenges my own Islamophobia, I remain uncertain how to argue that being queer and Muslim will 'get better'. *My* past, as it has informed this project, is therefore far from perfect. In English grammar, the past imperfect tense describes an action we were going to achieve, but in fact remained incomplete. *We were going to have gay liberation but we didn't get it.* My intention was to clarify some understandings about why we do not really have a full queer liberation and contribute to the critiques of the ways in which queer politics is being drawn into Islamophobia. I think I have achieved that, not necessarily in a way that satisfies queer, post-colonial or Muslim politics in their various forms, but nonetheless, I have come some way towards an intellectual understanding that I hope contributes usefully to current politics. However, I am left only at beginnings and in that sense, not even halfway through the work that needs to be done, what needs to follow.

There is no 'future imperfect' tense in English grammar, since we can only assert what we intend to do rather than know that it will not, in fact, be completed. But I have suggested that it is possible to imagine a 'future imperfect' in our politics; a way of moving towards 'liberations' from both homophobia and Islamophobia that renders visible and rejects the assumptions of modernizing momentums and outcomes, and accepts the intersecting context in which our politics must develop. One that is not based on the conceits of the West and, in rejecting that basis, recognizes the privileges that queer politics enjoys in particular circumstances over Muslim populations and politics. We are so far from being able to imagine a dialogue but part of the reason for that is that both queer and Muslim forms of political engagement currently reiterate the triangulation of mutual exclusivity. Queer Muslim consciousness and visibility will make these positions less and less tenable, and more, much more is needed to enable that to happen, both in Western countries and in Muslim majority ones. But that is not all that needs to happen: Western queer politics and Muslim politics also need to arrive at a terrain of dialogue, from different routes and positions of privilege. All of these factors will produce a future imperfect that is full of tension, but we must begin. We are, both, actually quite good at beginnings. Queers of all stripes always choose a beginning when we reject the heteronormative; either publicly or in our private sexual worlds, we are beginning what we know will be a struggle. Most Muslims are also well versed in the importance of beginning a task, often invoking Allah's blessing, sometimes because we know that there is struggle ahead. Can we then, both begin to struggle together?

Appendices

Sources (all references are included below and in footnotes here and access to all websites reverified July 29, 2013).

1 LGBTIQ rights

The primary resource for laws regulating homosexuality and gender identity was the report produced for the International Lesbian, Gay, Bisexual, Trans and Intersex Association (ILGA), *State-Sponsored Homophobia, a World Survey of Laws: Criminalisation, Protection and Recognition of Same-Sex Love* (May 2013, available at http://ilga.org/ilga/en/article/1161). This was authored by Lucas Paoli Itaborahy and Jingshu Zhu. The authors indicate their sources are mainly government and NGO websites, focusing as they do on a precise account of legislation. Sources are listed clearly in the notes to this comprehensive document that is produced annually for the ILGA. Although it has its critics (see Chapter 4) ILGA 'is a world-wide network of national and local groups dedicated to achieving equal rights for lesbian, gay, bisexual, trans and intersex (LGBTIQI) people everywhere. Founded in 1978, it now has more than 700 member organizations. Every continent and approximately 110 countries are represented. Pan Africa ILGA, ILGA-Asia, ILGA-Europe, ILGA-LAC, ILGA-North America and ILGA-Oceania are regional chapters of ILGA. ILGA is to this day the only international non-governmental community-based association focused on fighting discrimination on grounds of sexual orientation and gender identity as a global issue'. (www.ilga.org).

2 LGBTIQ groups

Most countries on this list require organizations to register with the government to operate legally. This of course is a huge barrier, considering the illegality of same-sex sexual conduct and thus community organizations for LGBTIQ people. This makes it even harder for activists to educate and promote freedom of LGBTIQ people. To get around this, many of the organizations on this list are only web based, some of which keep a secretive email lists of LGBTIQ followers. Many of the web-based organizations maintain a mailing address overseas. Some of the websites are routinely hacked or blocked by state governments. This in turn promotes a culture of fear, further discouraging LGBTIQ people from gathering, even in private homes or secretive locations. This is by no means a comprehensive list since language barriers prevent me from accessing all available data. Rather, I have tried to deliver a brief sketch of activity in particular countries. Web sources are identified in the footnotes but again, many of these are temporary and access to a few has expired (noted in the footnotes).

Appendices 157

3 Muslim populations

Information on Muslim populations was taken from *The Future of the Global Muslim Population: projections for 2010–2030* (2011), published by the Pew Research Center, Forum on Religion and Public Life: 'This report was produced by the Pew Research Center's Forum on Religion & Public Life. The Pew Forum delivers timely, impartial information on issues at the intersection of religion and public affairs. The Pew Forum is a nonpartisan, non-advocacy organization and does not take positions on policy debates. Based in Washington, D.C., the Pew Forum is a project of the Pew Research Center, which is funded by The Pew Charitable Trusts. This report is part of the Pew-Templeton Global Religious Futures project, which is jointly and generously funded by The Pew Charitable Trusts and the John Templeton Foundation. The project analyzes religious change and its impact on societies around the world'. (2011: 3). Available at http://www.pewforum.org/The-Future-of-the-Global-Muslim-Population.aspx.

The report indicates 49 countries with majority Muslim populations in 2010 (>50%), comprising 1.2 billion or 74% of the total of 1.6 billion (the vast majority of the remainder – 23% – live in non-Muslim majority, less developed countries, with 3% living in the 'developed' West – Europe (bar Albania and Kosovo), North America, Australia, New Zealand and Japan). I have excluded Mayotte and its population of 200,000 which is not included in the ILGA report, probably because since 2011 it has become a department of France rather than a colony or independent country and thus its traditional Islamic laws are being replaced by the French civil code. Western Sahara is also excluded since it is a disputed state and most of its population of 500,000 continues to be governed by Moroccan politics and law, from which it has technically, but not legally, claimed independence.

4 Population figures

Taken from the United Nations Department for Economic and Social Affairs, Population Division. Various related reports available at http://esa.un.org/unpd/wpp/Documentation/publications.htm, but these figures are taken from the highlight report, *World Population Prospects: the 2010 Revision, Highlights and Advance Tables*.

5 Income levels

Income levels were drawn from the World Bank, 2010 GNI (gross national income) per capita in US dollars (formerly gross national product or GNP per capita). See www.worldbank.org or http://data.worldbank.org/indicator/NY.GNP.PCAP.CD/countries/1W?display=default. Income levels are categorized thus: 'Economies are divided according to 2010 GNI per capita, calculated using the World Bank Atlas method. The groups are: low income, $1,005 or less; lower middle income, $1,006–$3,975; upper middle income, $3,976–$12,275; and high income, $12,276 or more' (http://data.worldbank.org/about/

country-classifications). In a paper for the UN, Milanovic (2006) points out that the usual indicators do not account for income inequalities within countries and that there is much debate about whether consumption patterns are a more accurate indicator of actual income sources and capital (www.un.org/esa/desa/papers/2006/wp26_2006.pdf). There are numerous NGOs who have alternative figures, but none are wildly different from these indicators. Visual mapping is available at the World Bank site above but also – with similar income level categorizations – at http://ngm.nationalgeographic.com/2011/03/age-of-man/map-interactive.

Information on Gaza and the West Bank was taken from https://www.cia.gov/library/publications/the-world-factbook/docs/notesanddefs.html#2004 who had the latest estimate (2008) but given that the World Bank estimates only $1,250 in 2005 (their latest figures (see: http://data.worldbank.org/country/west-bank-and-gaza) this figure must be open to question.

Information on Turkish Cyprus is from a report on Economic and Social Indicators produced by the State Planning Organization of the self-declared Turkish Republic of Northern Cyprus – only officially recognized as a state by Turkey (http://www.devplan.org/Frame-eng.html).

6 Governance indicators and colonial history

There are any number of rankings and criteria used therein to assess the overall governance structure of a country. A comprehensive source is the World Bank's Worldwide Governance Indicators that provide details on each country along six dimensions of responsive government (http://info.worldbank.org/governance/wgi/index.asp) and I have used this where information from below is not available. However, none of the rankings is without its critics. For simplicity in this context, I have used the Economist Intelligence Unit's rankings that draw from a number of different other rankings and collates this data (available at www.sida.se/Global/.../EIU_Democracy_Index_Dec2011.pdf). Countries are then ranked out of 165 states as one of four types of regimes: full democracies; flawed democracies; hybrid regimes; and authoritarian regimes.

Colonial histories were drawn from a range of sources on the web but these are matters of common knowledge and easily verifiable through many different sources. The historical time span of colonization is the main information, rather than the more precise information of different forms of colonial rule. Many modern countries did not exist in their current state but I have concentrated on these as the most useful way of painting a broad picture. Inaccuracies and simplifications here are entirely my own.

Appendix A: Queer Rights in Muslim Majority Countries by Region

Table 1 LGBTIQ rights in Africa

Country and Population (2011) % Muslim (% of global Muslim total)	Laws regulating homosexuality Male/male (M/M) Female/female (W/W)	Governance ranking and type Colonial history	GNI per Capita income in dollars (2010)	LGBTIQ groups
Algeria 35.98 million 98% Muslim (2.1%)	M/M and W/W illegal 1966 Penal Code:[1] 'homosexual acts': imprisonment (2 months–2 years) *and* fine (500–2,000 Algerian dinars)	130 – Authoritarian Ottoman Empire 1516–1830 French 1830–1962	4,450	Abu Nawas, is secretive LGBTIQ group located in Spain where it began operating in 2008 after being denied the legal rights to work in Morocco in 2006.[2] Lexo Fanzine, a monthly lesbian online magazine.[3] Began operating in 2011. No known location. Alouen provides online resources for LGBTIQ people, focusing mainly on safe sex and HIV testing.[4] The website does not provide an office or mailing address.

(*continued*)

Table 1 Continued

Country and Population (2011) % Muslim (% of global Muslim total)	Laws regulating homosexuality Male/male (M/M) Female/female (W/W)	Governance ranking and type Colonial history	GNI per Capita income in dollars (2010)	LGBTIQ groups
Burkina Faso 16.97 million 58.9% Muslim (0.6%)	Both legal Never criminalized Equal age of consent	124 – Authoritarian French protectorate from 1896 until 1960 (known as Upper Volta until 1984)	550	LAMBDA Burkina Faso[5] The group focuses on HIV/AIDS treatment and stigma associated with HIV/AIDS. A report by the Swedish International Development Cooperation Agency on LMAMBDA Burkina Faso notes that the organization is '[is] primarily working with counselling and support, helping people to deal with senses of guilt (caused by the stigma from the rest of the society) ... they do not at this point have the capacity to reach out to the public or to advocate for the rights of LGBTIQ people'.[6]

Country	Laws	Rank/Regime	Number	Notes
Chad 11.53 million 55.7% Muslim (0.4%)	Both legal Never criminalized Unclear if equal age of consent	166 – Authoritarian French protectorate from 1900–1960	620	N/A
Comoros 0.75 million 98.3% Muslim (<0.1%)	M/M and W/W Illegal 1982 Penal Code:[7] Imprisonment (1–5) years *and* fine (50,000–1,000,000 francs); maximum penalty with minors	=126 – Authoritarian French colony from 1841–1975.	720	N/A
Djibouti 0.91 million 97% Muslim (0.1%)	Both legal Never criminalized [Note: some say it is de facto illegal since the country is run under Islamic law][8] Equal age of consent	=147 – Authoritarian French colony 1896–1967	1,270 (2009)	N/A
Egypt 82.54 million 94.7% Muslim (4.9%)	M/M illegal W/W unclear Charged under laws against prostitution.	115 – Hybrid (lowest rank hybrid before authoritarian category) Ottoman Empire 1517–1882 Effective British protectorate from 1882–1952	2,420	Ehna Online Magazine (closed abruptly August 2012).[9]

(continued)

Table 1 Continued

Country and Population (2011) % Muslim (% of global Muslim total)	Laws regulating homosexuality Male/male (M/M) Female/female (W/W)	Governance ranking and type Colonial history	GNI per Capita income in dollars (2010)	LGBTIQ groups
The Gambia 1.77 million 95.3% Muslim (0.1%)	M/M and W/W illegal 1965 Criminal Code:[10] Charges under 'unnatural offenses' (also includes oral sex, anal sex and vulvar/anal penetration with object) Imprisonment (14 years)	132 – Authoritarian British and French control late 17th C to 18th C British control 1856–1965	450	N/A
Guinea 10.22 million 84.2% Muslim (0.5%)	M/M and W/W illegal 1998 Penal Code:[11] Imprisonment (6 months–3 years) *and* fine (100,000 to 1,000,000 Guinean Francs)	146 – Authoritarian French control 1890s–1958	400	N/A
Libya 6.42 million 96.6% Muslim (0.4%)	M/M and W/W illegal 1953 Penal Code: Charged with adultery ('with another person with their consent (outside marriage)'). Imprisonment (up to 5 years)	125 – Authoritarian Ottoman Empire 1551–1912 Italian control 1912–1943 Allied control 1943–1951	12,320 (2009)	N/A

Mali 15.84 million 92.4% Muslim (0.8%)	Both legal Never criminalized Equal age of consent	65 – Flawed French control from late 19th C–1960	600	The government actively refuses to recognize LGBTIQ groups, even if they are only focused on HIV/AIDS education for MSM. The government has prevented HIV/AIDS activists from meeting with MSM.[12]
Mauritania 3.54 million 99.2% Muslim (0.2%)	M/M and W/W illegal Between (Muslim) men: death by public stoning. Lesbian relations charged under 'outrage of public decency and Islamic morals': imprisonment (3 months–2 years) *and* fine (5,000–60,000 UM)	109 – Hybrid French control from late 19th C–1960.	1,030	N/A
Morocco 32.27 million 99.9% Muslim (2.0%)	M/M and W/W illegal Imprisonment (6 months–3 years) *and* fine (120–1,000 dirhams)	=119 – Authoritarian Coastal Spanish protectorate from 1884 then Spanish and French control from 1904-1956	2,850	Kifkify is Morocco's first LGBTIQ NGO. Operating from Spain for legal and security reasons, it runs a print and online gay magazine called *Mithly*.[13]

(*continued*)

Table 1 Continued

Country and Population (2011) %Muslim (% of global Muslim total)	Laws regulating homosexuality Male/male (M/M) Female/female (W/W)	Governance ranking and type Colonial history	GNI per Capita income in dollars (2010)	LGBTIQ groups
Niger 16.07 million 98.3% Muslim (1%)	Both legal Never criminalized Unequal age of consent (21)	110 – Hybrid French control 1922–1960	370	N/A
Senegal 12.77 million 95.9% Muslim (0.8%)	M/M and W/W illegal Imprisonment (1–5 years) *and* fine (100,000– 1,500,000 francs); maximum if with minor	93 – Hybrid Increasing gradual French control from 1577–1960	1,090	Association Prudence: A HIV/ AIDS advocacy group for men that focuses on men that have sex with men (MSM).[14]

Sierra Leone 5.98 million 71.5% Muslim (0.3%)	M/M illegal Offences against the person Act, 1861 W/W legal	106 – Hybrid British colony from 1787–1961 (initially for freed slaves).	340	Two LGBTIQ groups exist: (1) Dignity Association provides trainings for LGBTIQl activists and human rights organizations.[15] (2) Why Can't We Get Married.com – West African Chapter in Sierra Leone. The organization does not focus on LGBTIQ issues but more broadly on promoting 'peace, respect and understanding for everyone' and will consider LGBTIQ Human Rights later when the project has gained more 'credibility' in Sierra Leone.[16]
Somalia 9.56 million 98.6% Muslim (0.6%)	M/M and W/W illegal Imprisonment (3 months–3 years): (reduced by a third if 'act of lust different from carnal intercourse') Sharia law in south Somaliland still practices this penal code	Very poor indicators of governance on World Bank Reports British protectorate from 1888 Italian control 1889–1943 British control 1943–1960	N/A	Somali Gay Community, a group based in the UK which host a news and networking website.[17]

(continued)

Table 1 Continued

Country and Population (2011) % Muslim (% of global Muslim total)	Laws regulating homosexuality Male/male (M/M) Female/female (W/W)	Governance ranking and type Colonial history	GNI per Capita income in dollars (2010)	LGBTIQ groups
Sudan, before separation 44.63 million 71.4% Muslim (1.9%)	M/M and W/W illegal in both Sodomy: flogging and potential imprisonment (up to 5 years); second conviction guarantees imprisonment up to 5 years; third conviction carries either death sentence *or* life imprisonment 'Indecent acts': lashing, potential imprisonment (up to a year) *or* fine	153 – Authoritarian Ottoman Empire (Egypt) 1822–1880s. British and Egyptian influence and varying control from 1880s–1956	1,270	Based on a report from a Sudanese website called Rumat Alhadag, an LGBTIQ group called Freedom Sudan was established in 2006.[18] The group describes itself as a secretive organization.[19] The president of the organization escaped jail in 2011 with the help of his family and fled the country. He operates the website from abroad.[20] However, the organization's website is no longer available and I cannot confirm whether the group is still operational.
Tunisia 10.59 million 99.8% Muslim (0.6%)	M/M illegal W/W legal Charged with 'sodomy': imprisonment (3 years)	92 – Hybrid Ottoman Empire 1534–1881 French protectorate 1881–1956	4,160	The only organization is an online news site called, GayDay magazine.[21]

Table 2 LGBTIQ rights in Central Asia

Country and Population (2011) % Muslim (% of global Muslim total)	Laws regulating homosexuality Male/male (M/M) Female/female (W/W)	Governance ranking and type Colonial history	GNI per Capita income in dollars (2010)	LGBTIQ groups
Afghanistan 32.36 million 99.8% Muslim (1.8%)	M/M and W/W illegal 1976 Penal Code:[22] Charged with 'adultery' or 'pederasty' (in this terminology refers to two men regardless of age): imprisonment ('long') Sharia law technically in place	152 – Authoritarian 16th C – Mughal control 16th-18th C, divided regional control between Mughals and Safavid Empire 19th C consolidation of modern state but conflict with British and Russian Empires, resolved by 1920. 1979–1989 – Soviet dominated national government 2001– present, US-led invasion with gradual ongoing reduction of Western troops/advisors	410	N/A

(continued)

Table 2 Continued

Country and Population (2011) % Muslim (% of global Muslim total)	Laws regulating homosexuality Male/male (M/M) Female/female (W/W)	Governance ranking and type Colonial history	GNI per Capita income in dollars (2010)	LGBTIQ groups
Kazakhstan 16.21 million 56.4% Muslim (0.5%)	Both legal – 1998 Equal age of consent	137 – Authoritarian 19th C – effective Russian rule with direct colonization in 1890s Soviet republic under USSR 1922–1991	7,590	N/A
Kyrgyzstan 5.39 million 88.8% Muslim (0.3%)	Both legal – 1998 Equal age of consent	107 – Hybrid Russian control from 1876 Soviet republic under USSR from 1919–1991.	840	An NGO called Labrys was established in 2004 and officially recognized in 2006.[23] The NGO has an office in Bishkek. Among the organization's objectives is advocacy specifically for LGBTIQ people.[24] Details on reports Labrys submitted to the national government can be found here.[25] The Office also serves as a shelter for transgendered people and women who are victims of violence. It has at least once been raided by the state police.[26] Labrys, although based in Kyrgyzstan, writes reports in partnership with international human rights groups on sexual minorities in Turkmenistan, Azerbaijan and Uzbekistan.[27]

Tajikistan 6.98 million 99% Muslim (0.4%)	Both legal – 1998 Equal age of consent	151 – Authoritarian Absorbed by Russia from 1864–1885 Soviet republic under USSR from 1924–1991	800	N/A[28]
Turkmenistan 5.11 million 93.3% Muslim (0.3%)	M/M illegal Imprisonment (up to 2 years) W/W Legal	165 – Authoritarian Russian control from 1881 Soviet republic under USSR from 1924–1991	3790	N/A
Uzbekistan 27.76 million 96.5% Muslim (1.7%)	M/M illegal 1994 Criminal Code:[29] Imprisonment (up to 3 years) W/W Legal	164 – Authoritarian 19th C increasing Russian control Soviet republic under USSR from 1924–1991	1280	N/A

Table 3 LGBTIQ rights in West Asia ('Middle East' without North African countries)

Country and Population (2011) % Muslim (% of global Muslim total)	Laws regulating homosexuality Male/male (M/M) Female/female (W/W)	Governance ranking and type Colonial history	GNI per Capita income in dollars (2010)	LGBTIQ groups
Bahrain 1.32 million 81.2% Muslim (<0.1%)	Uncertain Decriminalized in 1976 with updated Penal Code, but can still be charged under vague morality laws[30]	144 – Authoritarian Portuguese control 1521–1602 Persian control 1602–1783 British protectorate from 1860–1971	18,730 (2008)	N/A
Iran 74.80 million 99.7% Muslim (4.6%)	M/M and W/W illegal 1991 Penal Code. Sodomy: death sentence Lesbianism: lashing; death sentence on fourth conviction	159 – Authoritarian Imperial power from 15th C Occupation by Russian and British in particular regions,1911–1921	4,520	No known organizations in Iran. The Iranian Queer Organization (Iranian Queer Railroad) operates in Toronto, Canada.[31]
Iraq 32.67 million 98.9% Muslim (1.9%)	Uncertain 1969 Penal Code reinstated in 2003, legally decriminalizing same-sex relations. However, reports of persecution persist[32]	112 – Authoritarian Ottoman Empire from 16th-early 20th C British mandate from 1920–1932 US led occupation from 2003–2011	2,340	No known groups in Iraq. A refugee organization called Iraqi LGBTIQ operates in London, UK.

Jordan 6.33 million 98.8% Muslim (0.4%)	Both legal 1951 Penal code? Equal age of consent	118 – Authoritarian Ottoman Empire 1516–1918 British mandate of Transjordan 1922–1946	4,340	N/A
Kuwait 2.82 million 86.4% Muslim (0.2%)	M/M Illegal Imprisonment (up to seven years) W/W unclear	122 – Authoritarian Ottoman Empire from 17th C – 1899 British protectorate 1899–1961	47,790	N/A
Lebanon 4.26 million 59.7% Muslim (0.2%)	M/M and W/W illegal 'intercourse against nature': imprisonment (up to one year)	94 – Hybrid Ottoman Empire from 16th–early 20th C French mandate 1920–1943	8,880	Helem, Sexual Health NGO focused on LGBTIQ health issues, as well as advocacy.[33] Helem operates a Community Center, open 6 days a week, providing low cost or free services to LGBTIQ people. There is also a library of books and films where anyone is welcome to relax in a non-judgmental atmosphere. Helem also run a 24-hour help line run by trained volunteers.
Oman 2.85 million 87.7% Muslim (0.2%)	M/M and W/W illegal Imprisonment (6 months–3 years)	134 – Authoritarian Portuguese control 1507–1650 Self-governing since 1750	18,260	N/A

(*continued*)

Table 3 Continued

Country and Population (2011) % Muslim (% of global Muslim total)	Laws regulating homosexuality Male/male (M/M) Female/female (W/W)	Governance ranking and type Colonial history	GNI per Capita income in dollars (2010)	LGBTIQ groups
Palestinian Territories 4.15 million 97.5% Muslim (0.3%)	M/M illegal British Mandate Criminal Code (1936) Imprisonment (up to 10 years) W/W legal	99 – Hybrid Ottoman Empire from 16th C–1922 British mandate 1922–1948 1948 Partition and civil war resulting in State of Israel and continuing disputes over status and land occupied by Israel	2,900 (estimate for 2008 cited in the CIA World Fact Book but World Bank 2005 estimate is at only 1,250)	Aswat, a lesbian group maintains an active website but does not disclose whether they have a physical office or meeting space.[34] Another group, alQaws, is a 'community-based and grassroots organization that works with LGBTIQQ Palestinians throughout Israel and the Palestinian occupies territories'. The group maintains an office in Jerusalem, Israel (on the Israeli side of the 1967 border).
Qatar 1.87 million 77.5% Muslim (0.1%)	M/M and W/W illegal Prescribed with adultery/ Zina laws	138 – Authoritarian 1783–1868 part of Bahrain Ottoman control 1871–1916 British protectorate 1916–1971	121,700 (cited in Pew Report, see sources above)	N/A

Saudi Arabia 28.08 million 97.1% Muslim (1.6%)	M/M and W/W illegal Sharia law	161 – Authoritarian Tribal history with Ottoman loyalties from 16th C until 1918 Unified in 1932	16,190 (2009)	N/A
Syria 20.77 million 92.8% Muslim (1.3%)	M/M and W/W illegal Imprisonment (up to 3 years)	=157 – Authoritarian Ottoman Empire from 1516–1920 French protectorate 1920–1946	2,750	N/A
Turkey 73.64 million 98.6% Muslim (4.6%)	Both legal 1858 Equal age of consent	88 – Hybrid Ottoman imperial power from 13th C until 1918.	9,890	Kaos GL.[35] 'the organisation has been publishing the journal *KAOS GL* (now a quarterly publication) since its founding. The group operates the KAOS Cultural Center, which hosts cultural activities, meetings, and showings of films. The center also houses a LGBTIQ history library.'[36] Turkey also has Gay Pride events.[37] There are other LGBTIQ organizations, such as Lambdaistanbul.[38] Turkish courts have also affirmed the right of LGBTIQ organizations to exist openly.[39]

(continued)

Table 3 Continued

Country and Population (2011) % Muslim (% of global Muslim total)	Laws regulating homosexuality Male/male (M/M) Female/female (W/W)	Governance ranking and type Colonial history	GNI per Capita income in dollars (2010)	LGBTIQ groups
UAE 7.89 million 76% Muslim (0.2%)	M/M and W/W illegal Laws against adultery	149 – Authoritarian Portuguese control early 16th C Ottoman Empire 16th C–1892 British protectorate 1892–1971	41,930	Facebook group: Gay, Lesbian, Bisexual & Transsexual Rights in the UAE.[40]
Yemen 24.80 million 99% Muslim (1.5%)	M/M and W/W illegal 1994 Penal Code Male/male relations: whipping *or* imprisonment (up to a year); married men sentenced to death by stoning Lesbian relations: Imprisonment (3–7 years, dependent on intent)	150 – Authoritarian Ottoman Empire mid 16th–mid 17th C. British rule in Aden from 1839 Ottoman rule in north from 1872–1918 British rule in south until 1967	1,070	N/A

Table 4 LGBTIQ rights in South and Southeast Asia

Country and Population (2011) % Muslim (% of global Muslim total)	Laws regulating homosexuality Male/male (M/M) Female/female (W/W)	Governance ranking and type Colonial history	GNI per Capita income in dollars (2010)	LGBTIQ groups
Bangladesh 150.49 million 90.4% Muslim (9.2%)	M/M and W/W illegal 1860 Penal Code:[41] Imprisonment (to life or to 10 years) *and* fine	83 – Hybrid Mughal Empire 16th–18th C Maratha Empire 19th C British informal rule from 1760s, formalized in 1857 until partition as East Pakistan in 1947.	700	LGBTIQ Bangladesh is a website with the aim of supporting LGBTIQ people in Bangladesh.[42] The website does not provide an address other than an email account. There is another website called, BoysOnlyBangladesh, that serves as a way for Bengali men to meet other men.[43]
Brunei 0.41 million 51.9% Muslim (<0.1%)	M/M illegal 2001 Penal Code:[44] Imprisonment (to 10 years) *and* fine W/W legal	Indicators are above average on the World Bank Report although this is not a democracy British protectorate 1888–1984	50,100 (cited in Pew Report, see sources above)	N/A

(*continued*)

Table 4 Continued

Country and Population (2011) % Muslim (% of global Muslim total)	Laws regulating homosexuality Male/male (M/M) Female/female (W/W)	Governance ranking and type Colonial history	GNI per Capita income in dollars (2010)	LGBTIQ groups
Indonesia 242.33 million 88.1% Muslim (12.7%)	Both legal in most places but unequal age of consent Penal Code (last amended 1999)[45] prohibits sex with minors Since 2002, Aceh province practices Sharia law for Muslims and prohibits homosexual acts	60 – Flawed Dutch informal control through Dutch East Indies Co., formalized from 1800s–1949.	2,500	There are several LGBTIQ groups in Indonesia. Arus Pelangi, formed in 2006, is a charity and community organization. The group maintains an office in Jakarta.[46] Indonesia is also home to the Q! Film Festival, often referred to as the only LGBTIQ film festival in the Muslim world. 2012 marks 10-year anniversary of the Q! Film Festival in Jakarta.[47] Indonesia is also home to the Ardhanary Institute, 'a centre for lesbian, bisexual, and transgender (LBT) research, publications, and advocacy based in Jakarta'.[48] The organization also operates a crisis centre.[49] The Institute Pelangi Perempuan, based in Jakarta, is a LBT group for women and youth.[50] Forum Komunikasi Waria Indonesia (OurVoice Indonesia), is an advocacy organization for LGBTIQ people.[51] I could not confirm whether the group maintains an office or centre.[52] Our Voice is another LGBTIQ organization that promotes LGBTIQ issues through online media.[53] GAYa NUSANTARA Community Center is located in Surabaya, a city located in East Java.[54]

Malaysia 28.86 million 61.4% Muslim (1.1%)	M/M and W/W illegal Charged under 'carnal intercourse against the order of nature' (includes anal and oral penetration): imprisonment (up to 20 years), potential whipping Sharia law in some states	71 – Flawed Portuguese control 1511–1641 Dutch control from 1641 but with increasing control of British from 1786 until 1963	7,760	N/A
Maldives 0.32 million 98.4% Muslim (<0.1%)	M/M and W/W illegal Uncodified Sharia law Male/male relations: banishment (9 months–1 year) *or* whipping Lesbianism: house arrest (9 months–1 year), reported sentencing of whipping	Above average indicators on World Bank Report British protectorate 1887–1965	5,750	N/A
Pakistan 176.75 million 96.4% Muslim (11%)	M/M illegal Imprisonment (life, or 2–10 years), potential fine W/W legal	105 – Hybrid Mughal Empire 16th–19th C British informal rule from 1760s, formalized in 1857 until partition as Pakistan in 1947.	1,050	N/A

Table 5 LGBTIQ rights in Europe

Country and Population (2011) % Muslim (% of global Muslim total)	Laws regulating homosexuality Male/male (M/M) Female/female (W/W)	Governance ranking and type Colonial history	GNI per Capita income in dollars (2010)	LGBTIQ groups
Albania 3.22 million 82.1% Muslim (0.2%)	Both legal Since 1995 Criminal Code Equal age of consent and ban on employment discrimination	87 – Hybrid Ottoman control from 15th C until 1912.	3,960	In the last three years, LGBTIQ issues 'suddenly became Albanian headlines when Prime Minister Sali Berisha (who is still in office) unexpectedly declared his support for same-sex marriage at a televised meeting of his ministers'.[55] Before the Prime Minister's unexpected announcement, there was very little or no coverage of LGBTIQ Albanians in the popular press or in the general public.[56] Today there are two LGBTIQ organizations who work to support legislative and social change: Alliance Against LGBTIQ Discrimination! and Pro LGBTIQ.[57] Both groups do not provide an office address. However, they do provide community services and programs which indicates a probability that they are for security reasons not disclosing the address online.[58]

Azerbaijan 9.31 million 98.4% Muslim (0.5%)	Both legal – 2000 Equal age of consent	140 – Authoritarian Russian control 1813–1918 Soviet republic under USSR 1920–1991	5,330	No known LGBTIQ organizations. The only available resources for LGBTIQ Azerbaijanis is a website started by a young LGBTIQ activist called Ruslan Balukhin.[59]
Kosovo 1.83 million 91.7 % Muslim (0.1%)	Both legal – 1994 Equal age of consent Ban on employment discrimination Constitutional ban on discrimination due to sexual orientation since 2008	Average indicators on the World Bank Report As part of Serbia, Ottoman control 15th C–1912. Austro-Hungarian Empire 1915–1918 Incorporated into Kingdom of Yugoslavia 1929–1941, conquered by Axis powers in 1941, then communist republic until 1991 separation as Serbia. Independence as Kosovo achieved in 2008 after civil war.	3,290	There are two official LGBTIQ organizations in Kosovo.[60] Libertas Kosovo provides a range of resources and services, including an LGBTIQ resource room/library, meeting space, weekly activities, counseling and advocacy, among other activities.[61] Qendra për Emancipim Shoqëror (Center for Social Emancipation) located in Pristina. 'QESh was founded in April 2005 as an association with the purpose of creating a safe/tolerant/gay-friendly environment for the LGBTIQQ community of Kosovo through awareness raising activities of general society and support activities for the LGBTIQQ community.'[62]

179

Appendix B: Queer Rights in Countries with Significant and Projected Muslim Populations

Table 1 LGBTIQ rights in countries with significant Muslim populations in 2010

Country and population (2011) % Muslim (% of global Muslim total)	Laws regulating homosexuality Male/male (M/M) Female/female (W/W)	Governance ranking and type Colonial history	GNI per Capita income in dollars (2010)	LGBTIQ groups
Benin 9.1 million 24.5% Muslim (2.26 million)	Both legal Unequal age of consent since 1947 amendment to Penal code of 1877 (21 for same sex)	76 – Flawed French control 1892–1960	780	N/A

Bosnia-Herzegovina 3.75 million 41.6% Muslim (1.56 million)	Both legal 1998–2001 (3 different regions decriminalized over this period) Equal age of consent Prohibition on employment discrimination since 2003	95 – Hybrid Ottoman Empire mid 15th C–1878. Austro-Hungarian Empire 1878–1918. Incorporated to Kingdom of Yugoslavia 1918–1941, conquered by Axis powers in 1941, then communist republic until 1992 independence.	4,770	The first LGBTIQ organization was founded in 2002 and gained official government recognition in 2004. The group, Organization Q, was the first LGBTIQ organization to gain government registration. Organization Q's mission is as follows: 'Organization Q works on the promotion and protection of the culture, identity, human rights and support to the LGBTIQ persons; elimination of all forms of discrimination and inequality based on sex, gender, sexual orientation, sexual identity, gender identity, gender expression and intersexual characteristics'. The group runs a large number of programs, including advocacy and educational activities, health studies and outreach (HIV/AIDS related work), workshops on safe-sex, human rights and LGBTIQ issues.[63] They are actively engaged in public and private proactive rights projects such as Pride festivals, parades (attempted), lobbying strategies, photo exhibitions, health and education seminars, participation in research and more.[64] Several other organizations exist throughout the country,[65] including Okvir, which also carries out workshops and social events.[66]

(continued)

Table 1 Continued

Country and population (2011) % Muslim (% of global Muslim total)	Laws regulating homosexuality Male/male (M/M) Female/female (W/W)	Governance ranking and type Colonial history	GNI per Capita income in dollars (2010)	LGBTIQ groups
China 1,347.57 million (1.35 billion) 1.8% Muslim (23 million)	Both legal since 1997 (includes Hong Kong and Macau) Equal age of consent	141 – Authoritarian Imperial power in 15th C to 20th C Republic 1912–1949 Communist Republic 1949–present	4,270	There are many LGBTIQ organizations in China, most of which are located in China's most populated eastern coastal regions. In Hong Kong alone, there are several LGBTIQ organizations, see this site http://hongkong.angloinfo.com/information/family/LGBTIQ/ for more information.[67] In Beijing, the LGBTIQ center provides a number of services to the LGBTIQ community, including cultural programs, educational services and youth and senior programming.[68]
Cyprus 1.12 million 22.7% Muslim (0.2 million)	Both legal since 1998 Equal age of consent since 2002	40 – Flawed Ottoman Empire 1570–1870 when leased to the British. 1914–1960 British control	29,430	Accept Cyprus, located in southern Nicosia is an LGBTIQ advocacy organization.[69]
Eritrea 5.42 million 36.5% Muslim (1.91 million)	M/M illegal W/W illegal Penal code of 1957 (inherited from Ethiopian rule)	154 – Authoritarian Italian control 1890–1941 British control 1941–1951 federation with Ethiopia	340	N/A

Ethiopia 84.73 million 33.8% Muslim (28.72 million)	M/M illegal W/W illegal Criminal code of 2004	121 – Authoritarian Constant invasions in modern period but not colonized apart from Italian annexation 1935–1941	390	The organization Rainbow Health Initiative Ethiopia's stated purpose is to provide health related services for MSM and LGBTIQ Ethiopians. Its mission is as follows: 'To advance the sexual health and rights of MSM and reduce stigma and discrimination associated with them by creating general awareness with the aim of empowering the MSM community and the society at large, advocating for the rights to good health, access to STI/HIV and AIDS related care and treatment in Ethiopia'.[70] As a health care NGO it also engages in advocacy for LGBTIQ Ethiopians (which would not be possible for a LGBTIQ organization since homosexuality is illegal). Through the 'We are all family' campaign, the NGO address stigma about HIV and homosexuality.[71]
Guinea Bissau 1.55 million 42.8% Muslim (0.71 million)	Both legal since 1993 Equal age of consent	157 – Authoritarian Portuguese control from mid 15th C–1974	590	N/A

(*continued*)

Table 1 Continued

Country and population (2011) % Muslim (% of global Muslim total)	Laws regulating homosexuality Male/male (M/M) Female/female (W/W)	Governance ranking and type Colonial history	GNI per Capita income in dollars (2010)	LGBTIQ groups
India 1,241.49 million (1.24 billion) 14.6% Muslim (177.29 million – third largest national Muslim population in the world)	Both legal since 2009 (does not apply in Jammu and Kashmir)	39 – Flawed 15th C–18th C Imperial power as Mughal Empire (originally through invasion from central Asia) and subsequent Maratha dynasty British, Dutch and Portuguese involvement from 16th C with British rule established in mid 19th C until partition and independence in 1947	1,330	There are several LGBTIQ organizations in India, many existing in metropolitan regions such as Mumbai and New Delhi. Gay Bombay is one organization that organizes social events in Mumbai. In Kolkata, the SAATHII LGBTIQ Support Center and reference library provides several services such as counseling for LGBTIQ people.[72] For a complete list of LGBTIQ organizations operating in India, see this website http://www.indiandost.com/gay_group.php.[73]
Ivory Coast (Cote d'Ivoire) 20.15 million 36.9% Muslim (7.96 million)	Both legal Unequal age of consent	142 – Authoritarian Gradual French control from mid 19th C to full colonization in 1893–1960	1,160	Arc-en-Ciel was the first organization in the Ivory Coast to conduct advocacy around HIV/AIDS and homophobia.[74] In 2010, the group Alternative Côte d'Ivoire was founded with the specific mission devoted to LGBTIQI rights.[75]

(The Former Yugoslav Republic of) **Macedonia** 2.06 million 34.9% Muslim (0.71 million)	Both legal since 1996 Equal age of consent	73 – Flawed Ottoman Empire 16th C–1912 Incorporation into Serbia 1912–1941, occupied by Axis powers until 1944 1944–1991 part of communist republic of Yugoslavia.	4,570	EGAL (Equality for Gay and Lesbians) is a LGBTIQ Organization group focused on HIV/AIDS advocacy. The group was founded on November 3, 2003.[76]
Mozambique 23.93 million 22.8% (5.34 million)	Both illegal Penal code of 1886 (Portuguese colonial era) amended in 1954	100 – Hybrid Portuguese influence and control from mid 16th C until 1974.	440	Mozambican Association for Sexual Minority Rights (LAMBDA) was founded 2006. The organization is located in Maputo. 'LAMBDA's mission is to promote the civic, human and legal rights of LGBTIQ citizens, through public awareness and education and advocacy.[77] LAMBDA's target groups are all LGBTIQI citizens, civil society organizations, political and governmental institutions, social groups, such as the youth, teachers, medical doctors, and the general public'.[78]

(*continued*)

Table 1 Continued

Country and population (2011) % Muslim (% of global Muslim total)	Laws regulating homosexuality Male/male (M/M) Female/female (W/W)	Governance ranking and type Colonial history	GNI per Capita income in dollars (2010)	LGBTIQ groups
Nigeria 162.47 million 47.9% Muslim (75.73 million – sixth largest national Muslim population in the world)	Both illegal Criminal code 1990 (some northern states have Islamic Sharia laws prescribing the death penalty)	119 – Authoritarian British influence from 1885 expanding to protectorate from 1901–1960.	1,180	ILGA notes that 'two major coalitions exist in Nigeria, with membership spanning from small LGBTIQI community groups, to national governmental and non-governmental institutions'.[79] 'Sexual Minorities Against HIV/AIDS in Nigeria (SMAAN). 'SMAAN is a network of MSM organizations established in the year 2007 for the main purpose of contributing to policy issues/matters affecting the rights of sexual minorities and sexual minorities living with HIV & AIDS in Nigeria, through coordination, analysis, training, networking, awareness campaign development and advocacy'.[80] I could not confirm the existence of the second group, the Coalition for the Defense of Sexual Rights in Nigeria. Another group worth noting is QAYN, the first lesbian led LGBTIQQ regional organization in West Africa.[81]

Russian Federation 142.84 million 11.7% Muslim (16.38 million)	Both legal since 1993 Equal age of consent since 1997	117 – Authoritarian Imperial power from 16th C–1917. Dominant country in communist USSR with effective control over member socialist republics and allies in the Warsaw Pact of Eastern European communist states.	9,900	The Russian LGBTIQ network is an umbrella organization representing 10 regional LGBTIQ organizations.[82] LGBTIQ Human Rights Project GayRussia.Ru organizes pride events.[83]
(United Republic of) **Tanzania** 46.22 million 29.9% Muslim (13.45 million)	Both illegal Criminal code of 1945, amended 1998	90 – Hybrid German control from late 19th C British mandate from 1918–1961	530	Wezesha was founded in 2009 with the general objective of advancing LGBTIQ equality and raising awareness of LGBTIQ issues.[84] Among its many objectives, Wezesha aims to raise awareness of HIV/AIDS stigma and homophobia.[85]
Turkish Cyprus (Only recognized as a state by Turkey, who invaded in 1974 – independence proclaimed in 1983) 0.3 million (disputed census 2011) 98% Muslim (0.3 million)	M/M illegal Imprisonment (up to 5 years) W/W legal	N/A	N/A	The Initiative Against Homophobia-Cyprus is located in the northern section of Nicosia in Greek Cyprus.[86] It is unclear from their website what the organization does or how it aims to achieve its objectives.

Table 2 LGBTIQ rights in countries with projected significant Muslim populations by 2030 (those reaching 20% Muslim population or 22 million)

Country and population (2011) % Muslim (% of global Muslim total)	Laws regulating homosexuality Male/male (M/M) Female/female (W/W)	Governance ranking and type Colonial history	GNI per Capita income in dollars (2010)	LGBTIQ groups
Israel 9.25 million 23.2% (2.14 million) 17.7% in 2010	Both legal since 1988 Equal age of consent since 2000 Prohibition on employment discrimination since 1992 Civil partnerships since 1994 Joint adoption legal since 2008	36 – Flawed Ottoman Empire from 1518 until 1918 British mandate of Palestine 1918–1948 when state established. Illegal occupation of Palestinian territory by state of Israel at present.	21,170	Israel: There are many LGBTIQ organizations in Israel: 'the AGUDA (1975), KLAF – lesbian feminist community (1987), the Open House in Jerusalem for pride and tolerance (1997), Hoshen – an educational organization for the LGBTIQ community (2004), IGY – Israel LGBTIQ youth organization (2004), Tel Aviv municipal LGBTIQ center (2008)'.[87]
Montenegro 0.64 million 21.5% (0.12 million) 18.5% in 2010	Both legal since 1977 Equal age of consent Prohibition on employment discrimination since 2010 (also prohibition on discrimination based on gender identity from this time)	74 – Flawed Ottoman Empire from 16th C until late 19th C with various periods of independent control. Incorporated into Kingdom of Serbia 1918–1941, then occupied by Axis powers until 1944. Then incorporated into communist republic of Yugoslavia until 1992	6,750	LGBTIQ Forum Progress: The mission of the organization is to create 'safe, inclusive, and stimulative surroundings for all LGBTIQ persons providing education possibilities, building community, public advocacy, political participation and increasing approach to different kinds of services that lead to quality of life and health'.[88] Montenegro Gay Portal is an LGBTIQ advocacy group.[89] It is unclear whether they maintain an office or meeting space.

Notes

Introduction

1. Those cultural Muslims among you must already be horrified (as my family are) that I have a domestic pet – perhaps even more so than by my homosexuality. Be reassured, however, that you have the last laugh. Jess the Wonder Dog was officially given permanent entry into Canada after her examination by a vet at the airport and has avoided subsequent renewals of visas, applications for permanent resident status and English language tests, unlike her owner.
2. Auto/biography is a term introduced by the feminist theorist Liz Stanley 'to contaminate the idea that a narrative produced by a self writing about itself, and one produced by a self writing about another being, were *formally* distinguishable from each other' (Broughton, 2000: 242).
3. This chapter was published in a slightly different version in the online journal *Nebula*, 5 (4): 1–25, December 2008, http://www.nobleworld.biz/ and I am grateful for permission to reproduce it here.
4. Two important theoretical contributions are Puar's *Terrorist Assemblages: Homonationalism in Queer Times* (2007) and Massad's *Desiring Arabs* (2008). Both are passionately argued studies and have been influential in my project although I deploy more traditional sociological and political approaches than their cultural/literary studies texts. I deal with these in greater detail in Chapters 4, 5 and 6.
5. Appendix A includes five tables on Queer Rights in Muslim Majority Countries by Region and Appendix B includes two tables on Queer Rights in Countries with Significant Muslim Populations.

1 In Search of My Mother's Garden: Reflections on Migration, Gender, Sexuality and Muslim Identity

1. I was based in Sociology at the University of Strathclyde in Glasgow, UK, from 1998 to 2007, having completed a PhD there on sexuality and democratic politics (the department is now defunct, eaten alive by quality assessment regimes in UK academia). In the winter term of 2005 I served as the visiting Libra Professor at the University of Maine in Farmington, Maine, USA. My appointment was in the Women's Studies department, and included delivering the annual Women's History Banquet lecture. As the focus was on women's history, I focused on changes I perceived in Muslim women's identities, from my perspective as a gay man. I found the change of location from my usual life gave me space to think through these issues, and perhaps I have returned to them now precisely because I have had another change of scene, this time moving to Canada in 2007, teaching in Sociology at Trent University.

2. Reviewing intellectual progress in the second edition of her book that laid out an intersectional framework, Hill Collins notes that by 'rejecting additive models of oppression, race, class and gender studies have progressed considerably since the 1980s. During that decade, African- American scholar-activists, among others, called for a new approach to analyzing Black women's experiences ... Intersectional paradigms remind us that oppression cannot be reduced to one fundamental type, and that oppressions work together in producing injustice (Hill Collins, 2000: 18). Hill Collins also argues for theoretical accounts based on researching and disseminating the experiences of those who inhabit the sites of intersection, enabling their points of view to be illuminated in order to contest established dominant perspectives. This locates her work and intersectional studies in general firmly in the feminist tradition of standpoint epistemology.
3. When Weeks talks of that 'damned morality' in his history of sexuality in Victorian Britain, he refers in large part to the emerging gender divisions that compelled bourgeois women to become the moral and spiritual symbols of their marriage, family, class and national culture (1989). Western women in contemporary times still wrestle with these issues of reputation and the dialectical demands of being sexual and morally pure, evidenced in research done on sexual behavior, often in the context of understanding the possibilities of negotiating safer sexual practices (see Holland et al, 1998, *The Male in the Head*, for example) and in socialization studies more generally (see Rahman and Jackson, 2010, chapter 10, for example).
4. I am talking here about the decision to live publicly as a gay man, which is an active choice, rather than how we understand sexuality as an innate identity. I discuss and critique the issue of essentialist explanations of sexual identity in greater depth later in the book.
5. Queer theory is a diverse approach to cultural studies that emerged in the late 1980s as an extension of lesbian and gay scholarship that 'newly corroborated the idea that any form of cultural production is inherently ambivalent' (Hoogland, 2000: 164). Queer analytical strategies and theories are keenly focused on the exposure and demystification of essentialized *ontologies* of gender and sexual identity. Hood-Williams and Cealey Harrison explain that the deferment of ontology is a major premise of queer: 'Hence, gender shifts from being a substantive ontological or foundationalist notion to one in which the attributes of gender are performative, socially temporal but re-iterated and, as Goffman might say, "giving off" the appearance of interiority' (1998: 76).
6. Born and raised in Bristol, England from 1968, and then living in Glasgow, Scotland, to study and then work as an academic, from 1989 to 2007. I then fled the British academic system for a job in Sociology at Trent University in Ontario, Canada, around 2 hours north-east of Toronto. The local town, Peterborough is fairly traditional, mostly white Canadian and with no public gay space but some gay visibility around the university and increasing ethnic diversity, mostly students from Toronto and from abroad.
7. See, for example, recent research by Dale et al. (2002) which focuses on the socio-economic situation of Bengali and Pakistani women in Britain, contextualizing this within the history of Bengali and Pakistani men who have, since immigration first started in significant numbers, remained in low-paid and unskilled jobs and businesses. This is recognized by Government Equality

bodies in the UK particularly in relation to the gender gap in pay: see the recent consultation and information gathering campaign, 'Moving Up?', details at http://www.equalityhumanrights.com/, showing that both Bangladeshi and Pakistani women (who are overwhelmingly Muslim) and Afro-Caribbean women suffer from greater pay inequalities than ethnic white women.

8. Britain's National Health Service was gloriously celebrated in dance during the somewhat eccentric narrative of British history presented to the world at the opening ceremony of the London 2012 Olympics. (see the official Olympics channel, http://www.youtube.com/playlist?list=PL5F64CC0D24B809F9). Whilst the ceremony included a famous Bristolian the engineer Isambard Kingdom Brunel, hammily embodied by Kenneth Branagh, there were some notable absences from Britain's history, but then I suppose it would have been impolite to mention slavery and colonialism when welcoming the world to the irrepressibly multicultural contemporary Britain.

9. Stuart Hall developed the application of Gramsci's theories on hegemony to contemporary political formations, focusing in particular on how Thatcherism in 1980s Britain was an articulation of neo-liberal values in contest with the accepted post-war social democratic consensus (1983, 1988). Elements of neo-liberal thought gradually became mainstream to the point where traditional socialist and social democratic parties incorporated these values, most obviously the British Labour Party under the leadership of Tony Blair (see Phillips, 1998, for example). The neo-liberal hegemony is contested, as Gramsci argued all hegemonic projects are, but in the latest era of globalization and the emergence of trans-national corporations and a trans-national capitalist class (particularly after the collapse of state socialist societies) there is a widespread acceptance of neo-liberal values. As Hall comments: 'The whole point about the Blair/Brown version of neoliberalism is that it became the common sense of the middle. In fact it became the common sense of the whole bloody society' (Davison et al, 2010: 27).

10. In his appropriately majestic biography of Queen Elizabeth II, Pimlott points out that this was not a successful trip for the British Head of State (originally published in 1997, a Diamond Jubilee edition was published in 2012 by HarperCollins).

11. On July 7, 2005, 4 British Muslims attacked the public transit system in London, in co-ordinated attacks that killed over 50 people.

12. A controversial public debate developed in the UK in autumn 2006 when the Leader of the House of Commons, Jack Straw, revealed that he asked veiled Muslim women to remove their veils when they came to see him as their constituency MP. The intersections of social interaction, ethnicity, religion, gender, terrorism and multiculturalism in this issue echoed previous debates in France (Ezekiel, 2006, Najmabadi, 2006) and sustained a lengthy discussion in British newspapers, television news and political programs, involving politicians, Muslims and, to a lesser extent, Muslim women who actually wore the veil. See the article 'Radical Muslims must integrate, says Blair' in the *Guardian* newspaper, p4, Saturday, December 9th 2006, for example and a range of opinions and some anecdotal evidence that it is young, radical Muslim women who choose the veil, easily accessed by searching www.bbc.co.uk/news. The debate also threw media attention on the case of a Muslim woman teaching assistant who was sacked for refusing

to remove her veil when male teachers were present, and who subsequently lost her employment tribunal case claiming discrimination on gender and religious grounds, although the tribunal agreed she had been 'victimized'. See Vakulenko's articles on the judicial responses to veiling and headscarves in Europe, in which she illuminates how Muslim women's agency to choose the veil is being denied by both the legal system and some feminists (2007a, 2007b), echoing Motha's discussion of how this issue presents a challenge to western feminism and secularism (2007). This issue is also prominent in Canada, with numerous instances of Muslim women being refused the right to wear 'Islamic' clothing, from a girl wearing a headscarf during a soccer match in Montreal in 2007, to a 'code of life' published by the town of Herouxville, in which the council encourages immigrants to adapt to Quebec life by 'not stoning women' or 'forcing' them to wear the veil. Ruby's small study of Canadian Muslim women illustrates the complexity of veiling as an issue that helps women to negotiate identity both within and out with their own community in relation to gender, ethnicity and religion (2008).
13. An American television cop show from the 1970s, hugely popular in the UK and stereotypical of its genre: two male 'buddies' fighting crime with a really cool car and incidental sexual relationships.
14. See Nasar Meer's study on these issues in Britain, *Citizenship, Identity and the Politics of Multiculturalism: The Rise of Muslim Consciousness*. Basingstoke: Palgrave Macmillan, 2010.
15. 'With the collapse of organised communism in 1989–1992, western politics lost its Other. During the last decade, Islam, and in particular fundamentalist Islam, has been constructed as the unambiguous enemy of western civilisation' (2002: 109).

2 Islam versus Homosexuality as Modernity

1. As with all of us writing on issues of sexual diversity, the use of terms is important in our attempts to be inclusive, and yet there is always the danger of universalizing experiences and identities within the apparent recognition of difference. I attempt to be precise where discussions are specifically of male and/or female homosexuality rather than of bisexual, trans or intersex, particularly since most of the specific research discussed in subsequent chapters does not include much evidence beyond those who identify as lesbian or gay, often articulated as 'queer'. LGBTTIQQ2SA is the acronym used by the 2014 World Pride Human Rights Conference Committee (of which I am a member) 'to represent a broad array of identities such as, but not limited to, lesbian, gay, bisexual, transsexual, transgender, intersex, queer, questioning, two-spirited, and allies' (see, www.wphrc14.com). However, for brevity I use LGBTIQ as the overall descriptor for sexual diversity politics and identities since this is now (one) common usage in academia, as is the term 'queer' although I discuss queer theory as a specific theoretical framework in Chapter 5.
2. That is precisely why Obama was forced into denying that he is a Muslim. The July 21, 2008 cover can be viewed at: http://www.newyorker.com/magazine/covers/2008. In the same week, lawyers for the Guantanamo detainee Omar

Khadr released videotape showing parts of his interrogation in 2003 by Canadian security officials. In Canada, public debate focused on why the Canadian Government had not requested Khadr's repatriation despite the fact that he is a citizen, and one who was legally a child (under Canadian law) at the time of his detention and only 16 when interrogated by Canadian officers. In the absence of such a request, the traditional Canadian (and Western) guarantees of human rights and due process were unavailable to Khadr. He was detained in Afghanistan in 2002, accused of killing an American soldier. A Federal court ruling on April 23, 2009 required the Government of Canada to request Khadr's repatriation to mitigate the violation of his rights that had occurred through his detention. The government appealed that ruling but lost. See http://www.cbc.ca/world/story/2009/01/13/f-omar-khadr.html. A further Government appeal to the Supreme Court resulted in a ruling in January 2010 that while Khadr's rights as a Canadian citizen had clearly been violated, the Federal Government's authority over foreign policy meant the Court could not compel the Government to request his repatriation. Khadr remained in Guantanamo after being sentenced there by military tribunal to 40 years in prison in October, 2010, although a pre-trial deal agreed that he would be able to request transfer back to Canada after the first year, and only serve seven years in prison afterwards. See http://www.cbc.ca/news/world/story/2010/11/01/omar-khadr-plea-deal.html. He was returned to Canada in September 2012, to a maximum security prison where he will remain until 2018 if he serves his full sentence.

3. Said's study, *Covering Islam*, (1981/1997) illustrates the American media constructions of Muslims and Islam. For more recent evidence, see Karim's study of negative representations of Islamic 'others' by Western media covering the two decades before 9/11, *Islamic Peril: Media and Global Violence* (2003), supported by Poynting and Mason's (2007) study that points out that anti-Muslim media representations had been consistent in the UK and Australia prior to 9/11 though such particular events do provide a spike effect; 'The Resistible Rise of Islamophobia: Anti-Muslim racism in the UK and Australia before 11 September 2001.' *Journal of Sociology*, 43 (1): 61–86. Khan's (2000) description of British Muslims prior to 9/11 also discusses the long-standing tensions over their immigration; 'Muslim Presence in Europe: The British Dimension – Identity, Integration and Community Activism.' *Current Sociology*, 48 (4): 29–43.

4. See Fukuyama's recent reflections on his thesis in which he maintains that liberal democratic governance remains the only viable choice, while acknowledging that neither its current operation, nor the capitalism it is based upon, are historical perfections of either; 'Twenty Years after "The End of History"', *New Perspectives Quarterly*, 27 (1): 7–10, Winter 2010.

5. Turner argues that Strauss was critical of Schmitt's emphasis on religion, suggesting instead that it was the tension *between* reason and religious thought that created the struggle that produced a properly moral and serious life. Strauss was nonetheless sympathetic to the political perspective contained within Schmitt's work, and both influenced neo-conservative thought, particularly in the USA (Turner, 2002: 108–109).

6. Modood points out that a strict 'ideological secularism' has not existed in most Western democracies but rather that they have developed a '… moderate secularism, by which I mean the relative autonomy of politics so that

political authority, public reasoning and citizenship does not depend upon shared religious conviction and motivation' (2013: 67).
7. In his afterword to the second edition of his book, Barber acknowledges that his argument has been seen as part of the civilizational discourse. 'For although I made clear that I deployed Jihad as a generic term quite independently from its Islamic theological origins, and although I insisted that Islam has itself both democratic and nondemocratic manifestations and potentials, some readers felt the term singled out Islam and used it in pejorative ways to criticize non-Islamic phenomena ... I owe them an apology and hope they will find their way past the book's cover to the substantive reasoning that makes clear how little my argument has to do with Islam as a religion or with resistance to McWorld as the singular property of Muslims.' (2001: 299).
8. Said's *Orientalism* (1978) is regarded as instituting the field of postcolonial studies, conceptualizing the necessarily symbiotic relationship between the creation of 'orientalist' knowledge and the colonization of Eastern peoples. Contemporary postcolonial theories continue this emphasis and further deconstruct the exclusivity of Western modernity (see Bhambra, 2007, for example). In the context of civilizational clash, Turner (2002) challenges the orientalism within these arguments along five dimensions: that there are affinities between religious fundamentalisms in both West and East and these are often global, connected and partly to do with economic inequalities providing a pool of willing recruits; fundamentalism is often mistakenly identified with traditionalism and the latter is argued as evidence of Islam being anti-modernity; Islam is not a monolithic religion and Muslim cultures also vary enormously; Islam exists in the West now through significant migration and thus cannot be cast as simply outside of Western culture; and finally, the dichotomy of friend/foe is tautological, producing the clash it purports to describe.
9. 'This revolution has transformed, and continues to transform, the entire world. But in considering it we must distinguish carefully between its long-range results, which cannot be confined to any social framework, political organization, or distribution of international power and resources, and its early and decisive phase, which was closely tied to a specific social and international situation. The great revolution of 1789–1848 was the triumph not of "industry" as such, but of *capitalist* industry; not of liberty and equality in general but of *middle class* or *"bourgeois" liberal society*; not of "the modern economy" or "the modern state", but of the economies and states in a particular geographical region of the world (part of Europe and a few patches of North America), whose centre was the neighbouring and rival states of Great Britain and France' (Hobsbawm, 1962: 1).
10. 'Whilst it would be quite misleading to suggest that the rise of Christianity effectively banished secular considerations from the life of rulers and ruled, it unquestionably shifted the source of authority and wisdom from the citizen (or the "philosopher-king") to other-worldly representatives. The Christian worldview transformed the rationale of political action from that of the *polis* to a theological framework.' (Held, 1987: 37). One should note though that *polis* based governance was already in decline long before the emergence of Christianity as a dominant political force, often co-existing

with or subordinate to imperialism in antiquity from the time of the Persian Empire in the 6th century CE.
11. For example, in his book *What Went Wrong? The Clash Between Islam and Modernity in the Middle East*, Lewis (2002) discusses secularism and the development of civil society as fundamental to Western modernity's triumph over Islamic societies from the Age of Enlightenment. However, his explanation for its development is limited to the influence of Christianity, with almost no discussion of how socio-economic transformations provided the context for significant changes in the era of modern capitalism that Hobsbawm describes, or any detailed recognition of the challenges of the Reformation or its affinity with capitalist liberal democracy. Thus, he argues that 'Secularism in the modern political meaning – the idea that religion and political authority, church and state are different, and can or should be separated – is, in a profound sense, Christian. Its origins may be traced in the teachings of Christ, confirmed by the experience of the first Christians; its later development was shaped and, in a sense, imposed by the subsequent history of Christendom. The persecutions endured by the early church made it clear that a separation between the two was possible; the persecutions inflicted by later churches persuaded many Christians that such a separation was necessary' (2002: 96).
12. See the many examples in Rogan's historical study (2009), *The Arabs*, for example, which details how democratic principles of equality and liberty were often used by nationalist movements for claims to sovereignty but were overwhelmingly denied by their Western, democratic, colonial masters. Similarly, the Western need to import oil overrode the desire to export democracy during the Cold War, post-colonial era although this did not prevent the use of democratization as a justification for the recent invasions of Afghanistan and Iraq (see Kepel, 2006).
13. Their introduction to this special edition of the journal *Ethnicities* explains that the articles are part of a larger research project on policies around multiculturalism and gender, including a summary report of policies across Europe, available through the LSE Gender Institute website, www2.lse.ac.uk/genderInstitute/pdf/NuffieldReport_final.pdf. *Gender Equality, Cultural Diversity: European Comparisons and Lessons*, (Dustin, 2006).
14. The original essay 'Feminism and Multiculturalism: Some Tensions' was published in *Ethics*, 108 (4): 661–684 in July, 1998. This was reprinted in a book the following year (Okin, 1999, *Is Multiculturalism Bad for Women?*) with brief supportive and critical essays from 15 respondents and a reply to these by Okin. I have quoted from the 1999 book.
15. Furthermore, in her response, Okin welcomes critiques but feels the need to point out to those she has offended that their offence can only be expressed in Western liberal societies. Her motives in making this point in response to such criticisms seem to me an attempt to remind some of us (Muslims?) that we should be grateful to be in the West. However, given that I am one of those so offended, perhaps I am being ungenerous and so I leave you to judge the following for yourselves: 'Before I continue to discuss specific areas of agreement and disagreement, I want to point out that this debate is taking place only because its participants live in liberal societies, whatever the many defects of these societies. It is clear that what I have written has

offended several of the respondents, but nonetheless all of our work can be published and discussed freely. In many countries, some of us would be in danger of being silenced, if not placed in physical peril, for expressing views such as we express here. And thus it seems to me somewhat odd that some respondents strike out at the liberal values that allow all of us to express ourselves on highly controversial subjects.' (1999: 118).

16. 'My object, however, is a multiculturalism without culture: a multiculturalism that dispenses with the reified notions of culture that feeds those stereotypes to which so many feminists have objected, yet retains enough robustness to address inequalities between cultural groups; a multiculturalism in which the language of cultural difference no longer gives hostages to fortune or sustenance to racists, but also no longer paralyses normative judgement.' (A. Phillips, 2007: 8).

17. Phillips admits to the complexity of sorting this out in policy terms in her conclusions, but the principles of protecting dissent and the crucial right of 'exit' from the group are clear, as is her call for a more intersectional understanding of the ontological existence of those within minority groups, as a way of ensuring rights, exit, and visibility of coercion. Unlike Okin, she therefore acknowledges the complexities of how culture operates, and resists any determinist sociological equation of culture with agency. However, as Brahm-Levey points out in his comparative review of new ideas on multiculturalism, Phillips remains uncertain when discussing 'choice versus coercion' as a sociological issue (2009). Moreover, Modood points out that Phillips' position actually requires a theory of group representation even though her emphasis is on individual rights within a particular group (2013: 155–157). I take up these issues in more detail in Chapter 6.

18. 'The recent animus is distinctive, perhaps, only in that is has been occasioned by a set of developments bound up with Muslim immigration to Western liberal democracies, and the coincident rise internationally of militant Islam. As a result, the intellectual and polemical critiques of multiculturalism are now witnessing public policy shifts rather more readily than they once did.' (2009: 76).

19. See Modood's discussion for a clear and detailed summary of the reactions to multiculturalism in Europe as a reaction to Muslim immigrant assertiveness and agency (2013, particularly Chapters 1 and 8).

20. This point is implied in Puar's argument, but her focus remains on sexuality rather than the underpinning formation of modernity (Puar, 2007: 3–11).

21. 'We deliberately use the term "gay" as opposed to "queer" or "LGBTIQQ". "Queer" alludes to a subject-position and politics that is marginal in the Dutch context (cf. Duyvendak, 1996), while lesbians and transgenders play a minor role in the discourses we examine.' (Mepschen et al., 2010: 963).

22. In their introduction to a special issue of *Sexualities* on the Queer Netherlands, Hekma and Duyvendak confirm this normalization but also point out the ambivalence towards public and non-monogamous homosexuality in Dutch society: 'The invisibility of homosexuality asked for by many Muslims is thus also demanded by many white Dutch, albeit in a different way: we accept you as long as we don't have to see that you exist or have to see what you do. For their part, lesbians continue to remain largely invisible in public life and the media' (2011: 627).

23. I will discuss this evidence in more detail in Chapters 3, 4 and 5, but, for example, a survey of Muslims in the US showed that 61 percent thought homosexuality should be discouraged (comparing to 38% for the general population), Pew Research Center (2007), *Muslim Americans: Middle Class and Mostly Mainstream*. Available through http://religions.pewforum.org/affiliations. Tilo Beckers points out that the World Values Survey shows that there is a lower average level of acceptance of homosexuality in Muslim cultures, arguing that this is a mix of religiosity and culture, 'Islam and the Acceptance of Homosexuality: The Shortage of Socioeconomic Well-Being and Responsive Democracy.' (2010). There has been a consistent opposition of Muslim majority states to the incorporation of sexual orientation within human rights legislation. See for example, Samar Habib, (2010a) 'Introduction' to Habib, *Islam and Homosexuality*; Joke Sweibel, 'Lesbian, gay, bisexual and transgender human rights: the search for an international strategy.' *Contemporary Politics* 15, 1 (2009): 19–35; and Matthew Waites, 'Critique of "sexual orientation" and "gender identity" in human rights discourse: global queer politics beyond the Yogyakarta Principles.' *Contemporary Politics* 15, 1 (2009): 137–156. However, as Jurgen Gerhards points out in his analysis of the European Values Survey, the majority of EU citizens do not support the acceptance of homosexuality, but with large variations between the more socio-economically 'modernized' states and those more recently acceded, 'Non-Discrimination towards Homosexuality: The European Union's Policy and Citizens' Attitudes towards Homosexuality in 27 European Countries.' *International Sociology*, 25, 1 (2010): 5–28.
24. See http://www.foxnews.com/story/0,2933,599202,00.html, for the account from Fox and you can visit Gutfield's own political blogsite to see details of the proposal at http://www.dailygut.com/?i=4696.

3 Problematic Modernization: The Extent and Formation of Muslim Antipathy to Homosexuality

1. Scott Kugle's work remains a major contribution to thinking through the religious basis of Islamic views of homosexuality, demonstrating how both the Quran and the hadith tradition are routinely cited as authoritatively condemning homosexuality (2010: 22–24).
2. See, for example, http://www.theglobeandmail.com/news/national/toronto/cardinal-thomas-collins-opposes-students-calling-clubs-gay-straight-alliances/article2445850/.
3. The Iranian President's visit to Columbia University, and the criticisms he faced from Columbia President Lee Bollinger were widely and internationally reported. See http://abcnews.go.com/US/story?id=3642673.
4. See, for example, http://www.politico.com/news/stories/0112/72016.html.
5. Sweibel (2009) provides a detailed account of the institutional strategies and processes that led European LGBTIQ NGOs to their success at mainstreaming sexual orientation into the emerging human rights and anti-racial discrimination practices of the EU in the 1990s, contrasting this with the lack of similar success at the UN.

6. Kosovo is one nation that is within Europe but not officially a member of the EU since its legal status is still in dispute following the end of the Balkan war of the 1990s. Kosovo became a UN and then EU protectorate by the war's end and declared independence in 2008 but homosexuality has been legal since 1994, well before any EU influence.
7. The list of signatories can be found at the end of the document 'The Yogyakarta Principles: Principles on the Application of International Human Rights Law in Relation to Sexual Orientation and Gender Identity' available as a pdf at http://www.yogyakartaprinciples.org/principles_en.htm. None were involved as representatives of their national governments but rather as individuals or NGO representatives.
8. The resolution can be found at http://ilga.org/ilga/static/uploads/files/2011/6/17/RESOLUTION%20L9rev1.pdf. The report was delivered in November 2011, *Discriminatory laws and practices and acts of violence against individuals based on their sexual orientation and gender identity*, available at http://www.ohchr.org/EN/Issues/Discrimination/Pages/LGBT.aspx. These pages also provide links to the UN's response to the Yogyakarta Principles and this recent activism at the UN, in the form of a booklet establishing member state obligations to protect the rights of LGBTIQ peoples, *Born Free and Equal: Sexual Orientation and Gender Identity in International Human Rights Law*. For a thorough review of cases and decisions in human rights law, see Hamzic (2011).
9. This was prepared by the Islamic Council and presented to the Muslim World League (http://en.themwl.org/), then UNESCO. The Muslim World League still exists but it has been superseded in political terms but the Organization of Islamic Co-operation (see note 10). The declaration is available on various websites and reprinted as Salem Azzam, Secretary General (1998): Universal Islamic declaration of human rights, *The International Journal of Human Rights*, 2:3: 102–112
10. This IGO, founded in 1969, is the second largest after the UN and currently comprises 57 member states (all Muslim majority nations and some with significant Muslim populations) and is now called the Organization on Islamic Co-operation. Its approach to human rights is based on Islamic teachings (as witnessed in the Cairo Declaration) and its current statement on these issues reads thus:

> The Member States of the OIC face many challenges in the 21st century and to address those challenges, the third extraordinary session of the Islamic Summit held in Makkah in December 2005, laid down the blue print called the Ten-Year Program of Action which envisages joint action of Member States, promotion of tolerance and moderation, modernization, extensive reforms in all spheres of activities including science and technology, education, trade enhancement, and emphasizes good governance and promotion of human rights in the Muslim world, especially with regard to rights of children, women and elderly and the family values enshrined by Islam. (http://www.oic-oci.org/page_detail.asp?p_id=52)

> The OIC's Council of Foreign Ministers also decided to create the Islamic Educational, Scientific and Cultural Organization (ISESCO) in 1979 which has a number of publications and reports referring to gender, development

and education, but nothing on sexuality, homosexuality or either connected to rights (http://www.isesco.org.ma/index.php).

11. 'In the run up to the most recent CHOGM in Perth, Australia, in October 2011, there was extensive lobbying. The Commonwealth Human Rights Initiative organized a *Civil Society Statement of Action on the Decriminilisation of Same Sex Conduct in the Commonwealth* .... addressed to both the Secretariat and Member States ...' (Lennox and Waites, 2013a: 36) in Corinne Lennox and Matthew Waites (eds)(2013b), *Human Rights, Sexual Orientation and Gender Identity in the Commonwealth: Struggles for Decriminalisation and Change* (London: School of Advanced Study).

12. Since 1999, the AU has been the successor organization to the Organization of African Unity, founded in 1963. The actual Charter of Human Rights is not available at their website (www.au.int/en) but is posted on the website of the Court of Justice (http://www.african-court.org/en/index.php/documents-legal-instruments). There is no mention of homosexuality or LGBTIQI but rather an apparently traditional emphasis on the family in Article 18: 'The family shall be the natural unit and basis of society. It shall be protected by the State which shall take care of its physical health and morals ... The State shall have the duty to assist the family which is the custodian or morals and traditional values recognized by the community.'

13. Member nations include ten African countries listed in Appendix A, table 1 (Mauritania, Morocco, Algeria, Tunisia, Libya, Egypt, Sudan, Djibouti, Comoros, Somalia) and all those listed from West Asia in Appendix A, table 4, except Iran and Turkey (www.arableagueonline.org/wps/portal/en/home_page). The Arab Charter for Human Rights is concerned with heterosexuality, prioritizing the family thus in Article 33:

    1. The family is the natural and fundamental group unit of society; it is based on marriage between a man and a woman. Men and women of marrying age have the right to marry and to found a family according to the rules and conditions of marriage. No marriage can take place without the full and free consent of both parties. The laws in force regulate the rights and duties of the man and woman as to marriage, during marriage and at its dissolution.
    2. The State and society shall ensure the protection of the family, the strengthening of family ties, the protection of its members and the prohibition of all forms of violence or abuse in the relations among its members, and particularly against women and children (http://www1.umn.edu/humanrts/instree/loas2005.html?msource=UNWDEC19001&tr=y&auid=3337655, this is a reprint of the Charter which is not accessible via the Arab League website).

14. Member states: Azerbaijan, Armenia, Belarus, Georgia, Kazakhstan, Kyrgyzstan, Moldova, Russia, Tajikistan, Turkmenistan, Uzbekistan and Ukraine.

15. The World Values Survey is an international network of social scientists who collect, collate and analyze data on beliefs and attitudes produced from representative samples at the national level to engage in cross-national and

longitudinal comparison. Data is organized into waves of 4 year time periods, beginning in 1981, and is drawn from around 80 countries. The European Values Survey was the original project and formed the model for wider global comparisons conducted since the second wave (www.worldvaluessurvey.org).
16. In an older study, Bonilla and Porter's longitudinal secondary analysis of American survey data shows a similarly high disapproval among the black population in general, which they speculate may be related to African American Christian religious values, although the original data they draw from does not indicate religious identification (1990: 448).
17. The other age cohorts are as follows: 65% disapproval in 25–34yrs; 55% in 35–44yrs; 54% in 45–54yrs; 50% in 55plus years. Policy Exchange is an independent think tank focused on UK policies and governance although Meer argues that it has an anti-Muslim bias given that its founders and researchers have been associated with publications and political positions that are critical of Muslim identity politics (see Meer, 2010: 193). This report relied on a survey of a representative sample of 1003 British Muslims and 40 qualitative in-depth interviews with younger British Muslims (see http://www.policyexchange.org.uk/publications/category/item/living-apart-together-british-muslims-and-the-paradox-of-multiculturalism).
18. See http://www.socialcohesion.co.uk/publications.php?page_id=2 for the full report. This is a UK based think tank, and although it is non-partisan, many of its publications are concerned with Islamic cultures in the UK in relation to security issues.
19. See the news report at http://www.guardian.co.uk/uk/2009/may/07/muslims-britain-france-germany-homosexuality. The information was taken from the *Gallup Coexist Index, 2009: A Global Study of Interfaith Relations*, which compared data on Muslims in the UK, France and Germany, available at http://www.gallup.com/strategicconsulting/en-us/worldpoll.aspx. This project draws from Gallup's worldwide polling data to disseminate information through the Coexist Foundation, the Gallup Center for Muslim Studies and the Muslim West Facts Project.
20. Demos is a non-partisan think tank based in the UK. This report, *A Place for Pride*, can be accessed at http://www.demos.co.uk/publications/aplaceforpride. The report is based on focus groups conducted with a representative sample of around 2000 British residents although the precise number of Muslims within this is not given.
21. Siraj describes her sample thus: '33 men and 35 women, aged between 15 and 70 years (median 35.6). In total, there were 50 married participants (24 couples, and 2 individual participants who were married but their spouse was not interviewed), 12 were single, 4 divorced, 1 separated and 1 was in a relationship. The ethnic composition of the sample was as follows: Pakistani, 38; Iraqi, 6; Indian, 6; British, 4; Egyptian, 3; Moroccan, 3; Other, 8. My sample was composed mainly of middle class participants, who were highly educated, and many of whom were in middle class professional occupations.' (2009: 47).
22. The Survey questionnaires for all the various waves, including the sixth, are available at http://www.worldvaluessurvey.org/wvs/articles/folder_published/article_base_116.
23. See Beckers (2010) for a brief description of the story of Lot that appears in all traditions. For a comprehensive and detailed engagement with Muslim scripture, see Kugle (2010).

24. See both the Appendix here for rankings of governance and a recent project on national laws that protect sexual orientation and gender identity (http://www.icj.org/sogi-legislative-database/). This project is a collaboration between the International Committee of Jurists and the Faculty of Law at the University of Toronto.
25. The implications of this explanation of modernization for queer rights strategies are discussed in Chapter 6.

4 Traditions and Transformations of Muslim Homo-eroticism

1. See the tables in the Appendix for country specific information.
2. My knowledge is limited to English language publications but among those, see Murray and Roscoe, *Islamic Homosexualities*, and Bruce Dunne, (1990). 'Homosexuality in the Middle East: an Agenda for Historical Research.' *Arab Studies Quarterly*, 12 (3–4): 55–82.
3. Epstein's is one of the first discussions of how gay politics in the USA adopted an 'ethnic identity' in its pursuit of civil rights and how this political move reinforced the idea of an essentialist gay identity, although he argues that 'ethnic' culture contains both ideas of an essential self, and notions of culturally learned and transmitted practices that together form the basis of ethnic identification (1992).
4. 'Any attempt to understand Islamic homosexualities, therefore, needs to begin with a survey of the sexual patterns of the societies it encountered. These societies, occupying the region from the Mediterranean to insular southeast Asia, have consisted largely of agrarian-based cities interconnected through trade, cultural exchange, and sometimes empires for millennia-hence Toynbee's designation of the region as a single culture area he termed the Oikoumene, the classical Greek term for the inhabited or "civilized" world.' (Roscoe, 1997: 55).
5. Murray argues that the slave groups of Mamluk and Ottoman Kullar were recruited in childhood (and even that some communities offered up their sons for this role) and then trained to serve the respective Sultan or Empire. Their ownership by the ruling Sultan, and the legal prohibition on transmitting their accumulated wealth (since they were salaried) was an attempt to create a one-generational group whose only interests and benefits could come from serving their ruler, rather than accumulating power through wealth for their families, thus preventing the emergence of powerful, rich families who might usurp the Sultan. Thus, they were slaves who had a high degree of access to their rulers and social status within that court, although not outside in the general population. See his chapters, 'Male Homosexuality; Inheritance Rules, and the Status of Women in Medieval Egypt: the Case of the Mamluks.' Chapter 9 (1997a) and 'Homosexuality among Slave Elites in Ottoman Turkey.' Chapter 10 (1997b) in Murray and Roscoe, *Islamic Homosexualities*.
6. Vanita argues that this variety challenges the orthodox Foucauldian view of homosexuality as an identity that only emerged through Western forms of knowledge and only in the West in the 19th century. However, she is not claiming that the Western homosexual is universal, but rather that other

forms of identities existed to describe stable homoerotic behaviors in these cultures prior to the 19th century. She also acknowledges that while India as a coherent national culture is a modern phenomenon, the literary traditions they present demonstrate both sufficient interdependence and commonality to mark out a coherent unit of study (2000: xv).
7. 'In Mir's ghazals (love poems), different male youths, including the sons of Sayyids, Brahmans, Mughals, Turks, gardeners, soldiers, masons, firework makers, washermen, moneychangers, boatmen, flower sellers, musicians, singers, goldsmiths, physicians, perfumers, and even sons of judges (qazis) and law-givers are included among "bazaar boys"' (Kidwai, 2000: 108).
8. See note 3 for a definition of the term 'Oikoumene'.
9. He also criticizes the lack of accuracy in translations used to make their arguments and conclusions. This is for those scholars who can read Arabic to assess, but of course it is a serious charge because of its implications about whether we accurately understand representations of Muslim sexuality in literature, juridical accounts and Islamic theology.
10. 'It is in the realm of the emergent agenda of sexual rights that made its appearance in the United States and other Western countries in the late 1960s and began to be internationalized in the 1980s and 1990s that talk of sexual practices in the rest of the world, including the Arab world, would be introduced to the international human rights agenda and would be coupled with "civilized" and "uncivilized" behaviour. This *incitement to discourse* on sexual rights outside the United States and Western Europe necessitated that human rights organizations and advocates incorporate existing anthropological knowledge of the non-Western world. This was central for the purpose of constructing the human subjects – or, more precisely, objects – of human rights discourse. In the course of such "international" human rights activism, two prime victims of human rights violations in Arab countries emerged and/or were created: women and "homosexuals".' (Massad, 2008: 37).
11. Human rights increasingly became part of the shift to neo-liberal practices in economic development by dominant organizations such as the IMF and World Bank, characterized as the Washington Consensus that emerged in the 1990s (Springborg, 2009). Although the overriding emphasis in governance was securing property rights and efficient market systems, this created a discourse in which 'good governance' was broadly conceived and thus permitted an increasing use of the provision and protection of human rights as both goal and criteria for assessing 'development' in poorer countries, including Muslim ones in the Middle East and North Africa (Khan, 2009; Springborg, 2009). A revised 'Washington consensus' developed by the World Bank in 2008 increased explicit recommendations of good governance as central to successful economic progress (Henry, 2009).
12. Arno Schmitt's work was heavily criticized by Massad as a key example of orientalist writing on Islam and sexuality and he was given space to rebut these claims in *Public Culture*, the journal that published Massad's first shot at the Gay International. See Vol. 15, no. 3 for both Schmitt's defence (587–591) and Massad's brief rebuttal (593–594), (Fall 2003).
13. See the discussion in Chapter Three of the UN's current position on sexuality, including note 8.

14. See, for example, the two books by David Rayside discussing the emergence of LGBT issues onto the national American agenda in the 1980s and their problematic progress since then, *On the Fringe: Gays and Lesbians in Politics*. (Ithaca, NY: Cornell University Press, 1998) and *Queer Inclusions: Continental Divisions: Public Recognition of Sexual Diversity in Canada and the United States*. (Toronto: University of Toronto Press, 2008). Both are comparative in method and demonstrate in detail the relative lack of sustained progress at a policy level in the American context in comparison to other Western states.
15. Although the *New York Times* reported that a US$3m fund had been dedicated to implementation (within an overall US$51.6 billion budget for 2012–2013 [http://www.state.gov/r/pa/prs/ps/2012/02/183808.htm]). Clinton also acknowledged that LGBTIQ people still suffered discrimination in the USA (http://www.nytimes.com/2011/12/07/world/united-states-to-use-aid-to-promote-gay-rights-abroad.html?pagewanted=all). The Federal Supreme Court has only very recently ruled on same-sex marriage, striking down the Defense of Marriage Act (that prevented same-sex marriage recognition) in June 2013. See, http://www.nytimes.com/2013/06/27/us/politics/supreme-court-gay-marriage.html?pagewanted=all&_r=0.
16. Massad critiques the Gay International and its '... exercise of political power to repress, if not destroy, existing non-Western subjectivities and produce new ones that accord with Western conceptions ... My point here is not to argue in favour of non-Western nativism and of some blissful existence prior to the epistemic, ethical, and political violence unleashed on the non-West, as facile critics would have it, but an argument against a *Western nativism* armed with a Rousseauian zeal intent on forcing people into "freedom," indeed a Western nativism that considers assimilating the world into its own norms as ipso facto "liberation" and "progress" and a step toward universalizing a superior notion of the human' (2008: 42). However, he provides little elaboration in his book on contemporary formations of same sex eroticism that are not derived from literature. Given that his study is quite clearly primarily one of literature and its associated discourses, it is perhaps unfair to expect more social scientific 'evidence' but his polemic against the decidedly non-fictional Gay International raises a reasonable expectation that we might be given more insight into contemporary Arab homo-eroticism.
17. Chan (2009) and Obendorf (2013) point out the similarities with Singapore's construction of 'Asian' values (another British colony) and see the Human Rights Watch report on the legacies of British colonial sodomy laws (chapter 3 in Lennox and Waites, 2013b, or see the full version at: http://www.hrw.org/reports/2008/12/17/alien-legacy-0).
18. Williams' chapter in Habib's collection (2010) is largely based on his own experiences of acting as 'expert witness' in asylum cases in the USA. His approach, while attempting to recognize the historical diversity in Malaysian culture, does not question the concept of homosexuality as it is manifested in Malaysia, or the ways in which it is conceptualized in US policy, making him, no doubt, a manifestation of Massad's 'Gay International'.
19. Please refer to the discussion of this term in Chapter 5.
20. Research on the Caribbean has also illustrated the reality of postcolonial homophobic nationalisms. See for example, Alexander (1994) and Wahab (2012) on Trinidad and Tobago, Gaskins comparison of these with the Bahamas, Jamaica (2013) and Blake and Dayle on Jamaica (2013).

21. 'While the explicit interpretive bias linking the emergence of the miracle/modernity in Europe to an innate sense of superiority may be rejected by contemporary theorists, the specialness of the West as a "factual" matter – that is, as something that happened that needs explanation – remains firmly in place ... insofar as the civilization of modernity is seen to entail the modernity of civilizations, and however differently other civilizations may then express "their" modernity, there is a clear understanding of Western modernity as the original form and form that achieved expression *without relations to others*' (2007: 70).

5 Queer Muslims in the Context of Contemporary Globalized LGBTIQ Identity

1. A consistent focus throughout is his challenge to the pessimistic 'moral decline' thesis of social conservatives and so his arguments and evidence are framed specifically to counter this view: 'Against such settled pessimism, even despair, I want to offer not so much optimism as a realistic and forward-looking appreciation of the changes in sexual and intimate life that are transforming everyday life and the rapidly globalizing world we inhabit' (2007: ix).
2. Yunel Escobar played for the Blue Jays in 2012 and had stenciled 'Tu Eres Maricon' on his eye guards – translated as 'You are a Faggot'. The fall-out is described below:

    > The Blue Jays suspended their 29-year-old shortstop for three games on Tuesday, As part of his discipline, Escobar will also undergo sensitivity training and participate in an outreach effort 'to help educate society about sensitivity and tolerance to others based on their sexual orientation,' according to the club.
    >
    > Escobar's lost salary, approximately $30,000, will be donated by the Jays to You Can Play – a project co-founded by Patrick Burke, son of Maple Leafs GM Brian Burke, to support equality for gay athletes – and the Gay & Lesbian Alliance Against Defamation. (http://www.thestar.com/sports/baseball/article/1258364--blue-jays-yunel-escobar-to-address-homophobic-slur)

3. Weeks says that he offers 'almost at random, the following' and then lists and briefly describes these 'unfinished revolutions' (2007: 7–15).
4. Weeks acknowledges the Foucauldian critique of subjectivity but he rejects these in favor of focusing on the optimistic possibilities of selfhood as elaborated by Giddens and argues that there is convincing evidence of change in social attitudes and the construction of relationships to justify rejecting a critique of subjectivity as only a manifestation of continuing inequalities of power (2007: 130–133).
5. Again, a small group of 14 from a variety of Arab countries, see Kramer (2010: 154–155) for demographic details of the subjects.
6. This is the term used to describe lesbian women who present as more masculine than *lesbi* although Blackwood points out that these terms are not directly comparable to English concepts (2005a: 223).
7. Wong speculates that the term originated with a description for young alternative men:

    > Interestingly, even though 'Punk kids' was used to label young boys who embraced punk culture at that time, such labeling was re-appropriated

by masculine-looking women who desire women as a distinctive identity marker of their gender identification and sexual preference. Most importantly, the visibility of the 'Punk kids' in the capital city in turn attracted other women who desire women in the rural areas, small towns or other cities to migrate to Kuala Lumpur, believing that they would be more accepted there.

I suspect that the term 'Punk kids' eventually evolved to become the local term '*Pengkids*' with the influence of the Malay language. (2012: 438)

8. Again, my knowledge is limited to those studies published in English.
9. A support group based on the web but with some limited presence in North American cities: 'Al-Fatiha is dedicated to Muslims of all cultural and ethnic backgrounds who are lesbian, gay, bisexual, transgender, intersex, queer, and questioning or exploring their sexual orientation and/or gender identity (LGBTIQQQ), and their families, friends and allies' (http://www.al-fatiha.org/).
10. Jaspal's study also suggests that queer Muslims also internalize the religious and cultural homophobia of their own communities (2012: 85).
11. Kugle's work, *Homosexuality in Islam* (2010), represents a thorough religious discussion in which he acknowledges that confronting sexual diversity for Muslim communities is a difficult task, largely because of religious frameworks.
12. See websites at www.al-fatiha.org; http://www.salaamcanada.org/; http://www.safraproject.org/; http://www.naz.org.uk/.
13. Hamzic also puts forward the term 'alterspace' in the context of queer Muslims, as a combination of hybridity and the emergence of a 'third space' but again, my preference for intersectionality rests with the importance of standpoint to is methodology although the theoretical terrain of his concept is similar to that of intersectionality:

> Our communities claim their origins through varying historical narratives, which may or *may not* have any links with the two analysed hegemonic discourses [Islamic theopolitical reductionism and Neo-liberal Homonormativity]. Their tapping into these discourses, for instance through performance and re-appropriation, comes usually out of bare necessity, out of a *strategic* choice, rather that out of a heart-felt 'belonging.' Their alterity is thus doubly asserted, as *resistance* and *incongruity*. (2012: 31)

14. Puar's analysis rejects intersectionality as a useful theoretical perspective because she argues that it repeats identitarian frameworks, preferring instead to imagine queer futures as assemblages (2007: 204). My project is somewhat more mundane, focusing more on the identity categories of queer Muslims as credible identity experiences that challenge current institutionalized versions of identity.
15. Butler is discussing this discourse in this article, and identifies its manifestations here as largely modernity as 'secular time' (2008).

6 The Politics of Identity and the Ends of Liberation

1. I am drawing here on what Fuss describes as the dynamic of the norm and the other, or how normative forms of identity achieve their disciplinary

dominance by both containing and externalizing ambiguity through an 'inside/out' process: '... heterosexuality secures its self-identity and shores up its ontological boundaries by protecting itself from what it sees as the continual predatory encroachments of its contaminated other, homosexuality' (1991: 2). The distinction here is that gay rights are now partially inside, partially outside in terms of Western civilizational positioning, although I suggested in Chapter 2 that they remain mostly absent.
2. Lennox and Waites point out that the British Government is continuing with this strategy, threatening to link aid to respect for human rights, and that some NGOs such as the London based Human Dignity Trust risk being seen as imposing Western ideas of queer identity and rights (2013a: 39–42).
3. See http://www.ohchr.org/EN/Issues/Discrimination/Pages/LGBT.aspx, for the booklet establishing member state obligations to protect the rights of LGBTIQ peoples, *Born Free and Equal: Sexual Orientation and Gender Identity in International Human Rights Law*.
4. Although she is clearly focused on American imperialism rendered through sexual exceptionalism and thus includes the leviathan of the West. However, I discuss the broader basis of this sexual exceptionalism in Chapter 2.
5. Massad consistently focuses on specifically Islamist discourses against sexual diversity, but the evidence presented in Chapters 3 and 4 demonstrates a wider basis to Muslim homophobia. See also the recent report on attitudes to homosexuality by the Pew Research Centre which include ten Muslim majority nations and Nigeria in its 39 country survey and headlines the fact that secular and affluent countries demonstrate a significantly higher acceptance of homosexuality and highlights the high levels of disapproval in Muslim nations (Pew, 2013, *The Global Divide on Homosexuality*). I have criticized the conceptual and empirical basis of these large scale surveys in Chapter 3, while acknowledging that the wider spread of evidence available gives a clear indication that Muslim communities are not accepting of homosexuality.
6. See Stuart Hall (1992) for the classic statement of this cultural process, 'Encoding/Decoding' reprinted in Hall, S. et al. (eds) *Culture, Media, Language* from the original 1977 publication at Birmingham Centre for Contemporary Cultural Studies. I am also drawing here on Whannel's idea of media vortextuality (2002: 206) although his emphasis is on temporally limited media events in celebrity culture.
7. See the conclusion to Chapter 2.
8. See Bhambra (2007: 152–155).
9. Despite the lack of actual scientific evidence for an innate 'cause' of homosexuality, the 'appalling appeal of nature' remains the dominant cultural framework for understanding gender and sexuality (Jackson and Rees, 2007). Not only is this true in 'scientific' realms, but translates into popular culture, including gay culture, as demonstrated by the worldwide pop hit from Lady GaGa, 'Born this Way', released in 2011 with the following lyrics: 'No matter gay, straight or bi Lesbian, transgendered life I'm on the right track, baby I was born to survive'.
10. See note 6.
11. Haring's work features in *Power to the Imagination: Artists, Posters and Politics*; an exhibition mounted at the Hamburg Museum fur Kunst und Gewerbe in 2011.

12. See the discussion in Chapter 4.
13. This 'dilemma' is engaged with positively by Young and others who have sought to recognize and resolve it as a tendency in multiculturalism but, as Modood points out, the essentialism of culture and identity that can result from political organization has also provoked a negative assessment of multicultural politics and policies (2013, Chapter 5).
14. See Waites (2009) for a thorough critique of these concepts in international law.
15. As quoted in Chapter 4, Habib puts it thus in the context of Arab cultures:

> The critiques of culturally insensitive approaches to sexual practices in the Arab world have overlooked their own insensitivity to the very real struggles of homosexual people in the Arab world (regardless of whether such a term is universally identified with, these individual are in the least aware of their inherent difference and exclusion from the socially sanctified sexual currencies of marriage and children). (Habib, 2010a: xviii)

16. See Klug's (2012) review *essay in Ethnicities*, which gives a useful overview of contemporary research on Islamophobia and argues that this concept has become an accurate, if broad, way to think about the variety of ways in which Muslims and Muslim cultures are represented and politicized in contemporary times.

7 Beginnings

1. See Richard Toye's history (2010), *Churchill's Empire: The World That Made Him and The World He Made*, for his account of the great man's love of empire.
2. Boellstorff has a useful summary of seven key issues in researching contemporary sexuality in the context of globalization, arguing that these demonstrate that we can no longer think of the local versus the global. His substantive issues are: histories of globalization and sexuality; globalization and intersectionality; feminism and the gendering of globalization; the globalization of heterosexualities; HIV/AIDS; sexuality online; globalization, sexual rights and citizenship (2012). He includes intersectionality as one of these key issues, but I have argued somewhat beyond that point, that the contemporary modernity is intersectional in full measure.
3. See, for example, De Leeuw and Van Wichelen on the Dutch Integration Exam (2012), Muhleisen et al., (2012) on the use of sexualities within Norwegian immigration testing, and Michalowski's analysis of the variable content of citizenship tests and promotion of social norms within Austria, Germany, the Netherlands, the UK and USA (2011).
4. See Puar's discussion of Israeli pinkwashing in her account of the censorship she suffered after accusations of anti-Semitism at a conference in Germany, 2010 (2011).
5. This process is much broader than Muslim cultures and therefore cannot be reduced to an exclusively Islamic response, although there are numerous Muslim examples such as the organized resistance to SOGI rights at the UN.

Canada's current Foreign Affairs minister regularly condemns other nations on queer rights issues, as have the US and British Governments. Lennox and Waites cite the negative response of the Ghanian President to such demands made by the British Prime Minister in the context of the Commonwealth, demonstrating precisely that such interventions reiterate the process of triangulation of Western exceptionalism and so reify the discrete positionality of Western and non-Western nations on this issue (2013a: 37–38). See other examples of this process in the rest of the collection by Lennox and Waites (2013c), particularly those focused on the Caribbean, and various chapters in Weiss and Bosia (2013a), particularly the one by Kaoma on African examples (2013).

6. Even in the case of the EU, no sanctions have been used to impose queer rights, but rather a combination of hard law mandates, 'soft law' policies, elite socialization and transnational activist dialogue have furthered the mainstreaming of queer issues and policy change (Kollman, 2009).
7. See, for example, the various chapters on development politics and sexual rights in Lind (2010b).
8. See http://www.ohchr.org/EN/Issues/Discrimination/Pages/LGBT.aspx, for the booklet establishing member state obligations to protect the rights of LGBTIQ peoples, *Born Free and Equal: Sexual Orientation and Gender Identity in International Human Rights Law*.
9. Modood details the institutional processes that this would involve in much more detail than I have space for (see chapter 4, 2013), but his preference is for active civil society development, rather than a state led, top down, incorporation of religious groups. I support this view because the former is much more likely to produce more Muslim groups centered on gender and sexuality.
10. See, http://www.cbc.ca/news/canada/montreal/story/2013/06/15/quebec-montreal-turban-ban-announcement.html.
11. I am conscious that I am not detailing the huge debates around gender and multiculturalism, particularly the central issue of whether some rights, such as gender equality, override the recognition of cultural practices that undermine those rights. My position is that rights of non-discrimination are the fundamental ones, but that cultural recognition that does not contravene these are part of the framework of social justice, drawing broadly on Phillips position of multiculturalism as primarily protecting individual rights of difference (2007) but with Modood's qualification that we are, in fact, recognizing group rights if, in practice, we are recognizing religious-ethnic claims for funding and autonomy (2013).
12. See the contributions in Habib (2010b), for example.
13. See, http://www.itgetsbetter.org/pages/about-it-gets-better-project/.

Appendices

1. See http://www.premier-ministre.gov.dz/images/stories/dossier/Codes/code_p%E9nal.pdf, date accessed July 15, 2013.
2. See http://www.abunawasdz.org/nous/, date accessed July 15, 2013.
3. See http://lexofanzine.jimdo.com/, date accessed July 15, 2013.

Notes 209

4. See http://www.alouen.org/, date accessed July 15, 2013.
5. 'Due to fear of persecution from the authorities it is not registered as an LGBTIQ organization, but as an organization that works for protection of marginalized and estranged individuals'.' – 'HRBA and the rights of LGBTIQ persons in Burkina Faso.' Revised 2011-01-30. A report by SIDA (Swedish International Development Cooperation Agency). See http://www.ucalgary.ca/sw/ramsay/africa/niger-burkina-faso.htm, date accessed July 15, 2013.
6. Ibid.
7. See http://www.comores-droit.com/code/penal, date accessed July 15, 2013.
8. See http://www.globalgayz.com/gay-life-in-djibouti-africa/2047/, date accessed July 15, 2013.
9. Eman El Shenawi, Al Arabiya News, see http://english.alarabiya.net/articles/2012/08/24/233994.html, date accessed July 15, 2013.
10. See http://www.ilo.ch/dyn/natlex/docs/SERIAL/75299/78264/F1686462058/GMB75299.pdf, date accessed July 15, 2013.
11. See http://www.unhcr.org/refworld/docid/44a3eb9a4.html, date accessed July 15, 2013.
12. 'There were no publicly visible lesbian, gay, bisexual, and transgender (LGBTIQ) organizations in the country. The free association of LGBTIQ organizations was impeded by a law prohibiting association "for an immoral purpose;" in 2005 the then governor of the District of Bamako cited this law to refuse official recognition of a gay rights association. On April 13, in Bamako, police prevented homosexual activists from assembling on the margins of a conference concerning HIV/AIDS in the homosexual community.' See http://www.state.gov/j/drl/rls/hrrpt/2009/af/135964.htm, date accessed July 15, 2013.
13. See http://www.gaymaroc.net/, date accessed July 15, 2013.
14. See http://www.huffingtonpost.com/joseph-vellone/growing-up-gay-in-senegal_b_1858428.html, date accessed July 15, 2013.
15. See http://www.globalrights.org/site/PageServer?pagename=www_africa_sierra_leone, date accessed July 15, 2013.
16. See http://westafricachapter.blogspot.ca/, date accessed July 15, 2013.
17. See http://www.somaligaycommunity.org/, date accessed July 15, 2013.
18. See http://frlan.tumblr.com/post/9881846421/LGBTIQi-rights-in-sudan-history-and-analysis, date accessed July 15, 2013.
19. See http://ethiolgbt.blogspot.ca/2011/07/sudanese-lgbt-group-post-first-video.html, date accessed July 15, 2013.
20. See http://changingattitude.org.uk/archives/4222, date accessed July 15, 2013.
21. See http://www.globalrights.org/site/DocServer/Shadow_Report_Tunisia.pdf, date accessed July 15, 2013. for the website itself, visit: http://gaydaymagazine.wordpress.com/, date accessed July 15, 2013.
22. See http://aceproject.org/ero-en/regions/asia/AF/Penal%20Code%20Eng.pdf/view, date accessed July 15, 2013.
23. See http://www.globalgayz.com/gay-life-in-kyrgyzstan/2192/, date accessed July 15, 2013.
24. See http://labrys.kg/index.php?cat=3, date accessed July 15, 2013.
25. See http://www.globalgayz.com/homosexuality-in-kazakhstan/395/, date accessed July 15, 2013.
26. See http://www.unhcr.org/refworld/topic,4565c22547,45a51a252,4809b9b01e,0,,,KGZ.html, date accessed July 15, 2013.

27. http://kyrgyzlabrys.wordpress.com/2008/09/10/labrys-writes-reports-on-sexual-and-reproductive-rights-in-azerbaijan-turkmenistan-and-uzbekistan/, date accessed July 15, 2013.
28. The U.S Department of State Report on Human Rights in Tajikistan reports that there are no country specific LGBTIQ organizations. see http://www.state.gov/j/drl/rls/hrrpt/2010/sca/154487.htm, date accessed July 15, 2013.
29. http://www.legislationline.org/documents/id/8931, date accessed July 15, 2013.
30. For instance, the British Foreign & Commonwealth Office still advises that homosexuality is illegal. See http://www.premier-ministre.gov.dz/images/stories/dossier/Codes/code_p%E9nal.pdf, date accessed July 15, 2013.
31. See http://english.irqr.net/about-our-work-what-we-do/, date accessed July 15, 2013.
32. See http://www.hrw.org/node/85050, date accessed July 15, 2013.
33. See http://www.helem.net/, date accessed July 15, 2013.
34. See http://www.aswatgroup.org/en/content/who-we-are, date accessed July 15, 2013.
35. See http://www.kaosgl.com/anasayfa.php, date accessed July 15, 2013.
36. See http://en.wikipedia.org/wiki/KAOS_GL, date accessed July 15, 2013.
37. See http://www.hurriyetdailynews.com/default.aspx?pageid=438&n=istanbul-becoming-proud-of-pride-week-2011-06-19, date accessed July 15, 2013.
38. See http://www.lambdaistanbul.org/s/, date accessed July 15, 2013.
39. See http://www.alarabiya.net/articles/2010/04/30/107290.html, date accessed July 15, 2013.
40. See the Facebook page: https://www.facebook.com/LGBTIQRightsUAE date accessed July 15, 2013. Contact: LGBTIQuae@hush.com. Read, An Open Letter to the UAE | NowPublic News Coverage http://www.nowpublic.com/world/open-letter-uae#ixzz26UiBXe6z, date accessed July 15, 2013.
41. See http://bdlaws.minlaw.gov.bd/sections_detail.php?id=11&sections_id=3233, date accessed July 15, 2013.
42. See http://lgbtbangladesh.wordpress.com/, date accessed July 15, 2013.
43. See http://groups.yahoo.com/adultconf?dest=%2Fgroup%2FBoysOnlyBangladesh%2F, date accessed July 15, 2013.
44. See http://www.agc.gov.bn/agc1/images/LOB/PDF/Cap22.pdf, date accessed July 15, 2013.
45. See http://www.unhcr.org/refworld/country,,,LEGISLATION,TMP,4562d8cf2,3ffbcee24,0.html, date accessed July 15, 2013.
46. See http://www.aruspelangi.or.id/visi-misi/, date accessed July 15, 2013.
47. See http://www.thejakartaglobe.com/lifelived/q-film-fest-raises-awareness-on-LGBTIQ-issues/548004, date accessed July 15, 2013.
48. See https://www.hivos.nl/dut./community/partner/50008059, date accessed July 15, 2013.
49. See http://ardhanaryinstitute.org/hal-tentang-kami.html, date accessed July 15, 2013.
50. See http://www.pelangiperempuan.or.id/profil/, date accessed July 15, 2013.
51. See http://www.thejakartaglobe.com/myjakarta/my-jakarta-hartoyo-general-secretary-of-ourvoice-indonesia/525651, date accessed July 15, 2013.
52. The website provides email and phone addresses but no physical address: http://www.ourvoice.or.id/id, date accessed July 15, 2013.

53. See http://www2.thejakartapost.com/news/2012/12/19/making-their-voices-heard.html, date accessed July 22, 2013.
54. See http://gaya-nusantara.blogspot.ca/2012/12/making-their-voices-heard.html, date accessed July 22, 2013.
55. See http://www.huffingtonpost.com/american-anthropological-association/albania-gay-rights_b_1497865.html, date accessed July 22, 2013.
56. Ibid.
57. http://historia-ime.com/en/english/123-albanian-LGBTIQ-organizations-disatisfied-with-the-anti-discrimination-commissioner.html, date accessed July 22, 2013.
58. For the 'Alliance Against Discrimination!' see http://www.aleancaLGBTIQ.org/index.php/sq/rreth-nesh, date accessed July 22, 2013. For Pro LGBTIQ see http://www.pinkembassy.al/en/LGBTIQ-albania, date accessed July 22, 2013.
59. See http://www.gay.az/, date accessed July 22, 2013. More information on the state of LGBTIQ visibility and LGBTIQ rights can be found here: http://www.pinknews.co.uk/2012/05/27/feature-the-truth-about-gay-life-in-azerbaijan-outside-of-the-eurovision-song-contest/, date accessed July 22, 2013.
60. See http://www.unpo.org/article/15295, date accessed July 22, 2013.
61. See http://libertas-kos.org/, date accessed July 22, 2013.
62. See http://www.qeshkosova.org/rrethqesh/, date accessed July 22, 2013.
63. See http://www.queer.ba/?q=en/content/organization-q, date accessed July 22, 2013.
64. See http://www.globalgayz.com/europe/bosnia/gay-life-in-bosnia-and-herzegovina/, date accessed July 22, 2013.
65. See http://www.globalgayz.com/gay-life-in-bosnia-and-herzegovina/2293/, date accessed July 22, 2013.
66. See http://www.okvir.org/, date accessed July 22, 2013.
67. See http://hongkong.angloinfo.com/information/family/LGBTIQ/, date accessed July 22, 2013.
68. http://www.LGBTIQcenters.org/Centers/China/1107/Beijing-LGBTIQ-Center.aspx. The centre's English website (though still under construction) can be found here: http://www.bjLGBTIQcenter.org/en/index.asp, date accessed July 22, 2013.
69. See http://www.acceptcy.org/node/240, date accessed July 22, 2013.
70. See http://www.rainbow-ethiopia.org/about-us, date accessed July 22, 2013.
71. See http://www.rainbow-ethiopia.org/programs, date accessed July 22, 2013.
72. See http://saathii.org/gensex/calcutta/counsel.html, accessed in March 2013 but not working in July 2013.
73. See http://www.indiandost.com/gay_group.php, date accessed July 22, 2013.
74. See http://www.globalgayz.com/gay-life-in-ivory-coast-an-interview/385/, July 22, 2013.
75. See http://ilga.org/directory/en/detail?o_id=5478, date accessed July 22, 2013.
76. See http://www.egal.org.mk/en/za_nas.htm, date accessed July 22, 2013.
77. See http://www.globalgayz.com/africa/mozambique/, date accessed July 22, 2013.
78. http://www.amsher.net/Default.aspx?alias=www.amsher.net/lambda, accessed in March 2013 but not working in July 2013.

79. See http://ilga.org/ilga/en/countries/NIGERIA/Movement, date accessed July 22, 2013.
80. http://www.amsher.net/Default.aspx?alias=www.amsher.net/smawan, accessed in March 2013 but not working in July 2013.
81. See http://www.qayn-center.org/welcome-2/, date accessed July 22, 2013.
82. See http://en.wikipedia.org/wiki/Russian_LGBTIQ_network, date accessed July 22, 2013.
83. See http://translate.google.ca/translate?hl=en&sl=ru&u=http://www.gayrussia.ru/&prev=/search%3Fq%3DGayrussia.ru%26hl%3Den%26tbo%3Dd%26biw%3D1366%26bih%3D643&sa=X&ei=T4TeUJ4xo9rYBb_ugeAP&ved=0CDMQ7gEwAA, date accessed July 22, 2013.
84. See http://www.LGBTIQnet.dk/countries/africa/tanzania
85. See http://www.wezeshatz.org/?page_id=109, date accessed July 22, 2013.
86. See http://www.queercy.org/index.php, date accessed July 22, 2013. For Queer Cyprus Association's address, see http://ilga.org/directory/en/detail?o_id=4248, date accessed July 22, 2013.
87. See http://ilga.org/ilga/en/countries/ISRAEL/Movement, date accessed July 22, 2013.
88. See http://LGBTIQprogres.me/en/o-nama-2/, date accessed July 22, 2013.
89. See http://archive.globalgayz.com/europe/montenegro/juventas-and-montenegro-gay-portal-2/, date accessed July 22, 2013.

Bibliography

ABC news: http://abcnews.go.com/US/story?id=3642673. Accessed June 29, 2013.
Abdulhadi, R. (2010). 'Sexualities and the Social Order in Arab and Muslim Communities'. Ch. 20 in Habib, S. (ed.), *Islam and Homosexuality, Vols 1 and 2*. Santa Barbara, CA: Praeger.
Abraham, I. (2009). '"Out to Get Us": Queer Muslims and the Clash of Sexual Civilization in Australia'. *Contemporary Islam* 3 (1): 79–97
—— (2010). '"Everywhere You Turn You Have to Jump into Another Closet": Hegemony, Hybridity, and Queer Australian Muslims'. Ch. 17 in Habib, S. (ed.), *Islam and Homosexuality, Vols 1 and 2*. Santa Barbara, CA: Praeger.
Adam, B., Duyvendak, J. W. and Krouwel, A. (eds) (1999). *The Global Emergence of Gay and Lesbian Politics: National Imprints of a Worldwide Movement*. Philadelphia: Temple University Press.
Adamczyk, A. and Pitt, C. (2009). 'Shaping attitudes about homosexuality: The role of religion and cultural context'. *Social Science Research*, 38: 338–351.
Afary, J. (2009). *Sexual Politics in Modern Iran*. Cambridge and New York: Cambridge University Press.
African Court on Human and Peoples' Rights: http://www.african-court.org/en/index.php/documents-legal-instruments. Accessed June 29, 2013.
African Union ('AU in a Nutshell'): http://www.au.int/en/about/nutshell. Accessed June 29, 2013
Ahmed, S. (2011). 'Problematic Proximities: Or Why Critiques of Gay Imperialism Matter'. *Feminist Legal Studies*, 19: 119–132.
Alexander, M. J. (1994). 'Not Just (Any)Body Can Be a Citizen: The Politics of Law, Sexuality, and Postcoloniality in Trinidad and Tobago and the Bahamas'. *Feminist Review*, 48: 5–23.
Ali, M. (2003). *Brick Lane*. London: Doubleday.
Al-Fatiha, http://www.al-fatiha.org/
Al-Sayyad, A. A. (2010). '"You're What?": Engaging Narratives from Diasporic Muslim Women on Identity and Gay Liberation'. Ch. 16 in Habib, S. (ed.), *Islam and Homosexuality*, Vols 1 and 2. Santa Barbara, CA: Praeger.
Altman, D. (1980). 'What Changed in the 70s?'. Ch. 4 in Gay Left Collective (eds), *Homosexuality, Power and Politics*. London: Allison and Busby.
—— (1993 [1971]). *Homosexual Oppression and Liberation*. New York: New York University Press.
—— (2001). *Global Sex*. Chicago and London: University of Chicago Press.
Anderson, R. and Fetner, T. (2008). 'Economic Inequality and Intolerance: Attitudes toward Homosexuality in 35 Democracies'. *American Journal of Political Science*, 52 (4): 942–958.
Anderton, C. L., Pender, D. A. and Asner-Self, K. K. (2011). 'A Review of the Religious Identity/Sexual Orientation Identity Conflict Literature: Revisiting Festinger's Cognitive Dissonance Theory'. *Journal of LGBT Issues in Counselling*, 5: 259–281.

Bibliography

Arab League: www.arableagueonline.org/wps/portal/en/home_page. Accessed June 29, 2013.
—— human rights charter: http://www1.umn.edu/humanrts/instree/loas2005.html?msource=UNWDEC19001&tr=y&auid=3337655. Accessed June 29, 2013.
Association of South East Nations (ASEAN): http://www.aseansec.org/. Accessed June 29, 2013.
Awwad, J. (2010). 'The Postcolonial Predicament of Gay Rights in the *Queen Boat* Affair'. *Communication and Critical/Cultural Studies*, 7 (3): 318–366.
Azzam, S. (1998). 'Universal Islamic declaration of human rights'. *The International Journal of Human Rights*, 2 (3): 102–112.
Babayan, K. and Najmabadi, A. (2008). *Islamicate Sexualities: Translations across Temporal Geographies of Desire*. Cambridge: Harvard University Press.
Barber, B. (2001). *Jihad vs McWorld*. New York: Ballantine Books.
Baudh, S. (2013). 'Decriminalization of consensual same-sex sexual acts in the South Asian Commonwealth: struggles in context'. Ch. 10 in Lennox, C. and Waites, M. (eds) (2013b), *Human Rights, Sexual Orientation and Gender Identity in the Commonwealth: Struggles for Decriminalisation and Change*. London: School of Advanced Study.
Bauman, Z. (2000). *Liquid Modernity*. Cambridge: Polity Press.
—— (2005) *Liquid Life*. Cambridge: Polity.
BBC news: www.bbc.co.uk/news
Beauvoir, S. de (1949/1972) *The Second Sex*. Harmondsworth: Penguin.
Beckers, T. (2010). 'Islam and the Acceptance of Homosexuality: The Shortage of Socioeconomic Well-Being and Responsive Democracy'. Ch. 4 in Habib, S. (ed.), *Islam and Homosexuality, Vols 1 and 2*. Santa Barbara, CA: Praeger.
Beckett, C. and Macey, M. (2001). 'Race, Gender and Sexuality: the Oppression of Multiculturalism'. *Women's Studies International Forum*, 24 (3–4): 309–319.
Bereket, T. and Adam, B. (2006). 'The Emergence of Gay Identities in Contemporary Turkey'. *Sexualities*, 9 (2): 131–151.
—— (2008). 'Navigating Islam and Same-Sex Liaisons Among Men in Turkey'. *Journal of Homosexuality*, 55 (2): 204–222.
Bhambra, G. (2007). *Rethinking Modernity: Postcolonialism and the Sociological Imagination*. Basingstoke: Palgrave Macmillan.
Blackwood, E. (2000). 'Sexuality and Gender in Certain Native American Tribes: The Case of Cross-Gender Females'. Ch. 8 in Williams, C. L., and Stein, A. (eds), *Sexuality and Gender*. Malden, MA: Blackwell.
—— (2005a). 'Transnational Sexualities in One Place: Indonesian Readings'. *Gender and Society*, 19 (2): 221–242.
—— (2005b). 'Gender Transgression in Colonial and Postcolonial Indonesia'. *The Journal of Asian Studies*, 64 (4): 849–879.
—— (2007) 'Regulation of Sexuality in Indonesian Discourse: Normative gender, criminal law and shifting strategies of control'. *Culture, Health and Sexuality*, 9 (3): 293–307.
—— (2010). *Falling into the Lesbi World: Desire and Difference in Indonesia*. Honolulu: University of Hawai'i Press.
Blake, C. and Dayle, P. (2013). 'Beyond cross-cultural sensitivities; international human rights advocacy and sexuality in Jamaica'. Ch. 17 in Lennox, C. and Waites, M. (eds) (2013b), *Human Rights, Sexual Orientation and Gender Identity in the Commonwealth: Struggles for Decriminalisation and Change* (London: School of Advanced Study).

Boellstorff, T. (2005a). 'Between Religion and Desire: Being Muslim and Gay in Indonesia'. In *American Anthropologist*, 107 (4): 575–585.
—— (2005b). *The Gay Archipelago: Sexuality and Nation in Indonesia*. Princeton: Princeton University Press.
—— (2007). *A Coincidence of Desires: Anthropology, Queer Studies, Indonesia*. Durham: Duke University Press.
—— (2012). 'Some notes on new frontiers of sexuality and globalization'. Ch. 12 in Aggleton, P., Moore, H. L. and Parker, R. (eds), *Understanding Global Sexualities: New Frontiers*. London and New York: Routledge.
Bonilla, L. and Porter, J. (1990). 'A Comparison of Latino, Black, and Non-Hispanic White Attitudes Toward Homosexuality'. *Hispanic Journal of Behavioral Sciences*, 12 (4): 437–452.
Bosia, M. J. (2013). 'Why States Act: Homophobia and Crisis'. Ch. 2 in Weiss, M. L. and Bosia, M. J. (eds), *Global Homophobia: States, Movements and the Politics of Oppression*. Chicago: University of Illinois Press.
Bracke, S. (2012). 'From "saving women" to "saving gays": Rescue narratives and their dis/continuities'. *European Journal of Women's Studies*, 19 (2): 237–252.
Brahm-Levey, G. (2009). 'What is Living and What is Dead in Multiculturalism'. *Ethnicities*, 9 (1): 75–93.
Broughton, T. (2000). 'Auto/biography and the Actual Course of Things'. In Cosslett et al. (eds), 2000, *Feminism and Autobiography: Texts, Theories and Methods*. London: Routledge.
Budhiraja, S., Fried, S. T. and Teixeira, A. (2010). 'Spelling it out; from alphabet soup to sexual rights and gender justice'. Ch. 8 in Lind, A. (ed.), *Development, Sexual Rights and Global Governance*. London and New York: Routledge.
Bullock, K. (ed.) (2005). *Muslim Women Activists in North America: Speaking for Ourselves*. Austin: University of Texas Press.
Butler, J. (2008) 'Sexual politics, torture and secular time'. *The British Journal of Sociology*, 59 (1): 1–23.
Callinicos, A. (2007). *Social Theory: a Historical Introduction*. Cambridge: Polity Press.
CBC news – on Omar Khadr: http://www.cbc.ca/news/world/story/2009/01/13/f-omar-khadr.html. Accessed June 24, 2013.
—— on Quebec Soccer Federation turban ban: http://www.cbc.ca/news/canada/montreal/story/2013/06/15/quebec-montreal-turban-ban-announcement.html. Accessed July 28, 2013.
Chan, P. C. W. (2009). 'Shared values of Singapore: sexual minority rights as Singaporean value'. *International Journal of Human Rights*, 13 (1–2): 279–305.
Chappell, L. (2006). 'Contesting Women's Rights: Charting the Emergence of a Transnational Conservative Counter-network'. *Global Society*, 20 (4): 491–520.
Commonwealth (statement on human rights): http://www.thecommonwealth.org/subhomepage/190707/. Accessed July 1, 2013.
Commonwealth of Independent States (CIS): http://www.cisstat.com/eng/cis.htm. Accessed June 29, 2013.
Connell, R. W. (1987). *Gender and Power*. Cambridge: Polity Press.
Cosslett, T., Lury, C. and Summerfield, P. (2000). 'Introduction' to Cosslett et al. (eds), 2000, *Feminism and Autobiography: Texts, Theories and Methods*. London: Routledge.
Dahlerup, D. (ed.) (1990) *The New Women's Movement: Feminism and Political Power in Europe and the USA*. London: Sage.

Dale, A., Shaheen, N., Kalra, V. and Fieldhouse, E. (2002). 'Routes into Education and Employment for Young Pakistani and Bangladeshi Women in the UK'. In *Ethnic and Racial Studies*, 25 (6): 942–968.

Davis, K. (2008). 'Intersectionality as buzzword: a sociology of science perspective on what makes a feminist theory successful'. *Feminist Theory*, 9 (1): 67–84.

Davison, S., Hall, S., Rustin, M. and Rutherford, J. (2010). 'Labour in a time of coalition'. *Soundings: A Journal of Politics and Culture*, 45: 19–31.

De Leeuw, M. and Van Wichelen, S. (2012). 'Civilizing Migrants: Integration, Culture and Citizenship'. *European Journal of Cultural Studies*, 15 (2): 195–210.

D'Emilio, J. (1993). 'Capitalism and Gay Identity'. Ch. 31 in Abelove, H., Barale, M. A. and Halperin, D. (eds) *The Lesbian and Gay Studies Reader*. New York: Routledge.

Dickemann, M. (1997). 'The Balkan Sworn Virgin: A Cross-Gendered Female Role'. Ch. 12 in Murray, S. and Roscoe, W. (eds), *Islamic Homosexualities: Culture, History and Literature*. New York: New York University Press.

Doring, J. (ed.) (2011). *Power to the Imagination: Artists, Posters and Politics*. Chicago: University of Chicago Press.

Duggan, L. (2002). 'The New Homonormativity: the Sexual Politics of Neoliberalism'. Ch. 7 in Castronovo, R. and Nelson, D. D. (eds), *Materializing Democracy: Toward a Revitalized Cultural Politics*. Durham; Duke University Press.

Dunne, B. (1990). 'Homosexuality in the Middle East: an Agenda for Historical Research'. *Arab Studies Quarterly*, 12 (3–4): 55–82.

Dustin, M. (2006) *Gender Equality, Cultural Diversity: European Comparisons and Lessons*. London: Gender Institute, London School of Economics and Political Science. Available at http://www.lse.ac.uk/collections/genderInstitute/NuffieldReport_final.pdf. Accessed June 24, 2013.

Economic Cooperation Organization (ECO): http://www.ecosecretariat.org/. Accessed June 29, 2013.

Equality and Human Rights Commission (UK): http://www.equalityhumanrights.com/

Elliott, A. (2001). *Concepts of the Self*. Cambridge: Polity Press.

El-Tayeb, F. (2012). '"Gays who cannot properly be gay": Queer Muslims in the neoliberal European City'. *European Journal of Women's Studies*, 19 (1): 79–95.

Engels, F. (1942) [1884]. *The Origin of the Family, Private Property and the State*. New York: International.

Epstein, S. (1992) 'Gay Politics, Ethnic Identity: The Limits of Social Constructionism'. Ch. 10 in Stein, E. (ed.), *Forms of Desire: Sexual Orientation and the Social Constructionist Controversy*. New York: Routledge.

Evans, D. (1993). *Sexual Citizenship: the Material Construction of Sexualities*. London: Routledge.

Ezekiel, J. (2006). 'French Dressing: Race, Gender and the Hijab Story'. *Feminist Studies*, 32 (2): 256–278.

Fekete, L. (2006). 'Enlightened fundamentalism? Immigration, feminism and the Right'. *Race and Class* 48 (2): 1–22.

Fox News: 'Glenn Beck: Greg Gutfeld Wants to Build Gay Bar Next to "Ground Zero" Mosque'. http://www.foxnews.com/story/0,2933,599202,00.html. Accessed June 24, 2013.

Fukuyama, F. (1992). *The End of History and the Last Man*. New York: Free Press.

—— (2010). 'Twenty Years after "The End of History"'. *New Perspectives Quarterly*, 27 (1): 7–10.

Fuss, D. (1991). 'Inside/Out', introduction to Fuss, D. (ed.), *Inside/Out: Lesbian Theories, Gay Theories*. New York: Routledge.
Gallup (2009) *Gallup Coexist Index, 2009: A Global Study of Interfaith Relations*. Available at http://www.gallup.com/se/127907/Gallup-Center-Muslim-Studies.aspx. Accessed June 29, 2013.
Gandhi, N. M. (2012). 'Siraat-e-Mustaqeem or the Straight Path'. *Journal of Lesbian Studies*, 16: 468–484.
Gaskins Jr, J. (2013). '"Buggery" and the Commonwealth Caribbean: a comparative examination of the Bahamas, Jamaica and Trinidad and Tobago'. Ch. 16 in Lennox, C. and Waites, M. (eds) (2013), *Human Rights, Sexual Orientation and Gender Identity in the Commonwealth: Struggles for Decriminalisation and Change*. London: School of Advanced Study.
Gerhards, J. (2010). 'Non-Discrimination towards Homosexuality: The European Union's Policy and Citizens' Attitudes towards Homosexuality in 27 European Countries'. *International Sociology*, 25 (1): 5–28.
Giddens, A. (1990). *The Consequences of Modernity*. Palo Alto, CA: Stanford University Press.
—— (1991). *Modernity and Self-Identity: Self and Society in the Late Modern Age*. Cambridge: Polity Press.
Gilman, C. (1998) [1898] *Women and Economics*. New York: Dover Press.
Globe and Mail: 'Cardinal Thomas Collins opposes students calling clubs "gay-straight alliances"'. http://www.theglobeandmail.com/news/toronto/cardinal-thomas-collins-opposes-students-calling-clubs-gay-straight-alliances/article2445850/. Accessed June 29, 2013.
Greenberg, D. F. (1988). *The Construction of Homosexuality*. Chicago: University of Chicago Press.
Guardian: 'Muslims in Britain have zero tolerance of homosexuality, says poll'. http://www.guardian.co.uk/uk/2009/may/07/muslims-britain-france-germany-homosexuality. Accessed June 29, 2013.
Gutfield, G. 'The Daily, Glut, Greg Gutfield'. http://www.dailygut.com/?i=4696. Accessed June 24, 2013.
Habib, S. (2010a) 'Introduction' to Habib, S. (ed.), *Islam and Homosexuality, Vols 1 and 2*. Santa Barbara, CA: Praeger.
—— (2010b) (ed.) *Islam and Homosexuality, Vols 1 and 2*. Santa Barbara, CA: Praeger.
Haddad, Y. Y. (ed.) (1991). *The Muslims of America*. Oxford and New York: Oxford University Press.
Hall, S. (1983). 'The Great Moving Right Show'. In Hall, S. and Jacques, M. (eds), *The Politics of Thatcherism*. London: Lawrence and Wishart.
—— (1988). *Thatcherism and the Crisis of the Left: the Hard Road to Renewal*. London: Verso Books.
—— (1992). 'Encoding/Decoding'. Ch. 10 in Hall, S., Hobson, D., Lowe, A. and Willis, P. (eds), *Culture, Media, Language*. New York and London: Routledge.
Hamzic, V. (2011). 'The Case of "Queer Muslims": Sexual Orientation and Gender Identity in International Human Rights Law and Muslim Legal and Social Ethos'. *Human Rights Law Review*, 11 (2): 237–274.
—— (2012). 'The Resistance from an Alterspace: Pakistani and Indonesian Muslims beyond the Dominant Sexual and Gender Norms'. Ch. 2 in Nynas, P. and Yip, A .K. T. (eds), *Religion, Gender and Sexuality in Everyday Life*. Farnham, Surrey; Ashgate Publishing.

Haritaworn, J. (2012). 'Women's rights, gay rights, and anti-Muslim racism in Europe: Introduction'. *European Journal of Women's Studies*, 19 (1): 73–78.

Hekma, G. and Duyvendak, J. W. (2011). 'Queer Netherlands: a puzzling example'. *Sexualities*, 14 (6): 625–631.

Held, D. (1987). *Models of Democracy*. Cambridge: Polity Press.

—— (1993). (ed.) *Prospects for Democracy: North, South, East, West*. Cambridge: Polity Press.

Hennessey, R. (2000) *Profit and Pleasure*. New York: Routledge.

Henry, C. M. (2009). 'Towards an Islamic Model for the Middle East and North Africa? '. Ch. 5 in Springborg, R. (ed.), *Development Models in Muslim Contexts; Chinese, 'Islamic' and Neo-Liberal Alternatives*. Edinburgh: Edinburgh University Press.

Hill Collins, P. (2000). *Black Feminist Thought: Knowledge, Consciousness and Empowerment*. Boston: Unwin Hyman. 2nd edition (1st edition 1990).

Hobsbawm, E. (1962). *The Age of Revolution*. London: Weidenfeld and Nicholson

—— (1975). *The Age of Capital*. London: Weidenfeld and Nicholson.

Holland, J., Ramazanoglu, C., Sharpe, S. and Thomson, R. (1998). *The Male in the Head: Young People, Heterosexuality and Power*. London: Tufnell Press.

Hood-Williams, J. and Harrison, C. (1998) 'Trouble with Gender'. *Sociological Review*, 46 (1): 73–94.

Hooghe, M., Dejaeghere, Y., Claes, E. and Quintelier, E. (2010). '"Yes, But Suppose Everyone Turned Gay?": The Structure of Attitudes toward Gay and Lesbian Rights among Islamic Youth in Belgium'. *Journal of LGBT Youth*, 7: 49–71.

Hoogland, R. C. (2000). 'Fashionably Queer: Lesbian and Gay Cultural Studies'. In Sandfort, T., Schuyf, J., Duyvendak, J. W. and Weeks, J. (eds), *Lesbian and Gay Studies*. London: Sage, pp. 161–163.

Houston, K. (2012). 'When God is Not So Good: Corporate Religion contra New Social Movement'. Ch. 9 in Nynas, P. and Yip, A. K. T. (eds), *Religion, Gender and Sexuality in Everyday Life*. Farnham, Surrey; Ashgate Publishing.

Human Rights Watch (2013). 'This alien legacy: the origins of "sodomy" laws in British colonialism'. Ch. 3 in Lennox, C. and Waites, M. (eds) (2013b), *Human Rights, Sexual Orientation and Gender Identity in the Commonwealth: Struggles for Decriminalisation and Change* (London: School of Advanced Study).

—— for full report, see http://www.hrw.org/reports/2008/12/17/alien-legacy-0. Accessed July 3, 2013.

Huntingdon, S. P. (1993) 'The Clash of Civilizations?', *Foreign Affairs* 72(3): 22–48.

—— (1996) *The Clash of Civilizations: Remaking of World Order*. New York: Touchstone.

Inglehart, R. (2008). 'Changing Values among Western Publics 1970 to 2006'. *West European Politics*, 31 (1–2): 130–146.

Inglehart, R. and Baker, W. (2000). 'Modernization, Cultural Change and the Persistence of Traditional Values'. *American Sociological Review*, 65 (1):19–51.

Inglehart, R. and Norris. P. (2003). *Rising Tide: Gender Equality and Cultural Change Around the World*. New York: Cambridge University Press.

Inglehart, R. and Welzel, C. (2005). *Modernization, Cultural Change and Democracy*. New York: Cambridge University Press.

—— (2010). 'Changing Mass Priorities: The Link between Modernization and Democracy'. *Perspectives on Politics*, 8 (2): 551–567.

International Lesbian, Gay, Bisexual, Trans and Intersex Association (ILGA) (various documents available): www.ilga.org. Accessed June 29, 2013.
Islamic Educational, Scientific and Cultural Organization (ISESCO): http://www.isesco.org.ma/index.php. Accessed June 29, 2013.
Itaborahy, L. P. and Zhu, J. (2013). *State-Sponsored Homophobia, a world survey of laws: criminalization, protection and recognition of same-sex love*. ILGA, available at http://ilga.org/ilga/en/article/1161. Accessed June 24, 2013.
It Gets Better, http://www.itgetsbetter.org/pages/about-it-gets-better-project/. Accessed July 29, 2013.
Jackson, P. A. (2009). 'Capitalism and Global Queering: National Markets, Parallels Among Sexual Cultures, and Multiple Queer Modernities'. *GLQ*,15 (3): 357–395.
Jackson, S. (2011). 'Heterosexual hierarchies: A commentary on class and sexuality'. *Sexualities*, 14 (1): 12–20.
Jackson, S. and Rees, A. (2007). 'The Appalling Appeal of Nature: The Popular Influence of Evolutionary Psychology as a Problem for Sociology'. *Sociology*, 41 (5): 917–930.
Jaspal, R. (2012). 'Coping with Religious and Cultural Homophobia: Emotion and Narratives of Identity Threat among British Muslim Gay Men'. Ch. 5 in Nynas, P. and Yip, A. K. T. (eds), *Religion, Gender and Sexuality in Everyday Life*. Farnham, Surrey; Ashgate Publishing.
Jivraj, S. and de Jong, A. (2011). 'The Dutch Homo-Emancipation Policy and its Silencing Effects on Queer Muslims'. *Feminist Legal Studies*, 19: 143–158.
Kaoma, K. J. (2013). 'The Marriage of Convenience: The U.S. Christian Right, African Christianity and the Postcolonial Politics of Sexual Identity'. Ch. 4 in Weiss, M. L. and Bosia, M. J. (eds), *Global Homophobia: States, Movements and the Politics of Oppression*. Chicago: University of Illinois Press.
Karim, K. H. (2003). *Islamic Peril: Media and Global Violence*. Montreal: Black Rose Books.
Kepel, G. (2006). *The War for Muslim Minds: Islam and the West*. Cambridge, MA: Belknap Press.
Khan, B. (1997a) 'Not-So-Gay Life in Pakistan in the 1980s and 1990s', Ch. 20. In Murray, S. and Roscoe, W. (eds), *Islamic Homosexualities: Culture, History and Literature*. New York: New York University Press.
—— (1997b). *Sex, Longing and Not Belonging: A Gay Muslim's Search for Meaning*. Oakland, CA: Floating Lotus.
—— (2010). 'Longing, Not Belonging, and Living in Fear.' Ch. 2 in Habib, S. (ed.), *Islam and Homosexuality, Vols 1 and 2*. Santa Barbara, CA: Praeger.
Khan, M. (2009). 'Is "Good Governance" an Appropriate Model for Governance Reforms? The Relevance of East Asia for Developing Muslim Countries'. Ch. 9 in Springborg, R. (ed.), *Development Models in Muslim Contexts; Chinese, 'Islamic' and Neo-Liberal Alternatives*. Edinburgh: Edinburgh University Press.
Khan, Z. (2000). 'Muslim Presence in Europe: The British Dimension – Identity, Integration and Community Activism'. *Current Sociology*, 48 (4): 29–43.
Kidwai, S. (2000). 'Introduction to Part III'. In Vanita, R. and Kidwai, S. (eds) (2000), *Same-Sex Love in India: Readings from Literature and History*. Houndmills, Basingstoke: St. Martin's Press.
Klug, B. (2012). 'Islamophobia: A concept comes of age'. *Ethnicities*, 12 (5): 665–681.

Kollman, K. (2009). 'European Institutions, Transnational Networks and National Same-Sex Unions Policy: When Soft Law Hits Harder'. *Contemporary Politics* 15 (1): 37–53.

Kollman, K. and Waites, M. (2009) 'The global politics of lesbian, gay, bisexual and transgender human rights: an introduction'. *Contemporary Politics*, 15 (1): 1–17.

Korycki, K. and Nasirzadeh, A. (2013). 'Homophobia as a Tool of Statecraft: Iran and its Queers'. Ch. 8 in Weiss, M. L. and Bosia, M. J. (eds), *Global Homophobia: States, Movements and the Politics of Oppression*. Chicago: University of Illinois Press.

Kramer, M. (2010). 'Sexual Orientation: The Ideological Underpinnings of the Gay Advance in Muslim-Majority Societies as Witnessed in Online Chat Rooms'. Ch. 7 in Habib, S. (ed.), *Islam and Homosexuality, Vols 1 and 2*. Santa Barbara, CA: Praeger.

Kugle, S. S., al-Haqq. (2010). *Homosexuality in Islam: Critical Reflections on Gay, Lesbian, and Transgender Muslims*. Oxford: Oneworld Press.

Landry, D. (2011). 'Queer Islam and New Historicism'. *Cultural Studies*, 25 (2): 147–163.

Leak, G. K. and Finken, L. L. (2011). 'The Relationship Between the Constructs of Religiousness and Prejudice: A Structural Equation Model Analysis'. *The International Journal for the Psychology of Religion*, 21: 43–62.

Lennox, C. and Waites, M. (2013a). 'Human rights, sexual orientation and gender identity in the Commonwealth: from history and law to developing activism and transnational dialogues'. Ch. 1 in

—— (2013b). 'Conclusion' to Lennox, C. and Waites, M., *Human Rights, Sexual Orientation and Gender Identity in the Commonwealth: Struggles for Decriminalisation and Change*. London: School of Advanced Study.

—— (2013c) (eds). *Human Rights, Sexual Orientation and Gender Identity in the Commonwealth: Struggles for Decriminalisation and Change*. London: School of Advanced Study.

Lewis, B. (1990) 'The Roots of Muslim Rage'. *Atlantic Monthly*, 266 (3): 47–60.

—— (2002) *What Went Wrong? The Clash Between Islam and Modernity in the Middle East*. New York: Harper Perennial.

Lind, A. (2010a). 'Introduction: Development, global governance and sexual subjectivities'. In Lind, A. (ed.), *Development, Sexual Rights and Global Governance*. London and New York: Routledge.

—— (2010b) (ed.) *Development, Sexual Rights and Global Governance*. London and New York: Routledge.

London 2012 Olympics: 'The Olympic Channel'. http://www.youtube.com/playlist?list=PL5F64CC0D24B809F9

Long, S. (2009). 'Unbearable Witness: How Western Activists (Mis)Recognize Sexuality in Iran'. *Contemporary Politics*, 15 (1): 119–36.

Luongo, M. T. (2010). 'Gays under Occupation: Interviews with Gay Iraqis'. Ch. 5 in Habib, S. (ed.), *Islam and Homosexuality, Vols 1 and 2*. Santa Barbara, CA: Praeger.

Mahdavi, P. (2008). *Passionate Uprisings: Iran's Sexual Revolution*. Stanford, CA: Stanford University Press.

—— (2012). '"The personal is political and the political is personal"; sexuality, politics and social movements in modern Iran'. Ch. 3 in Aggleton, P., Moore,

H. L. and Parker, R. (eds), *Understanding Global Sexualities: New Frontiers*. London and New York: Routledge.
Massad, J. A. (2002). 'Re-Orienting Desire: The Gay International and the Arab World'. *Public Culture*, 14 (2): 361–385.
—— (2003). 'The Intransigence of Orientalist Desires: A Reply to Arno Schmitt'. *Public Culture*, 15 (3): 593–594.
—— (2008). *Desiring Arabs*. Chicago: University of Chicago Press.
McClintock, A. (1995). *Imperial Leather: Race, Gender and Sexuality in the Colonial Context*. London: Routledge.
McDermott, E. (2011). 'The world some have won: Sexuality, class and inequality'. *Sexualities*, 14 (1): 63–78.
McIntosh, M. (1996) [1968] 'The Homosexual Role'. In Seidman, S. (ed.), *Queer Theory/Sociology*. Oxford: Blackwell Publishers.
Meer, N. (2010) *Citizenship, Identity and the Politics of Multiculturalism: The Rise of Muslim Consciousness*. Basingstoke: Palgrave Macmillan.
Mepschen, P., Duyvendak, J. W. and Tonkens, E. (2010). 'Sexual Politics, Orientalism and Multicultural Citizenship in the Netherlands'. *Sociology*, 44 (5): 962–980.
Michalowski, I. (2011). 'Required to assimilate: the content of citizenship tests in five countries'. *Citizenship Studies*, 15 (6–7): 749–768.
Minwalla, O., Rosser, B. R. S., Feldman, J. and Varga, C. (2005) 'Identity experience among progressive gay Muslims in North America: A qualitative study within Al-Fatiha'. *Culture, Health & Sexuality* 7 (2): 113–128.
Modood, T. (2013). *Multiculturalism* (2nd edition). Cambridge: Polity Press.
Modood, T. and Ahmad, F. (2007). 'British Muslim Perspectives on Multiculturalism'. *Theory, Culture and Society*, 24 (2): 187–213.
Morgenson, S. L. (2010). 'Settler Homonationalism: Theorizing Settler Colonialism within Queer Modernities'. *GLQ*, 16 (1–2): 105–131.
Motha, S. (2007). 'Veiled Women and the Affect of Religion in Democracy'. *Journal of Law and Society*, 34 (1), March 2007: 139–162.
Muhleisen, W., Rothing, A. and Svendsen, S. H. B. (2012). 'Norwegian sexualities: Assimilation and exclusion in Norwegian immigration policy'. *Sexualities*, 15 (2): 139–155.
Murray, S. (1997a). 'Male Homosexuality; Inheritance Rules, and the Status of Women in Medieval Egypt: the Case of the Mamluks'. Ch. 9 in Murray, S. and Roscoe, W. (eds), *Islamic Homosexualities: Culture, History and Literature*. New York: New York University Press.
—— (1997b). 'Homosexuality among Slave Elites in Ottoman Turkey'. Ch. 10 in Murray, S. and Roscoe, W. (eds), *Islamic Homosexualities: Culture, History and Literature*. New York: New York University Press.
—— (1997c). 'The Sohari *Khanith*'. Ch. 16 in Murray, S. and Roscoe, W. (eds), *Islamic Homosexualities: Culture, History and Literature*. New York: New York University Press.
—— (1997d). 'Male Actresses in Islamic Parts of Indonesia and the Southern Philippines'. Ch. 17 in Murray, S. and Roscoe, W. (eds), *Islamic Homosexualities: Culture, History and Literature*. New York: New York University Press.
—— (1997e). 'Woman-Woman Love in Islamic Societies'. Ch. 5 in Murray, S. and Roscoe, W. (eds), *Islamic Homosexualities: Culture, History and Literature*. New York: New York University Press.

—— (1997f). 'The Will Not to Know: Islamic Accommodations of Male Homosexualities'. Ch. 2 in Murray, S. and Roscoe, W. (eds), *Islamic Homosexualities: Culture, History and Literature*. New York: New York University Press.

Murray, S. and Roscoe, W. (eds) (1997a). *Islamic Homosexualities: Culture, History and Literature*. New York: New York University Press.

—— (1997b) 'Introduction' to Murray, S. and Roscoe, W. (eds), *Islamic Homosexualities: Culture, History and Literature*. New York: New York University Press.

Muslim World League: http://en.themwl.org/. Accessed June 29, 2013.

Najmabadi, A. (2006). 'Gender and Secularism of Modernity: How Can a Muslim Woman be French?'. *Feminist Studies*, 32 (2): 239–255.

Naz project, http://www.naz.org.uk/

New Yorker: 'Covers: 2008'. http://www.newyorker.com/magazine/covers/2008.

New York Times, on Clinton's speech to the UN: http://www.nytimes.com/2011/12/07/world/united-states-to-use-aid-to-promote-gay-rights-abroad.html?pagewanted=all&_r=1&. Accessed July 3, 2013.

—— on recent US Supreme Court decisions: http://www.nytimes.com/2013/06/27/us/politics/supreme-court-gay-marriage.html?pagewanted=all&_r=0. Accessed July 3, 2013.

Obendorf, S. (2013). 'A few respectable steps behind the world? Gay and Lesbian rights in contemporary Singapore'. Ch. 8 in Lennox, C. and Waites, M. (2013b) (eds), *Human Rights, Sexual Orientation and Gender Identity in the Commonwealth: Struggles for Decriminalisation and Change*. London: School of Advanced Study.

Office of the High Commissioner for Human Rights (United Nations). *Born Free and Equal: Sexual Orientation and Gender Identity in International Human Rights Law*. Available at http://www.ohchr.org/EN/Issues/Discrimination/Pages/LGBT.aspx. Accessed July 27, 2013.

Okin, S. M. (1998). 'Feminism and Multiculturalism: Some Tensions'. *Ethics*, 108 (4): 661–684.

—— (1999). *Is Multiculturalism Bad for Women?* Princeton: Princeton University Press.

Organization of Islamic Cooperation (human rights declaration): http://www.oic-oci.org/english/article/human.htm. Accessed July 1, 2013.

Ouzgane, L. (ed.) (2006). *Islamic Masculinities*. London and New York: Zed Books.

Parekh, B. (2006). *Rethinking Multiculturalism: Cultural Diversity and Political Theory*. 2nd edition. Basingstoke: Palgrave Macmillan.

Parker, R. and Aggleton, P. (2012). 'From research to policy and practice'. Ch. 16 in Aggleton, P., Moore, H. L. and Parker, R. (eds), *Understanding Global Sexualities: New Frontiers*. London and New York: Routledge.

Peletz, M. G. (2006). 'Transgenderism and Gender Pluralism in Southeast Asia since Early Modern Times'. *Current Anthropology*, 47 (2): 309–340.

Pew Research Center (2007), *Muslim Americans: Middle Class and Mostly Mainstream*. Available at http://religions.pewforum.org/affiliations. Accessed July 27, 2013.

—— (2013). *The Global Divide on Homosexuality*. Available at http://www.pewglobal.org/2013/06/04/the-global-divide-on-homosexuality/. Accessed July 27, 2013.

Phelan, S. (1997). 'Introduction' to Phelan, S. (ed.) *Playing with Fire: Queer Politics, Queer Theories*. New York: Routledge.

Phillips, A. (1993). *Democracy and Difference.* Cambridge: Polity Press.
—— (2007) *Multiculturalism without Culture.* Princeton: Princeton University Press.
Phillips, A. and Saharso, S. (2008). 'The Rights of Women and the Crisis of Multiculturalism'. *Ethnicities,* 8 (3): 291–301.
Phillips, L. (1998). 'Hegemony and Political Discourse: The Lasting Impact of Thatcherism'. *Sociology,* 32 (4): 847–867.
Pimlott, B. (2012). *The Queen: Elizabeth II and the Monarchy.* London: Harper Press.
Plummer, K. (1995). *Telling Sexual Stories.* London: Routledge.
Policy Exchange (2007): 'Living apart together: British Muslims and the paradox of multiculturalism'. http://www.policyexchange.org.uk/publications/category/item/living-apart-together-british-muslims-and-the-paradox-of-multiculturalism.
Politico.com: 'Leon Panetta details deep defense cuts'. http://www.politico.com/news/stories/0112/72016.html. Accessed June 29, 2013.
Poynting, S. and Mason V. (2007). 'The Resistible Rise of Islamophobia: Anti-Muslim racism in the UK and Australia before 11 September 2001'. *Journal of Sociology,* 43 (1): 61–86.
Pronger, B. (1990). *The Arena of Masculinity: Sports, Homosexuality and the Meaning of Sex.* London: GMP Publishers.
Puar, J. K. (2007). *Terrorist Assemblages: Homonationalism in Queer Times.* Durham and London: Duke University Press.
—— (2011). 'Citation and Censorship: the Politics of Talking About the Sexual Politics of Israel'. *Feminist Legal Studies,* 19: 133–142.
Rahman, M. (2000). *Sexuality and Democracy: Identities and Strategies in Lesbian and Gay Politics.* Edinburgh: Edinburgh University Press.
—— (2009) 'Theorising Intersectionality: Identities, Equality and Ontology'. Ch. 14 in Grabham, E., Cooper, D., Krishnadas, J. and Herman, D. (eds) *Intersectionality and Beyond: Law, Power and the Politics of Location.* London: Routledge.
—— (2010). 'Queer as Intersectionality: Theorizing Gay Muslim Identities'. *Sociology,* 44 (5): 1–18.
Rahman, M. and Hussain, A. (2011). 'Muslims and Sexual Diversity in North America'. Ch. 15 in Rayside, D. and Wilcox, C. (eds) *Faith, Politics and Sexual Diversity in Canada and the United States.* Vancouver: UBC Press.
Rahman, M. and Jackson, S. (2010). *Gender and Sexuality: Sociological Approaches.* Cambridge: Polity Press.
Rayside, D. (1998). *On the Fringe: Gays and Lesbians in Politics.* Ithaca, NY: Cornell University Press.
—— (2008). *Queer Inclusions: Continental Divisions: Public Recognition of Sexual Diversity in Canada and the United States.* Toronto: University of Toronto Press.
—— (2011) 'Muslim American communities' response to queer visibility'. *Contemporary Islam,* 5 (2):109–134.
Rayside, D. and Wilcox, C. (eds) (2011a). *Faith, Politics and Sexual Diversity in Canada and the United States.* Vancouver: UBC Press.
—— (2011b). 'Introduction: The Difference that a Border Makes: The Political Intersection of Sexuality and Religion In Canada and the United States'. Ch. 1 in Rayside, D. and Wilcox, C. (eds) (2011a), *Faith, Politics and Sexual Diversity in Canada and the United States.* Vancouver: UBC Press.

Razack, S. (2008). *Casting Out: the Eviction of Muslims from Western Law and Politics*. Toronto: University of Toronto Press.
Ritchie, J. (2010). 'How Do You Say "Come Out of the Closet" in Arabic? Queer Activism and the Politics of Visibility in Israel-Palestine'. *GLQ*, 16 (4): 557–575.
Rizzo, H., Abdel-Hamid, A. and Meyer, K. (2007) 'The Relationships Between Gender Equality and Democracy: A Comparison of Arab Versus Non-Arab Muslim Societies'. *Sociology* 41 (6): 1151–1170.
Rogan, E. (2009). *The Arabs: A History*. New York: Basic Books.
Roscoe, W. (1997). 'Pre-Cursors of Islamic Male Homosexualities'. Ch. 3 in Murray, S. and Roscoe, W. (eds), *Islamic Homosexualities: Culture, History and Literature*. New York: New York University Press.
Rouhani, F. (2007). 'Religion, identity and activism: Queer Muslim diasporic identities'. Ch. 14 in Lim J., Brown, G. and Browne, K. (eds), *Geographies of Sexualities: Theory, Practices and Politics*. Aldershot: Ashgate Publishing.
Ruby, T. F. (2008). 'Listening to the Voices of Hijab'. Ch. 5 in Kimmel, M., Aronson, A. and Kaler, A. (eds), *The Gendered Society Reader: Canadian Edition*. Don Mills, ON: Oxford University Press.
Saed, K. (2005). 'On the Edge of Belonging'. Ch. 7 in Abdul-Ghafur, S. (ed.), *Living Islam Out Loud*. Boston, MA: Beacon Press.
Safi, O. (2003). 'Introduction: *the times they are a-changin'* – a Muslim quest for justice, gender equality and pluralism'. Safi, O. (ed.), *Progressive Muslims: on Justice, Gender and Pluralism*. Oxford: Oneworld Press.
Safra project, http://www.safraproject.org/
Said, E. (1985/1975). *Beginnings: Intention and Method*. New York: Basic Books.
—— (1978). *Orientalism*. New York: Vintage Books.
—— (1981/1997). *Covering Islam*. New York: Vintage Books.
Salaam Canada, http://salaamcanada.org/
Schmitt, A. (2003). 'Gay Rights versus Human Rights: A Response to Joseph Massad'. *Public Culture*, 15 (3): 587–591.
Schmitt, A. and Sofer, J. (eds) (1992). *Sexuality and Eroticism Among Males in Moslem Societies*. New York: Haworth Press.
Seidman, S. (1996). 'Introduction' to Seidman, S. (ed.), *Queer Theory/Sociology*. Oxford: Blackwell.
—— (2004). *Beyond the Closet: the Transformation of Gay and Lesbian Life*. New York: Routledge.
Shah, S. (2013). 'The Malaysian Dilemma: negotiating sexual diversity in a Muslim-majority Commonwealth state'. Ch. 9 in Lennox, C. and Waites, M. (eds), *Human Rights, Sexual Orientation and Gender Identity in the Commonwealth: Struggles for Decriminalisation and Change*. London: School of Advanced Study.
Shanghai Cooperation Organization (SCO): http://www.sectsco.org/EN/. Accessed June 29, 2013.
Sharlet, J. (2010). 'Public Displays of Affection: Male Homoerotic Desire and Sociability in Medieval Arabic Literature'. Ch. 3 in Habib, S. (2010b) (ed.), *Islam and Homosexuality, Vols 1 and 2*. Santa Barbara, CA: Praeger.
Simmons, G. Z. (2003). 'Are we up to the challenge? The need for a radical re-ordering of the Islamic discourse on women'. Ch. 9 in Safi, O. (ed.), *Progressive Muslims: on Justice, Gender and Pluralism*. Oxford: Oneworld Press.
Siraj, A. (2006). 'On Being Homosexual and Muslim: Conflicts and Challenges'. Ch. 11 in Ouzgane, L. (ed.), *Islamic Masculinities*. London: Zed Books.

—— (2009). 'The Construction of the Homosexual "Other" by British Muslim Heterosexuals'. *Contemporary Islam*, 3 (1): 47–57.
SOGI Legislative database: http://www.icj.org/sogi-legislative-database/. Accessed June 29, 2013.
South Asian Association for Regional Cooperation (SAARC): http://www.saarc-sec.org/. Accessed June 29, 2013.
Springborg, R. (2009). 'Conclusion: Not Washington, Beijing nor Mecca: The Limitations of Development Models'. In Springborg, R. (ed.), *Development Models in Muslim Contexts; Chinese, 'Islamic' and Neo-Liberal Alternatives*. Edinburgh: Edinburgh University Press.
Stanley, L. (2000). 'From "self-made women" to "women's made-selves"? Audit selves, simulation and surveillance in the rise of public woman'. In Cosslett et al. (eds), 2000, *Feminism and Autobiography: Texts, Theories and Methods*. London: Routledge.
Stoler, A. L. (2010). *Carnal Knowledge and Imperial Power: Race and the Intimate in Colonial Rule*. Berkeley, CA: University of California Press. 2nd edition.
Stulhofer, A. and Rimac, I. (2009). 'Determinants of Homonegativity in Europe'. *Journal of Sex Research*, 46 (1): 24–32.
Subrahmanyam, S. (1997). 'Connected Histories: Notes towards a Reconfiguration of Early Modern Eurasia'. *Modern Asian Studies*, 31 (3): 735–762.
—— (2005a). *Explorations in Connected Histories: Mughals and Franks*. New Delhi: Oxford University Press.
—— (2005b) *Explorations in Connected Histories: From the Tagus to the Ganges*, New Delhi: Oxford University Press.
Sweibel, J. (2009) 'Lesbian, gay, bisexual and transgender human rights: the search for an international strategy'. *Contemporary Politics*, 15 (1): 19–35.
Thorne, J. and Stuart, H. (2008). *Islam on Campus: a survey of UK student opinions*. Published by the Centre for Social Cohesion, London. See http://www.socialcohesion.co.uk/ for availability of reports.
Toronto Star: 'Blue Jays' Yunel Escobar suspended three games for homophobic slur'. http://www.thestar.com/sports/baseball/2012/09/18/blue_jays_yunel_escobar_suspended_three_games_for_homophobic_slur.html. Accessed July 9, 2013.
Toye, R. (2010). *Churchill's Empire: The World That Made Him and The World He Made*. New York: Henry Holt and Company.
Traub, V. (2008). 'The Past is a Foreign Country? The Times and Spaces of Islamicate Sexuality Studies'. Ch. 1 in Babayan, K. and Najmabadi, A. (2008), *Islamicate Sexualities: Translations across Temporal Geographies of Desire*. Cambridge: Harvard University Press.
Turner, B. S. (2002). 'Sovereignty and Emergency: Political Theology, Islam and America', *Theory, Culture and Society*,19 (4): 103–119. 2002.
—— (1990). 'Periodization and Politics in the Postmodern'. Ch. 1 in Turner, B. S. (ed.), *Theories of Modernity and Postmodernity*. New York and London: Sage, pp. 1–13.
United Nations Human Rights: 'Combatting discrimination based on sexual orientation and gender identity'. http://www.ohchr.org/EN/Issues/Discrimination/Pages/LGBT.aspx. Accessed June 29, 2013.
Vakulenko, A. (2007a). 'Islamic Dress in Human Rights Jurisprudence: A Critique of Current Trends'. *Human Rights Law Review*, Vol. 7, No. 4, pp. 717–739.
—— (2007b) '"Islamic Headscarves" and the European Convention on Human Rights; An Intersectional Perspective'. *Social and Legal Studies*, 16 (2): 183–199, 2007.

Valentine, G., Vanderbeck, R. M., Andersson, J., Sadgrove, J. and Ward, K. (2010). 'Emplacements: The Event as Prism for Exploring Intersectionality: a Case Study of the Lambeth Conference'. *Sociology*, 44 (5): 925–943.

Vanita, R. (2000). 'Preface' to Vanita, R. and Kidwai, S. (eds) (2000). *Same-Sex Love in India: Readings from Literature and History*. Houndmills, Basingstoke: St. Martin's Press.

Vanita, R. and Kidwai, S. (eds) (2000a). *Same-Sex Love in India: Readings from Literature and History*. Houndmills, Basingstoke: St. Martin's Press.

—— (2000b). 'Introduction to Part IV; Modern Indian Materials'. In Vanita, R. and Kidwai, S. (eds) (2000a), *Same-Sex Love in India: Readings from Literature and History*. Houndmills, Basingstoke: St. Martin's Press.

Wahab, A. (2012). 'Homophobia as the State of Reason: The Case of Postcolonial Trinidad and Tobago'. *GLQ*, 18 (4): 481–505.

Waites, M. (2008). 'Analysing Sexualities in the Shadow of War: Islam in Iran, the West and the Work of Reimagining Human Rights'. *Sexualities*, 11 (1–2): 64–73.

Waites, M. (2009). 'Critique of "sexual orientation" and "gender identity" in human rights discourse: global queer politics beyond the Yogyakarta Principles'. *Contemporary Politics* 15 (1): 137–156.

Walker, A. (1983). *In Search of Our Mother's Gardens: Womanist Prose*. New York: Harvest Books.

Weber, M. (2002). *Sociological Writings*. Edited by Wolf Heydebrand. New York: Continuum Press.

Weeks, J. (1989). *Sex, Politics and Society*, 2nd edition. Harrow: Longman.

—— (1996). *Invented Moralities: Sexual Values in an Age of Uncertainty*. Cambridge: Polity Press.

—— (2007) *The World We Have Won: The Remaking of Erotic and Intimate Life*. New York: Routledge.

Weiss, M. L. (2013). 'Prejudice before Pride: Rise of an Anticipatory Countermovement'. Ch. 7 in Weiss, M. L., and Bosia, M. J. (eds) *Global Homophobia: States, Movements and the Politics of Oppression*. Chicago: University of Illinois Press.

Weiss, M. L. and Bosia, M. J. (eds) (2013a). *Global Homophobia: States, Movements and the Politics of Oppression*. Chicago: University of Illinois Press.

—— (2013b). 'Political Homophobia in Comparative Perspective'. Ch. 1 in Weiss, M. L. and Bosia, M. J. (eds), *Global Homophobia: States, Movements and the Politics of Oppression*. Chicago: University of Illinois Press.

Welzel, C. and Inglehart, R. (2008). 'The Role of Ordinary People in Democratization'. *Journal of Democracy*, 19 (1): 126–140.

Westphal-Hellbusch, S. (1997). 'Institutionalised Gender-Crossing in Southern Iraq'. Ch. 15 in Murray, S. and Roscoe, W. (eds), *Islamic Homosexualities: Culture, History and Literature*. New York: New York University Press.

Whannel, G. (2002). *Media Sports Stars: Masculinities and Moralities*. London and New York: Routledge.

Williams, W. L. (2010). 'Islam and the Politics of Homophobia: The Persecution of Homosexuals in Islamic Malaysia Compared to Secular China'. Ch. 1 in Habib, S. (ed.), *Islam and Homosexuality, Vols 1 and 2*. Santa Barbara, CA: Praeger.

Wind-Cowie, M. and Gregory, T. (2011). *A Place for Pride*. London; Demos. Also can be accessed at http://www.demos.co.uk/publications/aplaceforpride.

Wollstonecraft, M. (1972[1792]) .'A Vindication of the Rights of Woman'. In M. Schneir (ed.), *Feminism: The Essential Historical Writings*, pp. 5–17. New York: Vintage Books.
Wong, Y. (2012). 'Islam, Sexuality, and the Marginal Positioning of *Pengkids* and Their Girlfriends in Malaysia'. *The Journal of Lesbian Studies*, 16: 435–448.
Woodiwiss, A. (2012). 'Asia, Enforceable Benevolence and the Future of Human Rights'. *Sociology*, 46 (5): 966–981.
World Pride Human Rights Conference, 2014. www.wphrc14.com.
World Values Surveys (cultural maps): http://www.worldvaluessurvey.org/wvs/articles/folder_published/article_base_54. Accessed June 29, 2013.
Yamani, M. (ed.) (1996). *Feminism and Islam: Legal and Literary Perspectives*. New York: New York University Press.
Yip, A. Kam-Tuck (2004). 'Embracing Allah and Sexuality? South Asian Non-Heterosexual Muslims in Britain'. pp. 294–310 in Jacobsen, K. A. and Pratap Kumar, P. (eds). *South Asians in the Diaspora*. Leiden: Brill.
—— (2005). 'Religion and the Politics of Spirituality/Sexuality: Reflections on Researching British Lesbian, Gay, and Bisexual Christians and Muslims'. *Fieldwork in Religion* 1 (3): 271–89.
—— (2007). 'Changing Religion, Changing Faith: Reflections on the Transformative Strategies of Lesbian, Gay, and Bisexual Christians and Muslims'. *Journal of Faith, Spirituality and Social Change* 1 (1): http://www.fsscconference.org.uk/journal/1-1.htm.
—— (2008a). 'The Quest for Intimate/Sexual Citizenship: Lived Experiences of Lesbian and Bisexual Muslim Women'. *Contemporary Islam*, 2 (2): 99–117.
—— (2008b). 'Researching Lesbian, Gay, and Bisexual Christians and Muslims: Some Thematic Reflections'. *Sociological Research Online* 13, 1: http://www.socresonline.org.uk/13/1/5.html.
—— (2009). 'Introduction to the special issue on Islam and Sexuality'. *Contemporary Islam*, 3 (1).
—— (2010). 'Coming Home from the Wilderness: An Overview of Recent Scholarly Research on LGBTIQ Religiosity/Spirituality in the West'. Ch. 2 in Browne, K., Munt, S. R. and Yip, A. K. T. (eds), *Queer Spiritual Spaces: Sexualities and Sacred Places*. Farnham, Surrey: Ashgate Publishing.
Yogyakarta Principles on the Application of International Human Rights Law in relation to Sexual Orientation and Gender Identity. http://www.yogyakartaprinciples.org/principles_en.htm. Accessed July 1, 2013.
Young, I. M. (1989). 'Polity and Group Difference'. *Ethics*, 99 (2): 250–274.
—— (1990). *Justice and the Politics of Difference*. Princeton: Princeton University Press.

Index

Abdulhadi, R., 86
Abraham, I., 108–11
Adam, B., 52, 107, 125
Adamczyk, A., 56, 57, 64
Afary, J., 104
African Charter on Human and People's Rights, 54
agency, 25, 71, 96–101, 115, 126, 192n. 11, 196nn. 17, 19
Age of Reason, 34
Ahmad, F., 46
Alexander, M. J., 203n. 19
Al-Fatiha, 103, 109, 110, 112, 205n. 8
Ali, M.
  Brick Lane, 13
alphabet soup approach, 143
Al-Sayyad, A. A., 109
alterspace, 205n. 12
Altman, D., 125, 126, 130–1
  Global Sex, 130
  Homosexual Oppression and Liberation, 130
Andersen, R., 64
Arab Charter for Human Rights, 199n. 13
Association of South East Asian Nations (ASEAN), 55
Awwad, J., 83, 88
Azzam, S., 198n. 9

Babayan, K., 75, 78, 103
Barber, B., 194n. 7
  Jihad vs McWorld, 33
Baudh, S., 140
Beauvoir, S. de, 19
Beckers, T., 56, 61, 197n. 23, 200n. 23
Bereket, T., 107
Bhambra, G., 30, 83, 88–9, 91–2, 124, 206n. 8
Blackwood, E., 87–8, 104–6
Blake, C., 203n. 19

Boellstorff, T., 106–7, 207n. 2
Bonilla, L., 200n. 16
Bosia, M. J., 91, 208n. 5
Brahm-Levey, G., 41, 196n. 17
Britishness, 15–16
Broughton, T., 12
Budhiraja, S., 143
Butler, J., 44, 116–17, 205n. 14

Cairo Declaration on Human Rights in Islam (1990), 54
Chan, P. C. W., 203n. 17
Claes, E., 58–9
Coatsworth, J., 51
colonialism, post-colonial cultures, and sexual regulation, 82–8
connected histories, 5, 6, 72, 124
  contemporary, 108–11
  homo-eroticism and, 88–97
  queer Muslims and, as modern intersectional subjects, 111–15
connected lives, 97
Cosslett, T., 25
critical hybridity, 110, 111

Dale, A., 190n. 7
Davis, K., 112, 113
Dayle, P., 203n. 19
de Jong, A.
  Strange Fruit, 147
De Leeuw, M., 207n. 3
democracy, as Western exceptionalism, 34–7
Demos
  A Place for Pride, 200n. 20
detraditionalization, 98, 99, 101, 126–8
disruptive intersectionality, 7
Duggan, L., 126
Dunne, B., 201n. 2
Duyvendak, J. W., 196n. 22

Economic Cooperation Organization (ECO), 55
Elliot, A., 99
El Tayeb, F.
  Strange Fruit, 147
emancipation, of women, 38
Enlightenment, 34
Environics survey (2006), 57
Epstein, S., 201n. 3
Escobar, Y., 204n. 2
essentialism, 7, 41, 77, 81–2, 84, 90, 97, 111, 126–31, 136, 142, 190nn. 4–5, 201n. 3, 207n. 13
Eurocentric view, 5, 73, 84, 91, 124
European Values Survey (EVS), 62–3, 197n. 23, 200n. 15

Fekete, L., 43
Fetner, T., 64
Fukuyama, F., 193n. 4
  The End of History and the Last Man, 30–1
Fuss, D., 205–6n. 1

Gallup report (2009), 58
Gaskins Jr, J., 203n. 19
gay capitals, 90–1
'Gay International', 78–82, 120, 203n. 16
gender, 17–21
  equality, secularism, and multiculturalism in context of, 37–42
  sexual diversity and, 77, 125, 126, 153–4
  see also individual entries
Gerhards, J., 62, 197n. 23
Giddens, A., 98–9, 204n. 4
globalization, 5–6, 19, 31, 93, 94–115, 124, 130–1, 191n. 9, 204n. 1, 207n. 2
Gramsci, A., 191n. 9
Gutfield, G., 46–7

Habib, S., 83–4, 197n. 23, 203n. 18, 207n. 15, 208n. 12
Hall, S., 191n. 9, 206n. 6
Hamzic, V., 198n. 8, 205n. 12

Harare declaration (1991), 54
Haring, K., 128, 206n. 11
Harrison, C., 190n. 5
hegemony, 25, 96, 110–11, 126, 153, 191n. 9, 205n. 12
Hekma, G., 196n. 22
Held, D.
  Models of Democracy, 35
hetero-nationalism, 152
heteronormativity, 1, 44, 79, 105, 107, 110, 111, 129, 132, 153, 155
heterosexual dominance, 132
heterosexuality, 18, 20, 25, 54, 58, 75, 77, 81, 87, 98, 99, 104, 106, 127, 206n. 1
Hill Collins, P., 114, 190n. 2
history, narratives, and narrators, 10–13
Hobsbawm, E., 35
homocolonialism, 6–8, 121–3
  beyond, 130–5
  in multiculturalism, 144–9
  political presumptions, 125–30
  test, for internationalized Western queer politics and consciousness, 138–44
  Western exceptionalism embracing through, 149–54
homo-eroticism (Muslim), 70–2, 124, 129
  colonialism, post-colonial cultures, and sexual regulation and, 82–8
  connected histories and, 88–92
  in historical and contemporary context, 4–6
  in traditional Muslim cultures, 72–8
  transformation through 'Gay International', 78–82
  beyond westernization, and Muslim identity politics, 92–3
homonationalism, 2, 44, 81, 114, 120–2, 136
homonormativity, 44, 111, 120–2, 126–7, 136

homophobia (Muslim), 4, 5, 7, 27, 28–9, 46, 48, 49, 59, 62, 64, 71–2, 76, 86, 88, 91, 96, 111, 114, 116, 119, 122–3, 128, 132, 133, 136, 146–7, 149, 151, 153, 154
  in contexts of modernity and Islamophobia, 66–9
homosexualization, *see* homo-eroticism (Muslim)
Hood-Williams, J., 190n. 5
Hooghe, M., 58–9
Huntingdon, S. P., 30, 37
  The Clash of Civilizations: Remaking of World Order, 30

identity politics and ends of liberation, 118–19
  dialogue and queer and, 135–6
  homocolonialism and beyond, 130–5
    political presumptions of, 125–30
  triangulation of Western exceptionalism and, 119–25
Inglehart, R., 60–1, 64
intersectionality, 12–13, 124–5, 132–4, 153, 205nn. 12–13, 207n. 2
  disruptive, 7
  modernity and, 111–17
  queer, 24–6
Islamic Educational, Scientific and Cultural Organization (ISESCO), 198n. 10
Islamophobia, 7, 8, 29, 54, 66–9, 122, 132–3, 144, 146–7, 152, 154, 207n. 16
  contemporary, 24
  Islam versus homosexuality as modernity, 27–9
  conceits of West and resistance of East and, 47–8
  democracy as Western exceptionalism and, 34–7
  equality and secularism versus multiculturalism in gender context and, 37–42
  Islamic otherness and, 29–34
  sexual diversity as marker of Islamic otherness and, 42–7

Jackson, P. A., 90–1
Jackson, S., 18, 99
Jaspal, R., 205n. 9
Jivraj, S., 147

Kaoma, K. J., 208n. 5
Karim, K. H.
  Islamic Peril: Media and Global Violence, 193n. 3
Khadr, O., 192–3n.2
Khan, B., 108
  Sex, Longing and Not Belonging, 103
Khan, Z., 193n. 3
Kidwai, S., 76
Klug, B.
  Ethnicities, 207n. 16
Kollman, K., 143
Korycki, K., 113
Kramer, M., 103, 204n. 5
Kugle, S. S., 151, 197n. 1, 200n. 23
  Homosexuality in Islam, 205n. 10

late modernity, 98–100
Lennox, C., 54, 142, 206n. 2, 208n. 5
lesbi, 104–6
Lewis, B., 31, 37–8, 45
  What Went Wrong? The Clash Between Islam and Modernity in the Middle East, 195n. 11
liberal democracy, 31, 127
liberalism, 33, 35–6, 46
Lind, A., 140, 208n. 7
Long, S., 104

McDermot, E., 99
Mahdavi, P., 104, 113
Mason, V., 193n. 3
Massad, J. A., 71, 78–86, 88–90, 93, 103, 121, 128, 202n. 12, 203n. 16, 206n. 5
  Desiring Arabs, 78
'matrix of domination', 114
Mepschen, P., 45, 66, 67
Michalowski, I., 207n. 3
migration, 13–15
moderate secularism, 193n. 6

modern capitalism, 32
modernity, 4–6, 14, 15, 50, 77, 82, 94, 97, 102, 114, 117–26, 133, 137–9, 149, 194n. 8, 195n. 11, 196n. 20, 204n. 20, 205n. 14, 207n. 2
  contemporary, 138
  economic, 61
  intersectional, 115–17
  Islam versus homosexuality as, 27–48
  late, 98–100
  liquid, 99
  misunderstanding of, 82–8
  modernization and, 2–4
  sexual, 6, 62, 72, 89, 93, 95
  sociological basis of homosexualization during, 88–92
  understanding Muslim homophobia in contexts of, 66–9
  universal, 139
  Western, 2, 4, 28, 32–3, 37, 47, 50, 61, 65, 69, 70, 89, 91–3, 99, 120, 123, 126, 137, 194n. 8, 195n. 11, 204n. 20
modernization, 37–8, 72, 76–7, 83, 84, 86, 89–91, 93–4, 97–8, 100–3, 106, 114–18, 123–4, 139, 151, 154, 201n. 25
  modernity and, 2–4
  problematic, 49–69
    complexities and reactions to homosexuality, 62–6
    explaining Muslim antipathy, 59–62
Modood, T., 46, 146, 193n. 6, 196n. 17, 207n. 13, 208nn. 9, 11
monoculturalism, 7, 112, 122, 123, 129, 144, 147, 152
moralism, 32
Motha, S., 192n. 11
Muhleisen, W., 207n. 3
multiculturalism, 16, 18, 22, 25, 28, 196nn. 16–19, 207n. 13, 208n. 11
Murray, S., 72, 73–5, 78, 85, 103, 201nn. 2, 5

Muslim antipathy to homosexuality, extent and formation of, 49–51
  explanation, through modernization thesis, 59–62
  modernization complexities and reactions to homosexuality and, 62–6
  Muslim homophobia in contexts of modernity and Islamophobia and, 66–9
  Muslim majority and minority populations, attitude of, 56–9
  Muslim regulation at national and international level, 51–6
Muslim World League, 198n. 9

Najmabadi, A., 75, 78, 103
Nasirzadeh, A., 113
National Health Service (NHS), 15
Naz, 110, 112
neoliberalism, 111, 126, 191n. 9

Obendorf, S., 203n. 17
Okin, S. M., 18, 39–41, 147, 195–6nn. 14–15
  'Feminism and Multiculturalism', 39
Organization of Islamic Conference (OIC), 54
Organization on Islamic Co-operation (OIC), 198nn. 9–10
otherness, 28
  Islamic, 29–34, 82, 122
  and sexual diversity, 42–7

Panetta, L., 51
Parekh, B., 135, 147
Peletz, M. G., 75, 85, 86
Pew Research Center, 57, 206n. 5
Phillips, A., 39, 41, 43, 196n. 17, 208n. 11
Pimlott, B., 191n. 10
Pitt, C., 56, 57, 64
political identity, essential context of, 125–30
political possibilities, 6–8
political subjectivity, 127
Porter, J., 200n. 16

post-colonialism, 5, 14, 26, 36, 71–2, 82–3, 85–9, 91–3, 105, 124, 194n. 8, 195n. 12, 203n. 19
Poynting, S., 193n. 3
Puar, J. K., 2, 44, 81, 121, 126, 136, 205n. 13, 207n. 4
Punk kids, 204–5n. 6

queer
  intersectionality, 24–6
  Muslims, 94–102
    connected histories as modern intersectional subjects and, 111–15
    intersectional modernity and, 115–17
    in Muslim majority cultures, 102–8
    in West, 108–11
  rights
    in countries with significant and projected Muslim populations, 180–8
    in Muslim majority countries, 159–79
  theory, 10, 12–13
  see also individual entries

Rahman, M., 82, 113–14, 190n. 6, 195n. 15
  Sexuality and Democracy, 150
Rayside, D., 46, 57, 203n. 14
Razack, S., 38
reflexive essentialism, 127
reflexivity, 6, 8, 11, 97–8, 100–1
relativist epistemology, 12
Ritchie, J., 111
Rogan, E.
  The Arabs, 195n. 11
Roscoe, W., 70, 72, 73–5, 78, 88, 103, 201nn. 2, 5
Ruby, T. F., 192n. 11

Saed, K., 108
Safi, O., 150, 152
Safra, 110
Saharso, S., 39, 43

Said, E., 8, 30, 83, 138
  Covering Islam, 193n. 3
  Orientalism, 194n. 8
Salaam, 110
Schmitt, A., 78, 193n. 5, 202n. 12
  Sexuality and Eroticism Among Males in Moslem Societies, 72
Schmitt, C., 31–3
Seidman, S., 12, 132
self-expression value, 63–4
  syndrome, 60
sexual citizenship, 98, 126
sexual diversity, 3–6, 8, 24, 27–9, 32, 36, 50, 54, 63, 65, 66–70, 72, 76–7, 79, 81–5, 92–3, 95, 97–101, 104, 113, 114, 116, 118–19, 121–6, 135, 142–4, 148–54, 205n. 10, 206n. 5
  acceptance of, 41, 43, 45, 66, 67, 123, 149, 153
  contemporary, 124
  gender and, 77, 125, 126, 153–4
  as key area of conflict, 46
  as marker of Islamic otherness, 42–7
  politics, 132–3, 137, 138, 150, 152, 192n. 1
  public, 97
  resistance to, 4, 122, 149
sexual liberation, 7, 46, 100, 102, 118–19, 128, 130, 139, 152
sexual orientation, 8, 52–4, 56, 76, 81–2, 135, 143, 150, 156, 197nn. 5, 23, 201n. 24, 204n. 2, 205n. 8
Sexual Orientation and Gender Identity (SOGI), 120
sexual politics, 34, 115, 120, 123, 124, 130–1
Shanghai Cooperation Organization (SCO), 55
Siraj, A., 58, 200n. 21
Sofer, E., 78
  Sexuality and Eroticism Among Males in Moslem Societies, 72
Stanley, L., 12, 14, 24
Strauss, L., 31–2, 193n. 5
Subrahmanyam, S., 92, 124
Sweibel, J., 197nn. 5, 23